The Alternative Career Guide to More Than 700

Certificate Programs,

Trade Schools, and Job

OPPORTUNITIES

✶ ✶ ✶ ✶

You're Certifiable

Lee and Joel Naftali

✳ ✳ ✳ ✳

A Fireside Book
Published by Simon & Schuster

FIRESIDE
Rockefeller Center
1230 Avenue of the Americas
New York, NY 10020

FIRESIDE and colophon are registered trademarks
of Simon & Schuster Inc.

Designed by Carla Bolte

Manufactured in the United States of America

10 9 8 7 6 5 4 3 2 1

Library of Congress Cataloging-in-Publication Data
Naftali, Lee.
  You're certifiable: the alternative career guide to more than 700 certificate programs, trade
schools, and job opportunities / Lee and Joel Naftali.
      p.   cm.
1. Vocational education—United States—Directories.   2. Trade schools—United
States—Directories.   3. Career education—United States—Directories.   I. Naftali, Joel E.
II. Title.
L901.N24   1999
378'.013'02573—dc21   98-55504
                                                                CIP

ISBN 0-684-84996-8

Acknowledgments

Many thanks to Becky Cabaza and Carrie Thornton at Fireside, and to our lovely and talented agent, Kathleen Anderson. Thanks to Paula Ross of the YPN Group. As always, thanks to our parents for their generosity, encouragement, and bewildering enthusiasm for our "career." And finally, thanks to all the schools listed in this book, both for responding to our requests for information and for offering such inspiring career training programs.

Contents

Introduction

✻ ✻ ✻ ✻

We used to think education came in two flavors: unprofitable-but-interesting—studying anthropology or literature—and profitable-but-tedious—studying medical transcription or engineering. If we only knew then what we know now. . . .

There are hundreds of vocational schools that are nothing like those late-night truck-driving commercials. There are hundreds that have nothing to do with data processing. There are hundreds that don't lead to boring, conventional, or meaningless jobs.

You *can* get more from a career than just a paycheck. You can work with your favorite things—animals, art, crafts, people, language—in your favorite ways—crafting, healing, performing, counseling, designing. And you can make a living doing it.

Would you like to be a horse masseuse? How about a hot-air balloon pilot or shamanic counselor? Maybe you're interested in fabric design, dog grooming, or hypnotherapy. Or you might enjoy an old-fashioned craft, like wooden boatbuilding, silversmithing, or saddlemaking.

There are vocational training programs covering all of these subjects—and many other uncommon, interesting trades. Some programs are quick and cheap. Some are expensive and lengthy. Some offer financial aid, some include housing, and some offer free retraining. Some are accredited by professional organizations; some accredit themselves.

But they all have one thing in common: not only do they teach interesting and alternative trades, they also teach potentially profitable careers. They teach you how to make money doing what you learned, how to use your newfound skills to attract and serve clients. Sure, the chances are that you won't become the world's first billionaire bookbinder, childbirth assistant, or art appraiser, but you will be able to pay the rent—and many of the careers taught by schools in this book can become very profitable indeed.

The Careers ❖ ❖ ❖

We included careers working with animals, art, people, crafts, food, the media, outdoor adventures, and more—all in ways that are at least a little extraordinary, a little more interesting or less conventional than the average career.

You might wonder what criteria we used to decide which subjects to include. Well, we developed a painstaking and rigorous test to ensure that we only included the most interesting and unconventional vocations. A career passed the test if, when we got information about it, we thought, "Gee, that's interesting and unconventional!"

Which is to say that inclusion of programs in this book is not exhaustive. We didn't include listings of individual massage schools; there are hundreds of them, and they're fairly easy to find (check out your local Yellow Pages or the massage school directories we mention on page 117). Instead, we included a listing of specialized bodywork methods (such as Hellerwork, Rolfing, and reflexology) and the associations that represent them. We included a number of farrier (horseshoeing) schools that horse people might think are pretty mundane, but we're not horse people, so we think they're unusual and teach an interesting way to make a living. We included chocolate-making and animation training programs, but not cooking schools and graphic design programs. If you're looking for programs such as those, don't worry: whenever a more conventional career doesn't quite fit into a chapter, we tell you where to go for more information.

The Schools . . .

Then there are the schools themselves. We tried to include all the schools that seemed to offer, or said they offered, vocational training.

We didn't evaluate the earning potential of the various vocations. We didn't research the size of the market or the average income of practitioners. Why? *Because there are people making a good living in every one of the careers listed in this book.* Certainly, some are less lucrative than others, and some may even be downright difficult. But we didn't want to say, "Well, there's no way someone's gonna make a living doing cat massage," when the truth is that someone has, in fact, built a multi-million dollar business based on animal massage.

People are making a living in every one of the alternative careers mentioned in this book. We spoke to those who are working as childbirth educators, herbalists, and blacksmiths. We spoke to people who are professional animal communicators, auric healers, and sex surrogates. If you find one of the more offbeat subjects most attractive, we only have one word of advice: If you're passionate about it, your chances of making a living are greatly increased. Know that someone else is doing it, and you can, too.

Many of the schools in this book are accredited. More are not. Some are accredited by professional organizations, some by the state, some by themselves. In some fields, accreditation isn't an option, and in many others, it's entirely beside the point. In a field like Feng Shui (an ancient Chinese art of placement and design), where apprenticeship has been the traditional mode of learning for a thousand years, accreditation from some newfangled organization seems silly. And, in fact, no such organization exists. Do you need to learn saddlemaking or dog training from an accredited school? No, just from skilled and professional teachers.

Of course, there are benefits of accreditation. In some of the health-related fields, it is quite important for credibility and, increasingly, to practice legally (in a field such as hypnotherapy, for example, there's a growing movement toward state-licensed practitioner standards). In other fields, accrediting bodies offer various benefits to accredited members, such as networking, lobbying, and continuing education. But if a book that focuses on alternative careers includes only accredited schools, it becomes a pamphlet. And an unhelpful one, at that.

Then there's certification. The vast majority of schools offer a certificate to students who complete their course of study. Then you can call yourself a "certified whatever." But the certification itself isn't the important thing. Being well trained, gaining the skills, knowledge, and self-confidence to do a good job and get paid a fair wage, those are the important things.

We tried to include only programs that are indeed vocationally oriented and prepare students for a profession. However, we did include some programs—notably in the crafts field—that teach both hobbyists and aspiring professionals. For example, while several of the wood-carving schools offer short-term classes for hobbyists, more serious students are encouraged to arrange with the instructors to develop professionally oriented projects and curriculum. Basically, if we were assured that the coursework was appropriate as career training, and the school struck us as interesting, we included it.

We covered only a few training programs offered by colleges and universities, because they're easy to find and tend not to be all that alternative. We included college-based programs only if they are in fields that don't have many training programs, or if education in the field is routinely college-based (such as in museum studies and publishing). Still, some colleges and universities offer great certificate courses: if you're looking for something a little more mainstream, check out the programs offered by your local institution of higher learning.

We also didn't include any degree programs. Although there are many excellent acupuncture and Oriental medicine programs, for example, we didn't include them because they lead to a master's degree. The same goes for a few alternative therapy careers (such as art and music therapy), and the occasional art-related degree program (in fine arts or filmmaking, for example). Although many of these careers are unconventional and can be very rewarding, we had to draw the line somewhere. But never fear, we did include information that tells you how to hunt down these programs if they're what you're interested in.

Finally, we let the schools speak for themselves as much as possible, by borrowing heavily from their brochures and catalogs when we wrote the entries. For most schools, this resulted in straightforward and understandable entries. But for some, it led to buzzwords and jargon: if you find an entry appealing but confusing, make sure you contact the school directly to clarify exactly what they teach.

The Disclaimers ◆ ◆ ◆

First, all the information in this book was correct when we wrote it. But that was then, and this is now. Schools and programs change every year—classes are updated, new courses are added, and costs increase. And sometimes, unfortunately, schools relocate or close. Second, although we're certain that most of the training programs are excellent, we do not endorse any of them.

That said, we encourage you to jump in. Find a couple of schools that look good and call them. Get on their mailing lists. If possible, visit them. Ask them questions. These schools are operated by people who care, by people who are doing what they love for a living. They'll be thrilled to discuss their school and their coursework with you (and if they're not, that's all you need to know). They'll tell you about employment or entrepreneurial possibilities for graduates. They'll give you the names of satisfied grads. They'll tell you the inside story on the challenges and rewards of their profession. Maybe they'll even convince you that theirs is the school that will train you to make a living in your perfect career.

What's in This Book ◆ ◆ ◆

This book is divided into two parts. Part I, which contains chapters 1 through 3, helps you select a subject, choose a career, pick a training program, and develop a plan to make money before you even start training.

Chapter 1 covers subjects. If, as you're reading these words, you haven't a clue where to find schools that teach your favorite subjects, this chapter will help you figure it out. It'll help you move from a general sense of what you like to do to a more specific understanding of which schools in this book match your preferences.

Chapter 2 covers careers and schools. First, it helps you determine the probable job satisfaction and potential income of your favorite careers. Then it explains how to evaluate the costs and benefits of all the possible training programs.

Chapter 3 covers money. This chapter prepares you to make money before you even enroll in a school. Follow the advice in chapter 3 and not only will you be happier investing your time and money in a training program, you'll also have a much easier time making a living after you graduate.

Part II, which contains chapters 4 through 14, is the meat of the book—the school listings. Each entry tells you what you'll learn, how long the training takes, what it costs, and whom to contact for more information. Chapters 4 through 14 cover Animals, Art and Design, Bodywork and Physical Health, Consulting and Counseling, Craft and Trade, Food and Drink, Herbal and Alternative Medicine, Media, Metaphysical Healing, Outdoors and Active, and Therapy.

For more details on individual chapters, check out chapter 1, in which we provide an easy-to-browse list of the contents of this book to help you pinpoint training programs of interest.

Beyond the Book • • •

We hope this book offers something more than the names and addresses of specific training programs, more than a snapshot of intriguing careers. We hope it opens up a whole world of unconventional, enjoyable, rewarding work and encourages you, whatever your interests, to find a life in which work and play are the same. Even if—heaven forbid— there *is* no training program for your dream career, take heart: if people are making a living with some of the more alternative careers in this book (and they are!), you can make a living doing what you love, too. Good luck.

Did We Miss You?

Although we're fairly certain we found every last alternative career training program in the United States (and a few beyond it), there's a remote possibility that we missed one or two. Or even three. If you know of a program or school that isn't listed in this book but should be, please let us know. Thanks.

Lee and Joel Naftali
P.O. Box 2066
Santa Barbara, CA 93120
JRNaftali@aol.com

You're
Certifiable

PART I

★★★★

Chapter I

★ ★ ★ ★

The Subjects of Your Affection

You're probably not planning to read this book cover to cover: it is, after all, a directory. In fact, you may have already glanced at the Contents and decided which sections to read and which to ignore. But that may not be such a cunning plan—this book is about *alternative* careers, and alternative careers, by their very nature, are hard to categorize.

Does horseshoeing go in Animals or Craft and Trade? Should Feng Shui be in Design or Consulting? Is beer brewing more appropriate in Food and Drink or Metaphysical Healing? Who knows? Some of the careers simply don't fit neatly into any one category. So the chapter and subject headings don't always reflect their contents with perfect accuracy.

Of course, you can be pretty confident that if you're interested in some sort of alternative design career, the Art and Design chapter is the best place for you. But it may not be the only place: other chapters contain design careers that aren't in Art and Design because they involve, for example, working with animals, crafts, or the media.

That's why we recommend that you read this chapter. It imposes order on the unconventional career chaos. It provides brief descriptions of all the chapters and subjects in this book, highlighting the hidden gems, unclassifiable careers, and cross-disciplinary trainings that you might otherwise overlook.

If you already know which type of alternative career suits you, this chapter will help you find appropriate training programs—even when they're tucked away in unexpected chapters.

On the other hand, maybe all you know is what you *don't* want—a buttoned-down, nine-to-five, regular job. Or maybe you have a dim picture of a suitable career, but no idea which training programs teach it. Or maybe you're just not sure what some of the chapter headings mean. What is Therapeutic Riding Instruction? What does Coaching and Life Guidance involve? And what's in those mysterious Miscellaneous sections?

If you have any of these concerns, we encourage you to read through all the chapter descriptions below, including those that don't immediately interest you. You may discover that teaching natural vision correction is exactly what you're looking for—even though it's in the Bodywork and Physical Health section and you recoil at the thought of physical contact with clients. Or you might find that, despite your lack of vocational direction, some of the schools are inexplicably fascinating. When that happens, follow up—you're probably stumbling toward your perfect career.

The Usual Subjects ✦ ✦ ✦

The following chapter descriptions tell you four things. First, they explain each of the section headings. Some, such as Floral Design and Animation, are fairly obvious. But others, such as Homeopathy and Feng Shui, are a bit more obscure—the descriptions will give you enough information to make an initial decision about the appeal of various careers.

Second, they list the careers in the Miscellaneous sections. These are often the most interesting, exciting, lucrative, and/or offbeat careers. If you're interested in a subject, we highly recommend that you read through the entire Miscellaneous section in that chapter.

Third, they refer you to other sections with similar careers. For example, in the Art and Design section, we suggest you check out the candymaking and cake-decorating schools—despite being in the Food and Drink chapter, they require art and design skills.

And, fourth, they explain a bit about what we haven't included. If a career you expected to find in a particular chapter isn't there, either it requires a degree or we felt it was too conventional. But if the career was sort of borderline—very alternative but requires a degree, or fairly conventional but with interesting, vocationally oriented training programs—the chapter description will provide resources that help you locate appropriate degree programs or career schools.

Animals

This chapter contains six sections:

- *Animal Massage:* working hands-on with horses, dogs, and cats to promote health, recovery from injury and surgery, and high performance.
- *Dog Training:* primarily teaching obedience and good behavior, some training of protection, assistance, and police dogs.
- *Horse Management:* managing stables, understanding horse care and nutrition, working with racehorses and even becoming a jockey.
- *Pet Grooming:* grooming dogs and cats, including special breed and show cuts, skin and coat care, and many clipper and scissors techniques.
- *Therapeutic Riding Instruction:* helping disabled people gain strength, balance, and self-confidence—and have fun—through horseback riding.
- *Miscellaneous:* working with exotic animals, pet sitting, and psychic animal communication.

Other animal careers can be found in Craft and Trade (horseshoeing and, to a lesser extent, saddlemaking) and Herbal and Alternative Medicine and Metaphysical Healing (both of which include schools that offer some classes in veterinary health).

Art and Design

This chapter contains four sections:

- *Floral Design:* arranging and creating bouquets, vases, centerpieces, and more for retail sales and events such as weddings, funerals, and parties.
- *Museum Studies and Art Appraisal:* working privately and for museums doing curatorial, educational, and archival work, and appraisal and evaluation of fine art, folk art, antiques, and other valuable objects.
- *Feng Shui:* promoting health, prosperity, and happiness in homes, businesses, and offices through the use of the ancient Chinese art of interior design and placement.
- *Miscellaneous:* primarily garden design and surface pattern design, which involves creating patterns for wallpaper, tablecloths, gift wrap, and other surfaces produced in volume.

We didn't include graphic design training programs in this section, as they are easy to find and fairly conventional (if you're interested in graphic design, you can find a list of schools in the resources mentioned on page 91). There are, as far as we can tell, no formal faux finishing career training programs—if you're interested in decorative or faux finishing, check out adult education programs at local colleges and universities or consider apprenticing to a practicing professional. Finally, the garden design section does not include regular landscape gardening programs—we focused more on "design" than "garden."

Other art and design careers can be found in Media (the animation and filmmaking sections), Food and Drink (the cake decorating trainings), Craft and Trade (almost all of the programs require some art and design skills), Diving (which includes underwater photography and video), and Animals (pet grooming).

Bodywork and Physical Health

This chapter includes four sections:

- *Bodywork:* providing massage, somatic education, and other methods of therapeutic or healing touch for relaxation and wellness, and to address specific health concerns.

- *Colon Hydrotherapy:* introducing water into clients' colons to flush out toxins, clear blockages, and promote general well-being.
- *Movement Training:* helping clients stand, walk, run, breathe, and move with more strength, balance, grace, and integrity to reduce chronic pain and promote health and self-confidence.
- *Natural Vision Correction:* teaching clients to improve their vision through physical and mental exercises and a variety of other techniques involving nutrition and visualization.

There are too many bodywork schools to list each one individually. Instead, the Bodywork section provides contact information for alternative bodywork associations that represent training schools teaching methods ranging from Aston-Patterning to Watsu.

Other bodywork and physical health careers can be found in Animals (Animal Massage and Therapeutic Riding Instruction), Consulting and Counseling (Birth, Pregnancy, and Labor Support, some of which involve infant and labor massage), and Metaphysical Healing and Therapy (both of which contain some programs that include elements of bodywork). Finally, Therapy includes several movement and dance therapy training programs that are somewhat similar to the movement training programs in this chapter.

Consulting and Counseling

This chapter contains five sections:

- *Birth, Pregnancy, and Labor Support:* teaching breast-feeding skills and infant massage and providing doula services, which include advocating for and supporting women before, during, and after childbirth.
- *Coaching and Life Guidance:* helping clients discover their career path, set goals, and achieve success.
- *Genealogy:* consulting about family histories, researching lineages, and lecturing and teaching about genealogy.
- *Graphology:* analyzing handwriting for self-discovery, personnel evaluation, and questioned document examination.
- *Miscellaneous:* couples' counseling, firewalk facilitating, playing live music in medical settings to promote health and comfort, astrological counseling, using bau-biologie to evaluate and improve the effect of buildings on health, and whole health education.

Other consulting and counseling careers can be found in Art and Design (Feng Shui), Food (macrobiotic counseling), Outdoors and Active (guiding and outdoor leadership) and Metaphysical Healing, Herbal and Alternative Medicine, and Therapy, all of which include some programs with elements of counseling and consulting.

Crafts and Trade

This chapter contains eight sections:

- *Boatbuilding and Yacht Design:* working hands-on to fabricate boats (particularly wooden boats), and using engineering, ergonomics, and other sciences to design them.
- *Bookbinding:* conserving old books and creating new ones, using techniques such as leather and metal binding, gold lettering, and embossing.
- *Horseshoeing:* using metalworking skills to create horseshoes, including therapeutic or corrective shoes.
- *Jewelry and Watchmaking:* designing, making, and repairing every kind of jewelry and watch (from diamond rings to cuckoo clocks to art jewelry to digital watches).
- *Piano Tuning and Musical Instrument Repair:* tuning, rebuilding, and repairing pianos and band instruments.
- *Violin and Guitar Making and Repair:* constructing and repairing violins, guitars, cellos, violas, and other stringed instruments.
- *Woodworking and Furniture Making:* creating artistic and functional furniture and other wood projects.
- *Miscellaneous:* blacksmithing, bladesmithing, jade carving, glassblowing and neon tube bending, saddlemaking, and sign making. There is also a handful of schools that offers certificate programs for aspiring craft artisans who want to work in wood, metal, fibers, and clay.

Food and Drink

This chapter contains three sections:

- *Beer Brewing:* working in a commercial or microbrewery.
- *Candymaking and Cake Decorating:* making chocolate and other confections and, well, decorating cakes.

- *Whole Foods and Macrobiotic Cooking*: cooking as personal chefs, for restaurants and caterers, conducting cooking classes, and offering macrobiotic counseling services.

Traditional cooking schools are not included in this section—if you're interested in becoming a chef or pastry chef, check out the books on page 225.

Herbal and Alternative Medicine

This chapter includes four sections:

- *Ayurveda*: helping clients use the ancient Indian art and science of healthful daily living to achieve balance, purity, and wellness.
- *Herbology*: identifying health problems and recommending both Western and traditional Chinese herbal preparations to address them. Some herbalists also prepare their own liniments, tinctures, and other remedies.
- *Homeopathy*: treating illness or disease with minute doses of herbs and other preparations that stimulate clients' abilities to heal themselves.
- *Miscellaneous*: using aromatherapy, flower essences, colorpuncture, and bioenergetics to promote health and healing.

This chapter does not include acupuncture and Oriental medicine training, because they are master's degree programs. If you're interested in getting a degree in alternative medicine, check out the resources on page 236.

Elements of herbal and alternative medicine can be found in careers in Metaphysical Healing (many work with herbs, aromatherapy, and elements of traditional Chinese medicine).

Media

This chapter contains four sections:

- *Animation*: preparing for entry-level careers in the animation business, doing 3D modeling, character development, texture mapping, storyboarding, etc.

- *Broadcasting*: working as an on-air personality (such as a DJ or sportscaster or meteorologist) or in a behind-the-scenes job.
- *Filmmaking*: directing, lighting, editing, and doing any number of other jobs on documentary, experimental, and commercial films.
- *Publishing*: understanding the basics of a variety of jobs in publishing—manuscript acquisition, editing, contract negotiation, and so on.

The Animation and Filmmaking sections don't include degree programs. If you're interested in a more formal animation training, check out the books on page 267. And if you're looking for a more thorough or academic film education, check out those on page 284.

Metaphysical Healing

This chapter contains one section:

- *Metaphysical Healing*: vibrational, energetic, spiritual, and psychic healing. In addition to teaching a wide variety of healing methods—such as auric healing, laying on of hands, gemstone healing, and etheric surgery—some of the programs in this chapter also emphasize secondary skills such as clairvoyant counseling, herbology, and nutrition.

Other metaphysical healing careers can be found in Animals (animal communication), Art and Design (Feng Shui, which includes elements of both metaphysics and health), Bodywork and Physical Health (several of the bodywork trainings are based on energetic systems), Consulting and Counseling (Holistic Coaching and Aura-Soma color consulting), Therapy (shamanic counseling and assorted other alternative therapy careers), and some of the Herbal and Alternative Medicine sections.

Outdoors and Active

This chapter contains three sections:

- *Diving*: underwater construction, salvage, testing, photography, and medicine.

- *Guiding:* river, ski, and mountain guiding, and outdoor leadership.
- *Miscellaneous:* balloon piloting and professional clowning.

There are many active alternative careers that we didn't include because they require that students already have a certain level of expertise: if you want to be a skydiving instructor, you ought to know a thing or two about parachutes. The trainings in this chapter—with just a few exceptions—accept students with little or no experience in their future field. This is also the only chapter in the book that includes careers that may be seasonal, such as river raft guiding. But it is possible, with a little imagination and tenacity, to guide year-round, or to combine several kinds of outdoor guiding careers into one *über*-career (such as alpine guiding in the winter, balloon piloting in the summer).

Other outdoor and active careers can be found in Animals (almost any animal career can be active, and dog training, horse management, horseshoeing, and therapeutic riding instruction are often outdoors), Art and Design (garden design), and, to a limited extent, Herbology (those programs that emphasize wildcrafting).

Therapy

This chapter contains three sections:

- *Breathwork and Rebirthing:* helping individuals, clients, and groups harness the therapeutic power of breath to transform and heal.
- *Hypnotherapy:* making helpful and therapeutic suggestions to help clients overcome blocks, break bad habits, achieve their potential, and move toward self-discovery and wholeness.
- *Miscellaneous:* a very wide variety of programs, including movement therapy, shamanic counseling, sexual surrogacy, astrology, focusing, rapid eye technology, and many other unique therapeutic modalities. Some are fairly conventional, some not at all. Some work with a specific population that has a particular problem—for example, children with neurological or muscular disabilities—and some work with the general population to increase self-awareness and happiness.

Alternative therapy programs that require master's degrees, such as music, art, and dance therapy, are not included. If you're interested in any of them, see page 327 for associations you can call for more information.

Other therapy careers can be found in Bodywork and Physical Health (many of the bodywork methods have emotional, as well as physical, effects), Consulting and Counseling (coaching and life guidance and graphology), and Metaphysical Healing (several of the programs teach intuitive, clairvoyant, or psychic counseling).

What to Do If Nothing's for You ◆ ◆ ◆

Those are the subjects. We hope that a handful—or more—of the programs intrigue, excite, or inspire you. But if none of the above really captured your fancy, try this:

First, browse all the entries. But don't expect the heavens to open the instant your eyes alight upon the perfect program. If a skill or technique or class catches your fancy, get more information. Your future vocational passion may be smoldering beneath the surface of a fairly cut-and-dried entry. If you're at all interested, call for a brochure or catalog.

Then, if you're still stuck, it's time to pull out the big guns: discover your passion or purpose. There are plenty of good books that help you do this. (We like *I Could Do Anything If Only I Knew What It Was* by Barbara Sher, *The Truth About You* by Arthur Miller and Ralph Mattson, and, always humbly, *Generation E* by us.) The clearer you are about your mission, your driving desire, the easier it is to find people, organizations, and training programs that support that mission. Oddly enough, the more narrowly you define what you want, the easier it is to achieve.

And, finally, find a program that's pretty close to what you want: a school that, while it's not perfect, does make you daydream for a passing moment and does have some attractive elements. Then take that almost-right program and make it entirely right. Focus on whatever interests you about the career and customize the training program for your own purposes. One of the benefits of working in an alternative field is that flexibility and innovation don't give people hives: there's plenty of room for your unique take on an already alternative career. Just because you can't find the perfect training doesn't mean you can't create it.

Chapter 2

✳ ✳ ✳ ✳

Evaluating
Schools and Careers

You've seen the whole range of alternative career schools. You know what's in all the sections. You understand what the more obscure training programs are teaching. And you're probably a bit overwhelmed. Not only do you not know which of the schools would be best for you, you haven't even decided on one career. Don't worry: This chapter will help you identify the best career for you and evaluate the merits (and otherwise) of specific schools.

Your first task is obvious—call or write for more information from each of the schools that interests you. Although it would make sense to avoid all the extra paperwork by pinpointing a career before getting information from schools that will ultimately be inappropriate, the information is free and can lead you to dismiss or focus on one career with a minimum of fuss. And many of the schools send information with helpful career tips—how large the market is, what and where the possible jobs are, and so on—that will help you narrow down your career search.

Also, the brochures, catalogs, and information sheets range from glossy four-color *objets d'art* to what looks like the final stand of mimeograph technology: you can get a fairly accurate feeling for a school from its marketing material. Still, some well-known and highly respected programs send information that appears to have been designed by a drunk baboon wielding a charred twig, so this should only be the beginning of your research.

Choosing a Career ◆ ◆ ◆

First determine exactly for which careers the various schools prepare you. You may think this is completely obvious: dog grooming school teaches you to be a groomer, cooking school to be a chef. But that's not always the case. For example, the dog grooming programs teach everything from being an assistant pet hygienist on up to owning your own grooming salon, and cooking trainings cover being a personal chef, a cooking teacher, a nutritional consultant, and working for a caterer, restaurant, or health center. As you pore over the catalogs you receive, tease out all the potential careers, not just the most obvious. Discard the uninteresting and otherwise inappropriate careers, and you have a list of your possible future vocational fields.

Do a little research on all of them. First check out magazines, Web sites, books. Get a sense of the field: Is it growing? What challenges is it facing? Does it seem to be cooperative or competitive? Is it too obscure to even find information about? Too conventional to be interesting? You can get a fairly strong sense of a profession from an afternoon spent at a bookstore, library, or on-line search engine, and that's all you need for background.

Then, for the careers that are still in the running, there are basically two questions you want to answer: Will you like working in the field? And will you make a living working in the field?

Predicting Job Satisfaction

You like animals. You like design. You like working with your hands. What could be better than pet grooming? Good question. But you don't have to spend thousands of dollars and months of study to find out that maybe, as you also like chocolate, you'd have been happier being a candymaker. Instead, you research your probable job satisfaction before getting involved in the field.

Talk to people who are already doing whatever it is you're considering being trained to do. Find them in the Yellow Pages. Search for them on-line. Ask friends and family for contacts. Once you locate a handful of people who are working in your prospective field, ask them anything and everything:

- How did they get involved in the field?
- Is it a good time to get started?
- What are the major obstacles and opportunities?
- How do they spend most of their time? (Sometimes this is very different from what you'd expect, given the name of the job. Owners of floral design shops may spend all their time marketing and almost none of it actually working with flowers, for example.)
- What are their favorite and least favorite parts of the job and the field?

And so on. Most people will be flattered that you're so interested in what they do, and will be happy to spend some time talking with you.

Then, if it's practical, ask if you can spend a couple of hours working for them (for free, of course). We can't recommend this highly enough. Nothing will give you a better sense of whether or not you'll like working in a particular field than working, if only briefly, in that field. Of course, the more time you spend, the more accurate a picture you'll get of the careers, but any time is better than none.

If hands-on interning is not practical (in therapy or bodywork, for example), but you're highly interested in the career, consider paying for a session or two to get a picture of the practitioner at work.

Researching Income Potential

After identifying a potentially satisfying career, you have to determine if it's lucrative enough to support you in the manner to which you would like to become accustomed. As we mentioned in the Introduction, there are people making a living in all of the careers in this book. But some are geared toward a comfortable living, and some are geared toward a more white-knuckled, pray-the-rent-check-doesn't-bounce lifestyle. Although it's true that what you get out of a career depends on what you put in—and people do make surprisingly good incomes in goofy-sounding careers—there are more- and less-profitable vocations.

Finding out where your future field falls on this spectrum requires just a touch more research.

If you're interested in a fairly well-established career (such as, for example, dog grooming or floral designing), the best place to start is at the reference desk of your local library. Reference librarians are an endless source of all that is good: ask them where to find information on salaries and wages for your field. If it's not too alternative, you'll have no trouble finding exactly what you want to know.

On the other hand, if you're thinking of going into something a bit less conventional, like balloon piloting, colon hydrotherapy, or saddlemaking, there is probably no information to be found. But that's okay. Because even if you did find some generic information in the library, the best way to get the real scoop is, again, to talk to people in the field.

You were already going to ask them about career satisfaction. Now you'll have just a few more questions regarding income potential. Ask them about:

- The job market. Are there more jobs than job hunters? What does an entry-level person get paid?
- The possibility of self-employment. What does it cost to get started? How difficult is it to find clients? How much can you expect to make in the first few years? Can you start a business part-time?
- Advice for additional income. How do people in the field make more money? If they were starting over, what would they focus on to help them get a good job or attract clients?

You may find that, while it's true that practitioners make $60 an hour, they tend to bill only ten hours a week. It's still a living, but it's not a six-figure, shiny-new-car living.

Finally, when you contact grads to research the schools (see Student Satisfaction, below), ask them the same questions—about both vocational and financial satisfaction.

By the time you finish your research, you'll most likely discover you've already made a decision. At some point, consciously or otherwise, you probably identified one or two careers that are clearly your favorites. If so, congratulations.

If not, spend some time evaluating all the information you received in light of what you know about yourself. Will you enjoy a career that requires much marketing? Is the ease or difficulty of a job hunt the most important factor for you? Do you want to avoid well-established fields, or does the chaos of an emerging field give you a rash? And consider satisfaction versus remuneration. It's all about your own priorities and preferences. Do as much research as you can, and follow your instincts.

Selecting Schools ◆ ◆ ◆

Once you've determined your single favorite field (or, if you're indecisive, your favorite two or three), focus on the schools themselves. There are six features—Cost, Location, Duration, Curriculum and Classes, Student Satisfaction, and Career Opportunities—that will help you evaluate schools and choose the best one for you.

Cost

The cost of a program shouldn't be its most important feature. We know it's tempting to skim through the listings and disregard everything that costs more than your upper limit, but we hope you don't. Some of the more expensive programs provide such thorough training that you're virtually guaranteed to make more money in the long run. And some of the cheaper programs . . . well, you get what you pay for. That's not to say that all of the more affordable programs are inferior to their expensive brethren: we just don't want price to be your first and last consideration.

But how do you attend a program that costs more than you can afford?

Many of the programs, and almost all the expensive ones, offer some sort of payment or installment plan, financial aid, work study, or at least accept credit cards. If the brochure or catalog mentioned a payment plan, we noted it in the listing. But even if the listing doesn't say anything about financing, you ought to ask. Things change, exceptions are made, and payment options vary. If a school does offer financing, seriously consider it—investing in your future career isn't such a terrible use of credit.

That's the good news. The bad news is this: we included the total cost—tools, supplies, fees, and assorted other expenses—if the school catalog or brochure mentioned them. If they didn't, we didn't. So always ask about tools, supplies, books, equipment, manuals, fees, registration costs, and any additional expenses.

Finally, if the school includes housing in their tuition, the listing says so. But even if the school provided the information, we didn't list all the possible housing options—motels, dorms, apartments—and what they cost. Most schools continually update housing lists and options. Ask them for current information.

Location

Within the subject activities, we organized the training programs by state. Obviously, it's easiest to attend a training near your home. Sometimes, though, the most attractive program will be in the least attractive place—thousands of miles away, in an urban sprawl or isolated hamlet. And you may not be able to travel any distance for a number of reasons—kids, a job you can't (yet) leave, and so on.

But we'll say it again: The most important thing is the quality of the education. If you'll be spending five or ten years happily working in your new career, how much does the couple of months you spent training in a distant city matter? If you simply can't do it, fine. But if your perfect training program is too far away for comfort, but not impossible, think seriously about making a short-term sacrifice.

However, you do have to factor in the costs: housing, travel, storage, and so on. Any good school will offer some help with the first of these. They'll send you lists of housing possibilities, ranging from in-school dorms to homestay situations to the rental section of the local classifieds. With the other expenses, you're probably on your own—just be sure they don't take you by surprise.

If you're interested in a program that's far away, long-term, and part-time, ask the school about the local job market—and ask if they'll introduce you to potential employers, preferably in the field you'll be studying.

Duration

The training programs range from weekend seminars to full-time, multiyear residential courses. If you're considering a brief program, you've got it easy—as long as you're certain you'll be willing to hang out a shingle or apply for a job without more comprehensive training. (We don't mean that you *shouldn't* be willing to do so. Just make sure you are.)

Some of the greatest benefits of short-term trainings are what they *don't* include: worry about making a living, finding housing, and missing work while enrolled in a lengthy program.

But you should also find out what they *do* include: What additional or advanced training is offered? What percentage of students go on to make a living in the career? Are there on-the-job training or apprenticeship opportunities if you're not entirely confident with your skills after completing the coursework? And does the program really prepare students to become practicing professionals or employable job candidates?

Longer programs have many benefits, too. In addition to the increased depth of instruction, students make a deeper commitment to the career and often develop deeper relationships with teachers and other students. You don't just toss away a year's worth of work because your first few months in your new job are rocky. And you can rely on the support of other graduates who are having the same problems and opportunities and want to share resources and newfound expertise.

Here are some questions to ask if you're considering a longer program: Is it full-time or part-time? If it's just evenings and weekends, can you hold a job while attending the training? If so, will the school help you find one in the field? Do students have access to tools, equipment, materials, and even instructors outside of class sessions? Are practice labs available? Can you begin to offer your services or products for sale before you finish the training?

Also note the difference between the number of hours of training and the program's overall duration. An intensive three-week course that meets fifty hours a week is almost certainly more comprehensive than a nine-month course that meets one weekend a month for six hours. Although the nine-month course may offer homework assignments, more time to absorb the material, and other benefits, the three-week course includes over three times more classroom instruction.

Curriculum and Classes

The backbone of every program is its curriculum and classes. So be sure you understand exactly what is offered before choosing a school. There are three questions you want answered: What's included? How is it presented? Who presents it?

The first question is straightforward. If you don't entirely under-stand what subjects are covered and what skills are taught after reading the listing in this book and the school's material, get on the phone. Ask exactly what you'll be taught. You want specifics. What skills will you learn? What techniques? What methods? Will you be introduced to people—employers, experts, workers—in the field? Is supervised prac-tice with clients available? Do students get to work on professional proj-ects? What extracurricular support is there? And so on.

Once you understand exactly what's involved, you want to know how it's taught. How do you like to learn? Through hands-on practice, lectures, demonstrations, independent study, group projects, or some combination? One student may love a school because it offers the opportunity to do self-directed work, make mistakes, and experiment. Another would hate the same program because it doesn't offer enough advice, direction, and supervision. Only you know your learning pref-erences, and it's your job to ensure that the school's teaching methods support them. So ask how they teach.

And while you're at it, ask about the student-teacher ratio. Many alternative training programs pride themselves on the small size of their classes: give them a chance to brag. If the classes aren't small, ask if and how you can expect to be given individual attention and instruction.

Finally, who teaches the classes? Is it the superstar director? Faculty members who are currently working in the field? Advanced students? Previous graduates? Ask who the instructors are, where they studied, and if they're working in the field as well as teaching about it. Ask if they are available to students during and after the training. Ask if they've been published or the subject of articles or books, and if they have, do a little reading.

Student Satisfaction

Bottom line: Does the training prepare students to get good jobs or build successful businesses? And the best way to find out is to ask the students themselves.

The programs should happily give you the names of some of their graduates (if they don't, beware). Of course, it's in their interest to refer you to students who liked the training and will give the program a good recommendation. But usually these students told the school they were willing to be quizzed about their situation. If you ask specific questions, you'll get specific answers, so don't be satisfied with generalized positive comments: quiz away.

Some schools provide the names of all the students who ever graduated, so don't be embarrassed to ask for more names if your school just offers two or three. And don't be embarrassed to call and get the information. It's your money, your time, and your future.

Here are some questions you can ask:

- Did you enjoy the training? How completely did it prepare you for real-world employment/self-employment?
- Would you go back to the same school if you had to do it over? What other schools have you heard good things about?
- What did you like most about the training? What did you like least? What would you change?
- Do you work full-time? How long did it take to get full-time work/build a strong client base?
- How much money do you make? (Go ahead and ask. Really.)
- What's the hardest part of making a living as a [whatever]? Does the school help with that?
- Does the school help with placement? Networking? What does it do for graduates?

And while you're talking to graduates about the school, don't forget to also ask questions about the career itself. How do they spend most of their time? Is there a growing demand for their services? Do they spend much time educating people about what they do, instead of being paid to do it?

Career Opportunities

Different training programs, even in the same subject, emphasize different careers. Some focus on preparing students for employment, some for self-employment. Some for one particular niche in a field, some for a more general practice. Make sure that your career goals and the program's career training are well matched.

For example, if you don't want the hassle of starting your own small business, you'll be frustrated in a program that teaches how to own and operate a mobile grooming van or a jewelry-making business. There are programs that emphasize employment in the grooming and jewelry fields that will be much more rewarding for you.

But beyond matching your goals and the school's training, you should also do a bit more career research. Ask the school about uncommon career opportunities. Ask what the most successful grads are doing. Ask what is unique about the way its program trains students for new careers.

For example, one student who graduated from an animal massage training course is now working at an aquarium, massaging walruses. Despite the fact that the schools focus on training students to massage horses, dogs, and cats, he's doing something completely unique. Every career has some interesting, obscure, possibly profitable niches: ask and maybe you'll find one that's perfect for you.

The Final Analysis

There are four final issues to consider when you're evaluating schools: credibility and accreditation, placement and marketing assistance, advanced and additional training, and legalities and licensing.

Some of the schools are directed by, or affiliated with, big names in the field: instant credibility. For example, if you're interested in becoming a shamanic counselor, the fact that the Foundation for Shamanic Studies is Michael Harner's organization will mean something to you. And the American Arts program at Sotheby's is, well, at *Sotheby's*.

Credibility can also be a result of accreditation. In the fields in which accreditation is available, you ought to evaluate the worth of the accreditation and the accrediting organization or organizations. Make a few phone calls to various schools and practitioners, check out a couple of articles on the career. In fields with certifying or licensing boards, people tend to have very strong opinions about which are good and which are less good. If it's at all important, you just have to ask.

Some of the schools offer formal placement and marketing assistance. They have job banks, employee contacts, marketing manuals, and so on. Find out which of the schools you're interested in offer this sort of service. But if your favorite schools don't offer graduate assistance, don't give up. You may be able to encourage them to begin a placement program, using you as a guinea pig. All of the schools have some contacts in the field. And all have engaged in some marketing efforts. If a formal program doesn't exist, ask them how they'll informally help you succeed after you graduate (and have some ideas ready).

Several schools allow graduates to retake their entire course of study for free. Others offer specialized trainings to students who've mastered the basics. It seems a bit premature, before even beginning the initial training, to think about advanced or additional training. But it's good to know what's available. At some point, the training that now seems esoteric and lofty may just be the next natural step in your ongoing education.

Finally, licensing and legal issues. Very few of the careers we list require licensing. But for those careers in which licensing is an issue, you've got to know where you stand. If you're interested in a career that involves touching your clients or, to a lesser degree, offering therapy or wellness-enhancing advice or supplements, you'll want to determine your legal standing. What can you say and not say? What can you treat and not treat? Do you need to be licensed, and by whom? Requirements vary by career, state, and year. Ask the schools for the most current information.

If you don't want to do all of the above, that's fine. But every question you ask, every article you read, and every bit of information you gather will ultimately help you make the right decision and be confident you've done so. Instead of starting a training program and worrying if it's the right one, and if you're even in the right field, you'll be able to focus on what's important: getting the best possible education.

Of course, there is one more thing to focus on: making a living in your new career. And that's covered in chapter 3.

Chapter 3

✶ ✶ ✶ ✶

Planning for Profit

You've identified your favorite subjects. You've researched the most interesting and potentially rewarding careers. And you've evaluated the training programs. Now comes the big question: How, exactly, will you make a living after you're trained?

Almost all of the programs focus more on teaching the subject than on training you to maximize your earning potential. That's not such a bad priority. And many schools do offer some instruction in financial matters—through placement programs, job-hunting seminars, marketing and small-business intensives, and so on.

But the best time to think about making a living in your new career is right now. Not only do you gain confidence about your training decision (or, equally valid, decide to abandon it entirely for another program), you also prepare to make money in the field. Your research today becomes money in the bank tomorrow. And that research covers three ways to make a living in your new career: employment, self-employment, and some combination of the two.

Get a Job ♦ ♦ ♦

What can you do before beginning a training program that will help you make money once you're fully certified and ready to roll? Three things: networking, focusing, and researching.

If you do nothing else, network. We can almost guarantee you a successful job hunt if, before you make the investment in a training program, you engage in a thorough shmoozing campaign. You'll meet potential employers, coworkers, experts, and allies of every description. Yes, these are the same people you spoke with while researching careers, but now you're (a) widening the net and (b) focusing on a career you *know* you want to enter.

So the first step is to identify as many people in the field as possible. Local employers, and the people who work for them, are a great place to start. But also contact employers in other locations, trade associations, newsletter or magazine columnists, authorities and experts, people with web sites, and even professionals in related fields.

Then call them. *Ask* if you can ask for their advice. Tell them your career plan. Ask for their feedback. Ask about local job opportunities, career possibilities, and so on.

And then listen. This step is the most difficult, particularly if you've already decided to go ahead with the training no matter what anyone says. And, frankly, you're most interested right now in making contacts. Still, these people are experienced in the field you want to enter. Listen to what they say, and consider acting on it.

The final step is this: *write* a thank-you note. We know it's old, stale advice. But it works. They'll remember who you are when you contact them again in the future. It just takes a minute, and it's polite, too.

If you do the above, what will you have accomplished? Lots. After you complete the training and are looking for a job, you'll be connected. You'll know people. They'll know people. And if you listened to their kind advice, they might even be a bit invested in you (only a bit, sure, but it all helps). Then, when you're looking for a job, ask them for leads. Maybe they'll be hiring. Maybe they'll know someone who is. Maybe they'll only know someone who might be. In any case, you'll be much better off than if you didn't make those connections early on.

The second way to increase your attractiveness to potential employers before completing your training is to focus your course of study.

When you're gathering advice and networking, ask what specialty or niche, what specific skills or techniques, are most appealing to prospective employers. If employers are looking for jewelry makers who can cut diamonds, or whole foods cooks who specialize in desserts, or doulas who provide both pre- and postpartum help, you want to know about it *before* you begin training. You can still study a broad range of subjects, but you will be able to focus on the most marketable skills. Ask what employers look for in new employees and then make sure you study those things.

Finally, research. The more you know about your field, the more attractive you are as a prospective employee. Read books on the subject, subscribe to magazines, trade journals, and newsletters, and even attend conferences or meetings if you can. Learn about the trends, politics, problems, philosophies, and potential of your field. If you're thinking of attending a publishing seminar, for example, and have been religiously reading *Publishers Weekly* for months, you'll be able to drop some names and speak to some issues that will pass right over the heads of your fellow students. If you'll be looking for work as a brewer, the knowledge you cull from *American Brewer* and *Modern Brewery Age* may well give you the extra job-seeking edge. And the time to start is now.

Hire Yourself ◆ ◆ ◆

The pretraining preparation for self-employment is much the same as that for employment: networking is extremely important, focusing on a niche market or service increases your earning potential, and researching gives you the extra edge. But there are differences.

Instead of networking with prospective employers, you'll be networking with future colleagues and prospective clients. Although some of them may not be thrilled with the additional competition, many of your future colleagues will be happy to help with advice, referrals, and all sorts of "been there, done that" guidance. If you start a conversation with them, you never know where it may lead: you could develop a mentor relationship, a marketing partner (wherein you share the costs and rewards of marketing), or just a supportive and informed friend. So call, chat, and connect—colleagues can be an extremely rewarding resource.

But the ultimate foundation of a business isn't colleagues. It's clients. And even though you won't be starting a marketing campaign and connecting with many individual clients, you can do some very valuable work.

How? ◆ ◆ ◆

Identify and connect with gatekeepers. What people or groups serve the same clients? Provide a similar benefit? Meet a related need? Where do your future clients gather? What groups or associations do they join? Those people, places, and groups are all gatekeepers to your future market, and they have valuable access to the people you want to serve.

So talk to them. Tell them what you're doing, ask for their advice, and thank them kindly. Then, once you're ready to get to work, you'll have a network of people who know and possibly even support you. You might get referrals, a note in a newsletter, a place to offer a class or demonstration, or any number of other benefits. Contacts are the lifeblood of small business—don't wait until you need them to begin cultivating them. Start now.

While focusing your training for self-employment, don't just emphasize marketable skills and techniques (as you would if you were interested only in employment). Define and narrow your market, too. It's called niche marketing, and it's one of the most powerful small business tools. In one sentence, it's this: Focus your business to serve one small (niche) population, meeting its very specific needs instead of trying to sell to everybody. This might sound backward: how can you make a more successful business with a smaller market? Shouldn't small businesses try to broaden and expand their markets, to sell to everybody? After all, that's what the multinational corporate overlords do, and they make a tidy profit.

But you're not them. For a small business, especially one just starting up, you'll make more money and serve more people if you focus on one small slice of the market. So instead of starting a business massaging animals, you focus on massaging racing dogs. Instead of paying equal attention to all facets of floral designing, you focus on funeral arrangements. Instead of learning to promote general health, you focus on working with children, or new mothers, or people with asthma. Then you'll know exactly who your market is and, equally important, they'll know exactly who you are.

You probably won't be able to make a decision about which niche market to serve until your training is under way. But always keep it in mind. Can you build a specialized kind of furniture, or furniture for people with special needs? Can you focus on offering Feng Shui consultations to small businesses or new home owners? Can you offer movement therapy to chronically ill people or actors? Niche marketing has made the difference between failure and success for many businesses. Let it work its magic for you.

One last bit of advice if you're considering self-employment: Don't be afraid of marketing. Many people who get into alternative careers equate marketing with used-car salesmanship. They think it's shallow, exploitative, expensive, and boring. And it can be. But it can also be honest, creative, affordable, and even a bit of fun—and it is absolutely vital for the success of your business. So if you'll be working for yourself, you must read at least several small business and marketing books. You may be the greatest piano tuner or spiritual healer in the country, but that doesn't pay the rent. Clients, attracted by marketing, pay the rent.

All of the Above ◆ ◆ ◆

Some of the training programs concentrate on preparing students for either employment or self-employment. The publishing programs, for example, tend to train students to get jobs in publishing, while most hypnotherapy programs assume students will be working for themselves. But in many of the careers, you don't need to choose one or the other. You can do a bit of both.

By combining employment and self-employment, you can get the benefits of both worlds: a secure paycheck, creative freedom, some self-direction, some supervision, part-time coworkers, and so on. If you have no clear preference, give some serious thought to finding a part-time job and starting a part-time business. In fact, it may be your best option even if you do have a clear preference for employment or self-employment.

Let's say you can't wait to go into business for yourself. You hate bosses, supervision, not being in charge. Still, easing slowly into self-employment is often the best way. You pay the rent with a part-time job while getting your business off the ground. You start marketing, attracting clients, building a reputation. Then, when you're truly ready, you can leave your job and devote yourself full-time to your business.

On the other hand, if you aren't at all interested in self-employment—the uncertainty, the risk, the solitude—you'll want to stick with a job. But if you're having trouble finding full-time work, consider taking on the occasional private client. Not only will the additional income help, but you may uncover hidden entrepreneurial passions as well.

Finally, flexibility is a virtue. Every field has many, often hidden, opportunities. You can write books or articles, organize conferences, start a newsletter, or found an association. You can consult, teach, or popularize. You can sell retail or wholesale, through catalogs or sales reps. If your career focuses on selling a service, you can develop a matching product, or vice versa. The possibilities go on. Although it's a fine place to start, don't limit yourself to doing the same work everyone else is doing. You bring your own interests, strengths, and expertise to the field: study it, work at it, master it, and make it your own.

PART II

★ ★ ★ ★

Chapter 4

✳ ✳ ✳ ✳

Animals

Animals are an American obsession—the horse and the pet industries generate billions of dollars every year. If you share the obsession, this chapter is for you. It introduces animal-related careers that range from the fairly conventional, such as dog grooming and training, pet sitting, and kennel and stable management, to the less common, such as animal massage, zookeeping, animal communication, and therapeutic riding instruction. These training programs prepare you to make a living with animals, whether you're interested in teaching, beautifying, managing, handling, or healing them.

Animal Massage ◆ ◆ ◆

Animal massage, though it sounds airy-fairy, can be a very solid career. If you love animals, healing, and working with your hands, you may have found your perfect vocation. Many practitioners specialize in horse massage—a strong market, particularly in areas associated with horse farms and the horse-racing industry. Others focus on massaging household pets, helping old or ill dogs and cats feel and heal better. Although several of the programs recommend that students take additional courses in human massage, they are not required.

TTouch International
P.O. Box 3739
Santa Fe, NM 87501
(800) 854-8326
(505) 455-2945
Fax: (505) 455-7233

TTouch International offers a professional TTouch Practitioner training and certification program. TTouch is a hands-on technique used to improve the physical, emotional, and mental health of companion animals. The training program teaches students to identify problems and implement creative solutions using bodywork, ground exercises, and techniques for specific issues such as fear, stress, barking, biting, trauma, and recovery from surgery and accidents. Other lessons cover pain-free grooming and how to train animals with understanding and compassion. Students also learn how to market their skills to meet the growing demand for alternative animal care.

TTouch International also offers advanced training to students who want to become TT.E.A.M. (TTouch Equine Awareness Method) Practitioners, who use TTouch techniques that encourage understanding and partnership with horses and resolve behavioral and physical difficulties. In addition to intensive workshops, the TT.E.A.M. training includes completing case studies and attending a refresher or advanced course every eighteen months.

How long it takes: TTouch Practitioner—2 years (6 8-day sessions)
TT.E.A.M. Practitioner—4 weeks

What it costs: TTouch Practitioner—$5,000
TT.E.A.M. Practitioner—$650

A payment plan is available.

Don Doran's Equine Sports Massage Programs
14735 Southwest 71 Avenue Road
Ocala, FL 34473
(352) 347-3747
Fax: (352) 347-8075

Don Doran offers two training programs: a professional course in Equine Sports Massage, and an Equi-Pressure practitioner course.

The Equine Sports Massage course teaches students to apply the principles of human sports massage on horses to relieve tension and stress, increase circulation, and reduce muscle fatigue. The curriculum includes courses in equine anatomy, physiology, kinesiology, and acu-pressure. Students learn hands-on applications of equine sports massage, contraindications, therapeutic techniques, neuromuscular therapy, mo-tion evaluation, stretching, pre- and postevent massage, alternative healing methods, and equine communication skills. Business skills such as networking and advertising are also taught.

The Equi-Pressure course teaches equine acupressure, which is the nonintrusive stimulation of specific energy points on a horse's body to maintain and restore vitality and health. The program trains students to use Equi-Pressure to give horses a competitive edge, stimulate good attitude, stamina, and health, locate and use the fourteen major energy channels of the horse's body, evaluate potential problem areas, and to combine Equi-Points with magnetic therapy.

Students work with many breeds of horses and a variety of equine health problems associated with racing, jumping, dressage, driving, endurance, and polo. Before attending the course, students must have a knowledge of horsemanship and feel comfortable working with horses. Although it is not a requirement of the program or the profes-sion, Don Doran suggests that students complete a human massage training program prior to or after completion of the equine massage training.

How long it takes: Equine Sports Massage course—100 hours in 12 days
Equi-Pressure course—6 days

What it costs: Equine Sports Massage Course—$1,395
Equi-Pressure Course—$695

Optissage
7041 Zane Trail Road
Circleville, OH 43113
(800) 251-0007
(614) 474-6436
Fax: (614) 474-2625

Optissage offers massage training programs for students who want to work with horses, dogs, and cats. Each of the courses covers the anatomy and physiology of the animal being studied, adapted massage techniques—including Swedish and sports massage techniques—acupressure points, massage theory, business practices, and animal behavior. The classes usually have eight or fewer students and two instructors, so each student gets personalized attention and the opportunity to perform hands-on work. For the canine and feline courses, students are encouraged to bring their own animals, although it's not required.

How long it takes: Equine program — 11 days
Canine program—6 days
Feline program—2 days

What it costs: Equine program—$1,600
Canine program—$598
Feline program—$199

Credit cards are accepted.

Equissage
P.O. Box 447
Round Hill, VA 20142
(800) 843-0224
(540) 338-1917

Equissage offers a certification program in equine sports massage. Students learn hands-on techniques that improve circulation, relax muscle spasms, enhance muscle tone, relieve tension, and increase range of motion in high-performance horses. The program covers the application of massage techniques and strokes, the physiology of muscles, the location of major muscles and muscle groups, and specific conditions that may affect horses due to strained, pulled, tired, or sore muscles. The program is geared to meet the increasing demand of racehorse and show horse owners and trainers for equine massage services that alleviate horses' stress and heal their sore and strained muscles.

How long it takes: 5 days

What it costs: $795

Credit cards are accepted.

Dog Training • • •

Most of the schools that teach dog training focus on obedience training for domestic dogs, teaching them to understand standard commands and stop unwanted behaviors. Others specialize in training police dogs, drug-sniffing dogs, or assistance dogs for the handicapped. This career could be right for you if you have a way with dogs—and, equally important, with their often less-trainable owners—and have had fun and success training your own dogs.

Affection Dog Training School
330 East Capella Avenue
La Habra, CA 90631
(888) 522-6463
(562) 697-0234

The school offers a professional dog trainer course that emphasizes specialized techniques for different dog temperaments. Subjects covered in the course include discipline, training principles, trainer attitude, interpreting canine body language, commands such as sit, heel, sit-stay, down-stay, come, stand-stay, and retrieve, and behavioral problems such as excessive barking, destructive chewing, digging, door dashing, fence jumping, and house soiling. Other topics include advertising, conducting training sessions with clients, evaluating canine temperament and trainability, and how to sell the training program to clients.

How long it takes: Class time is flexible, but students who attend full-time (meeting 4 times per week) can complete the course in 5 weeks.

What it costs: $2,500

A payment plan is available.

Dog Lovers
5000 Crenshaw Boulevard
Los Angeles, CA 90043
(213) 298-8811

Dog Lovers offers two training courses: Obedience Dog Training and Behavior Therapy, and Obedience and Personal Protection. The

Obedience Dog Training and Behavior Therapy course trains students to correct behavior problems such as digging, barking, and jumping, and trains dogs to obey such commands as sit, stay, heel, lie down, and come. In the Obedience and Personal Protection course, students learn to train protection dogs. The program includes classes in aptitude testing, guarding, breed personality, hand signals, basic retrieving, and attacking on command.

How long it takes:　Obedience Dog Training and Behavior Therapy—
6 months (full-time) or 12 months (part-time)
Obedience and Personal Protection—12 months (full-time) or 24 months (part-time)

What it costs:　Obedience Dog Training and Behavior Therapy—
$4,550
Obedience and Personal Protection—$8,500

Dog Lovers also offers pet-grooming courses. See Pet Grooming for information below in this chapter.

National Institute of Dog Training
Margolis Enterprises, Inc.
11275 National Boulevard
Los Angeles, CA 90064
(800) 334-3647
(310) 445-4671
Fax: (310) 312-1832
www.matthewmargolis.com

The institute offers instruction in dog training through a two-part home-study program. Part I teaches students to use love, praise, and affection to train dogs. They learn how to understand and communicate with dogs, and how to help families bond with them. Other subjects taught include breeds and classifications of dogs, temperament and personality testing, problem solving (including barking and housebreaking), training to heel, sit, come, and lie down, off-the-leash techniques, basic medical information, and dog nutrition. Part II teaches the business side of dog training, including instruction in marketing, setting prices, personal selling, developing a sales plan, conducting classes that serve as a marketing tool, and creating a newsletter that boosts your business. Students also receive a complete office procedures manual, staffing suggestions, and an employee handbook. An optional in-person review and certification program is available, as is a toll-free help line.

How long it takes: Correspondence course—students work at their own pace.

What it costs: $1,010

Several payment plan options are available.

Pro-Train Institute
3131 Protea Vista
Terrace Vista, CA 92084
(760) 941-4241
www.value-link.com/protrain.html

The Pro-Train Institute offers a complete professional dog-training course. The program covers Kennel Management, Obedience Dog Training, Protection and Police Dog Training, and Service Dog Training. The Kennel Management classes cover breeding, sanitation, grooming, nutrition, whelping, and handling techniques. The Obedience Dog Training section offers instruction in dog psychology, sociology, behavior modification techniques, puppy training, and how to run a dog obedience class. The Protection and Police Dog Training sessions cover personal protection, obstacle course training, training dogs in scent discrimination, tracking and trailing procedures, and agitation techniques. And, finally, in the Service Dog Training classes, students learn how to teach dogs to lead, go around obstacles, stop at curbs, travel in a straight line, ignore distractions, and build initiative, responsibility, and appropriate disobedience.

How long it takes: 500 hours

What it costs: $8,000
Cost includes room and board.

Credit cards are accepted and financing is available.

The Connecticut K-9 Education Center
239 Maple Hill Avenue
Newington, CT 06111
(203) 666-4646

The Connecticut K-9 Education Center offers three dog training and management courses: Kennel Management, Professional Dog Training, and Professional Guard and Attack Dog Training. The Kennel Management curriculum includes kennel design, equipment and supplies, maintaining kennel records, canine nutrition, breeding techniques, raising puppies, health and first aid, grooming, and basic obedience training. The program offers practical experience with kennel maintenance, care of pregnant bitches, laboratory procedures (such as fecal exams, mange scrapings, and heartworm checks), socializing young dogs, and handling fearful or nervous dogs.

The Professional Dog Training course offers students hands-on experience training dogs in basic and advanced obedience, public obedience, and obstacle course training (climbing, crawling, and jumping skills). Students also learn about various types of training equipment, public relations, behavior problems, canine psychology, puppy training, and safety precautions.

The Professional Guard and Attack Dog Training program teaches students to train personal protection dogs, area security dogs, and guard and attack dogs. This course is only for those who have mastered basic and advanced training skills.

How long it takes: Kennel Management—10 weeks
Professional Dog Training—14 weeks
Professional Guard and Attack Dog Training—
5 weeks

What it costs: Kennel Management—$2,850
Professional Dog Training—$2,850
Professional Guard and Attack Dog Training—
$1,450

Payment plans are available.

Alpha Canine Professional Dog Instructor Certification
P.O. Box 11322
St. Petersburg, FL 33733-1322
(813) 319-2900
Fax: (813) 398-0952

Alpha Canine offers a professional dog trainer program that covers On and Off Leash Obedience, and Behavior Modification. The On and Off

Leash Obedience classes teach students how to train dogs to follow commands (such as sit-stay, down-stay, come, sit, finish, and release), how to use hand signals, and how to time praise and corrections. The Behavior Modification classes teach students to identify and treat different types of unwanted behaviors, such as aggression, phobias, obsessive/compulsive behaviors, and separation anxiety. The program also covers canine history, psychology, and health, and introduces the business skills needed to start up a dog-training business: marketing and sales strategies, record keeping, and presentation and consultation techniques.

After completing the above, students may take postgraduate studies in aggression training, tricks and stunts, and assistance training for the physically impaired. Aggression training is designed to harness a dog's aggression and use it as a weapon for protection. Tricks and stunts training prepares students to teach dogs, well, tricks and stunts, for performances in the circus, theater, or television entertainment. And the assistance training course teaches how to train canine companions for physically impaired people who need canine assistance and companionship.

How long it takes: 6 months

What it costs: $5,995

Credit cards are accepted.

Academy of Canine Education
75-63 185th Street
Fresh Meadows, NY 11366
(718) 454-5800
Fax: (718) 264-0463

The academy offers a certificate program in professional dog training. Students receive hands-on training. They work with a variety of breeds to learn about dog temperament and instincts, learned behavior and socialization, and basic obedience training. The course also teaches hand signals, the proper use of correction and praise, how to housebreak dogs, and how to handle chewing, barking, aggression, and shyness. Other classes include Advanced Training, Protection Training, Dog Breeds, Vaccines/Common Ailments, Nutrition, Grooming, and Kenneling. Small business topics such as writing a business plan, customer relations, and working with clients are also covered.

How long it takes: Part-time—7 to 12 weeks
　　　　　　　　　　Full-time—4 weeks

What it costs:　$1,995

Payment plans are available.

Canines of America
New York Center for Dog Training and Clinical Behavior Therapy
89-10 Eliot Avenue
Rego Park, NY 11374
(718) 651-3840
Fax: (718) 651-7681
info@canines.com

Canines of America offers a program in Professional Dog Training. Students learn how to diagnose common behavior problems, develop treatment plans, work with clients and veterinarians, and obedience-train dogs in a humane but effective manner. Classes include Breed Identification, History of the Domestic Dog, Ethology and Behavior Modification, Learning and Development, Behavioral Pharmacology, Aggression, Phobias, and Obsessive Compulsive Behavior, Assessment, Diagnosis, and Treatment Program, Development of Dog Training Procedures and Technique, Puppy Training and Affecting Temperament Development, Instructor Skills Development, Animal Rescue, Kennel Management, Veterinary Medicine, and Developing a Training Plan.

How long it takes: 5 weeks

What it costs:　$3,000

Credit cards are accepted.

Canine Behavioral Institute
P.O. Box 1094
Marshalls Creek, PA 18335
(717) 588-1277
cbi2@ptd.net
www.pocc.com/~cbi

The institute offers a vocational course in dog training. The program first focuses on the basics of dog behavior and training and then allows students to explore individual interests. The curriculum is divided into four major fields: Canidology, Canine Sociology, Training, and Business Management. Canidology covers the history of the species, character and temperament, breeding, puppy growth, and health and nutrition. Canine Sociology includes anthropomorphism, human/canine relationships, and causes of and solutions to common behavior problems. Training teaches techniques, disciplining, obedience training, and advanced training techniques—including agility, protection, tracking, and ring sport. And Business Management covers business practices, sales, marketing, advertising, financial planning, and business plan development.

How long it takes: 12 weeks

What it costs: $3,995

School for Professional Dog Training
Kromerhaus Kennel
3247 Wimmer Road
Bethlehem, PA 18017
(610) 868-4009

The school offers a program in professional dog training that covers five subjects: Training, Grooming, Kennel Management, Police Protection and Security Training, and First Aid, Health Care, and Medical Care. The Training course covers obedience training, counseling dog owners, AKC showing, and agility training. The Grooming course introduces the fundamentals of dog and cat grooming, from basic baths to clips to grooming equipment. The Kennel Management course covers day-to-day kennel operations, record keeping, pet boarding, and dealing with employees. The Police Protection and Security Training course teaches students to train dogs for law enforcement agencies, prisons, and security firms. And the First Aid, Health Care, and Medical Care course covers health care and medical concerns, first aid for dogs, and what to have in a first aid kit for dogs and kennels. Other classes discuss bookkeeping, marketing, contracts, and other small business topics.

How long it takes: 1 month

What it costs: $3,500

West Virginia Canine College
P.O. Box 2078
Buckhannon, WV 26201
(304) 472-6691
Fax: (304) 472-6640

West Virginia Canine College offers a program in Dog Training. The curriculum includes obedience training, protection training, tracking and scent work, business ethics and management, conformation class and show ring etiquette, anatomy, nutrition, basic veterinary care, kennel management, protection dog training, personal protection training, and advanced tracking and man trailing. It also trains students to work with dogs on obstacle courses, which is designed to give dogs self-confidence.

How long it takes: 12, 8, or 4 weeks

What it costs: 12 weeks—$6,000
8 weeks—$4,200
4 weeks—$2,100

Payment plans and student loans are available.

Horse Management and Training ◆ ◆ ◆

The programs in this section teach a wide variety of skills, including stable management, riding and riding instruction, horse care and training, grooming, breeding, and even exercise riding and jockey skills. Because it doesn't focus on a single career, we recommend that, if you're looking for a horse-related job, you browse through all the listings. If you're interested in equine studies career trainings that lead to degree, call or write the Harness Horse Youth Foundation at 14950 Greyhound Court, Suite 210, Carmel, IN 46032, (317) 848-5132, and ask for *The Equine School and College Directory*.

Paradise Ranch Racing School
10268 LaTuna Canyon Road
Sun Valley, CA 91352
(818) 768-8708
Fax: (818) 252-4647

Paradise Ranch certifies Exercise Riders/Aspiring Jockeys, Grooms, and Racing Stable Managers/Aspiring Trainers. The Exercise Rider/ Aspiring Jockey course offers instruction in grooming and tacking the racehorse, mounting and dismounting, track terminology, track safety, posting and elevating, gaits, lengths of irons, seat and form, leg aids, use of weight as leverage, and use of stick. Other subjects taught include development of patience and confidence, communicating the horse's performance to the trainer, and the rules and regulations of racing.

The Groom training teaches students about tending and cleaning racehorses, recognizing leg problems, rubbing and bandaging, feeding and nutrition, medical treatments for lameness, understanding the body language of horses, and anatomy and conformation.

The Racing Stable Manager/Aspiring Trainer course offers instruction in horse care, training and conditioning, medication procedures and restrictions, horse race procedures (such as declarations and scratches and the claiming process), the client-trainer relationship, stable maintenance, and record keeping and scheduling.

How long it takes: Exercise Rider/Aspiring Jockey—1 to 3 months
Groom—1 to 3 months
Racing Stable Manager/Aspiring Trainer—1 to 3 months

The course length depends on the student's previous experience.

What it costs: Exercise Rider/Aspiring Jockey—$1,500 per month
Groom—$400 per month
Racing Stable Manager/Aspiring Trainer—$400 per month

Shasta College
11555 Old Oregon Trail
P.O. Box 496006
Redding, CA 96049
(916) 225-4660

Shasta College offers a certificate program in Equine Science that prepares students for work in horse training, horse grooming and care, and stable management. Core courses include Feeds and Feeding, Horsemanship, Horse Husbandry, Western and English Riding and

Training, Veterinary Practices, Horse Training, Agriculture Practices, Environmental Resources, Horseshoeing, and Horsepacking. Students are also required to take two career-planning courses.

How long it takes: 2 years

What it costs: State residents—$550
                     Nonresidents—$4,872
Financial aid is available.

College of Southern Idaho
Equine Program
315 Falls Avenue
Twin Falls, ID 83301
(208) 733-9554, ext. 2414
Fax: (208) 736-2136
jknight@evergreen2.csi.cc.id.us
www.csi.cc.id.us

The college offers a certificate training program in Horse Management that combines classroom learning and hands-on work. Classes include Basic Horseshoeing, Equine Nutrition, Equine Reproduction, Horse Health, Judging Horses, Anatomy of Unsoundness, Draft Horse Management, and Beginning, Intermediate, and Advanced English and Western Riding Skills. Students are also required to take Business Aspects of Raising Horses, which offers career planning for students interested in anything from starting a horse publication to becoming a horse breeder to working as a stable manager.

How long it takes: 1 year

What it costs: State residents—$1,650
                     Nonresidents—$3,650

Kentucky Horse Park
Education Department
4089 Iron Works Pike
Lexington, KY 40511
(800) 678-8813
(606) 259-4206
Fax: (606) 254-0253
www.horseworld.com/imh/kyhp/hp1.html

The Kentucky Horse Park offers two training programs: one in Equine Management and one in Equine Training and Development. The Equine Management program includes classes in stable management, horse care, anatomy, physiology, herd health, reproduction, mare and foal care, training, and riding. But students spend only a small portion of the day in the classroom. The majority of the training is spent caring for the many different breeds of horses at the park, each of which requires individual handling, feeding, grooming, and training.

The Equine Training and Development program is a work/study program that teaches the fundamentals of horse handling, care, and stable management. Students study and work on local farms to gain experience with different breeds of horses. Students who successfully complete the program are offered positions of employment on a Kentucky horse farm with a probationary period of six months.

How long it takes: Equine Management—5 months
Equine Training and Development—3 months

What it costs: Equine Management—$1,000
Equine Training and Development—$900

Pet Grooming ◆ ◆ ◆

If you're interested in becoming a pet groomer, you have plenty of training options: this is by far the largest section in the Animals chapter. These schools prepare students for careers that range from entry-level assistant pet grooming to owning and managing a groom shop. In addition to regular dog grooming, many schools teach cat grooming, show grooming, pet health issues, how to set up a mobile pet-grooming business, and other special skills. If you love animals, enjoy working with your hands, and have a flair for design, comb through the following training programs. Many of the pet-grooming schools offer some affordable housing options: be sure to call for more information if necessary.

Cal-A-Hi Dog Grooming School
282 Camino Norte
Chico, CA 95973
(916) 343-1554

Cal-A-Hi trains professional dog groomers. The program focuses on poodle, terrier, and cocker grooming, but also covers grooming of other pure and mixed breeds. The curriculum includes brushing, combing, bathing, dematting, cleaning ears, clipping nails, fluff drying, and clipping the face, feet, tail, and stomach. Courses cover such topics as dog anatomy and ear structure, first aid for dogs and groomers, pest extermination, skin disorders, handling or refusing aggressive dogs, shop design, breed styling for show dogs and pets, and tools of the trade. Some portion of each class is spent on grooming dogs for show.

How long it takes: 12 weeks

What it costs: $2,200

Payment plans are available.

Beaugay's School of Dog Grooming
385 First Street
Los Altos, CA 94022
(415) 948-4911

Beaugay's course offers hands-on experience grooming poodles, cockers, terriers, and mixed-breed dogs. Students learn drying techniques, shampooing, nail clipping, scissoring, dematting, undercoat raking, and finishing.

How long it takes: 8 weeks

What it costs: $1,700

Dog Lovers
5000 Crenshaw Boulevard
Los Angeles, CA 90043
(213) 298-8811

Dog Lovers offers four grooming courses: Pet Hygienist, All Breed Dog and Cat Grooming, Pet Poodle Grooming, and Grooming and Pet Shop Management. The Pet Hygienist course includes instruction in bathing, defleaing, ear cleaning, nail clipping, dipping, tooth care, trimming, and problem dog handling. The All Breed Dog and Cat Grooming training covers breed recognition, all-breed styling, dematting, handling, brushing and trimming, nails, dipping, flea and tick control, and tooth and ear cleaning. The Pet Poodle Grooming course covers poodle styling and care. The Grooming and Pet Shop Management course includes, in addition to grooming skills, instruction in pet health problems, customer etiquette, opening a new store, pricing, bookkeeping, sanitation, nutrition, stocking, and mobile shop setup.

How long it takes: Pet Hygienist—6 weeks (part-time)
All Breed Dog and Cat Grooming—6 months (full-time) or 12 months (part-time)
Pet Poodle Grooming—6 months (full-time) or 12 months (part-time)
Grooming and Pet Shop Management—12 months (full-time) or 24 months (part-time)

What it costs: Pet Hygienist—$495
All Breed Dog and Cat Grooming—$4,550
Pet Poodle Grooming—$2,495
Grooming and Pet Shop Management—$7,300

Dog Lovers also offers dog-training courses: See Dog Training.

The San Francisco SPCA Pet Grooming College
2500 Sixteenth Street
San Francisco, CA 94103
(415) 554-3000
publicinfo@sfspca.org
www.sfspca.org

The college offers pet-grooming training. Students work on shelter cats and dogs, learning proper bathing and grooming techniques while giving the animals a better chance at adoption. Privately owned dogs are also available, so students do learn to groom a variety of breeds. Courses include Brushing and Bathing, Eye, Ear and Foot Care, Clipper Rough Cut, Scissors Finish, Shop Procedure, Skin Care, General Health, Equipment Maintenance, and Cat Grooming. Class size is limited to six students.

How long it takes: 12 weeks

What it costs: $2,215

Classy Pet Grooming School
1542 West Eisenhower Boulevard
Loveland, CO 80537
(970) 667-2766

The school offers a professional grooming program designed to train students in the basic grooming skills for all breeds of dogs and some cats. The curriculum includes selection and care of equipment, safety and sanitation, animal psychology and temperament, proper handling and restraining, anatomy and physiology, skin disorders and parasites, first aid, cat grooming, shop operation, creative grooming, and practical experience. Specific skills taught include prepping, bathing, drying, finishing, scissoring, pricing, and record keeping.

How long it takes: 12 weeks

What it costs: $3,400

Credit cards are accepted.

The Connecticut K-9 Education Center
239 Maple Hill Avenue
Newington, CT 06111
(203) 666-4646

The center offers a Professional Dog Grooming training course. The program includes instruction in AKC breed identification, canine psychology, shop management, safety precautions, fluff drying, ear plucking and cleaning, parasite control, poodle clips (such as the Bikini, Bolero, Dutch Cut, Lamb Cut, and Puppy Cut), terrier cuts, and clipping and styling for mixed-breed dogs.

How long it takes: 10 weeks

What it costs: $2,850

Payment plans are available.

Edwardian School of Dog Grooming
16 Cross Street
New Canaan, CT 06840
(203) 966-4080

The Edwardian School offers a Professional Dog Groomer program. Subjects include anatomy, safety, sanitation, first aid, grooming basics, handling, brushing, combing, dematting, styling, setting patterns, bathing, drying, conditioning, grooming management, and finishing. If the school director feels that a student needs it, additional training is provided at no additional cost.

How long it takes: 10 weeks

What it costs: $3,200

All American School of Dog Grooming
2607 North Pine Hills Road
Orlando, FL 32808
(407) 293-5339

The All American School offers a Dog Grooming training course. The program includes classes on bathing, fluff drying, dipping, shampooing, clipper control and maintenance, grooming the face, stomach, and tush, stripping down, scissoring, setting patterns, and grooming poodle heads, feet, and teddy bear faces. Graduates are able to take a refresher course at no additional charge at any time within one year.

How long it takes: 10 weeks

What it costs: $1,525

Star Academy for Pet Stylists
2201 Southeast Indian Street, Unit C-6
Stuart, FL 34997
(561) 221-9330

Star Academy offers two levels of training: Basic All-Breed Grooming and professional master All-Breed Grooming Management.

The Basic All-Breed Grooming course teaches selection and care of equipment, safety and sanitation, first aid and CPR, anatomy, pest control, handling, clipping nails, cleaning ears, brushing, bathing, drying, clipping, scissoring, finishing, and cat grooming.

The Master All-Breed Grooming Management course teaches students to identify and groom every AKC breed, including advanced poodle grooming and creative grooming. Students also learn business management, retailing, boarding, and how to own and operate a professional grooming salon.

How long it takes: Basic All-Breed Grooming—11 weeks
Master All-Breed Grooming—19 weeks

What it costs: Basic All-Breed Grooming—$2,825
Master All-Breed Grooming—$4,450

Florida School of Dog Grooming
2315 North A Street
Tampa, FL 33609
(813) 254-2213

The Florida School of Dog Grooming trains professional dog groomers. The curriculum is divided into two sections: Grooming and Management. The Grooming courses cover basic equipment, bathing, flea dipping, cleaning ears, clipping nails, handling puppies and old dogs, poodle clipping, scissoring techniques (including styling and shaping the legs, body, topknot, mustache, and tail), caring for matted and tangled coats, and mastering pattern styling. The Management courses cover shop design, advertising, insurance, records and receipts, setting rates, bookkeeping, and boarding kennel management.

The school is also a working grooming salon, so students are able to work with customers and their pets in a professional setting. And the school also offers a refresher course at no additional charge for students who desire more training.

How long it takes: 12 weeks

What it costs: $2,825

A payment plan is available.

Academy of Dog Grooming Arts
1900 South Arlington Heights Road
Arlington Heights, IL 60005
(847) 228-5700
Fax: (847) 228-5700

The academy offers two professional training programs: Assistant Groomer and Professional Groomer.

The Assistant Groomer course trains students in the selection and care of equipment, safety and sanitation, dog anatomy and physiology, handling young, old, and aggressive dogs, skin disorders, parasites, bathing, drying, fur care, and animal CPR.

The Professional Groomer offers more advanced training in mixed breed poodle, terrier, spaniel, and long-hair breed styling, scissoring and finishing, cat grooming, and bow making. Other professional classes cover grooming the neglected pet, canine massage therapy, fluff and cage drying, and nutrition.

The academy also offers a Canine Cardiopulmonary Resuscitation seminar and a Shop Owner's course for those wishing to own or manage a grooming shop.

How long it takes: Assistant Groomer—6 weeks
Professional Groomer—13 weeks

What it costs: Assistant Groomer—$2,400
Professional Groomer—$3,900

The Nash Academy
857 Lane Allen Road
Lexington, KY 40504
(800) 788-5301
(606) 276-5301
Fax: (606) 277-1977

725 River Road
Edgewater, NJ 07020
(800) 788-5301
(201) 943-2710
Fax: (201) 945-2721

The Nash Academy's two schools each offers three levels of pet grooming training. Level I teaches brushing, combing, clipping nails, cleaning ears, preparatory clipping, bathing, drying, and basic finishing techniques. Level II teaches students to properly groom the most popular breeds of dogs (including poodles, cocker spaniels, and schnauzers) and cats. Level III trains students to perfect their grooming skills, increase their speed and efficiency, and concentrate on proper breed profile. Graduates of Level III may retake any of the trainings at no additional charge. The academy also offers a Japanese exchange program—students spend one month learning Japanese dog styling while living in Japan.

How long it takes: Level I—1 month
                         Level II—1 month
                         Level III—1 month

What it costs: Level I—$2,975
                         Level II—$1,000
                         Level III—$1,000

Payment plans and financing options are available.

Pedigree Career Institute
Harbor Mall, Route 1A
The Lynnway
Lynn, MA 01901
(800) 615-3647
(617) 592-3647
Fax: (617) 593-4454
info@pedigreecareer.com
www.pedigreecareer.com

The institute's Professional All-Breed Dog and Cat Grooming program is organized into four levels: Brushing and Bathing, Terriers and Sporting Breeds, Poodles and Non-Sporting Breeds, and Transition to Workplace. Brushing and Bathing covers the fundamentals of pet care, first-response medical procedures, muscular and skeletal anatomy, identifying specific coat textures and common skin and parasitic conditions, and selecting and applying appropriate shampoos and other products. The Terriers and Sporting Breeds course teaches breed profiles, history, origin, ancestry, coat texture, and general temperament of long- and short-legged terriers. It also offers instruction in clipping, scissoring, hand stripping, plucking, and carding. The Poodles and Non-Sporting Breeds course teaches a minimum of three poodle show trims and four poodle pet trims, grooming patterns for mixed-breed dogs, and handling and grooming cats. Specialty tools are introduced, and clipper and scissor techniques are emphasized. Transition to Workplace covers advanced grooming techniques such as drop coat scissoring, but focuses on teaching grooming shop management: starting and setting up a shop, purchasing, pricing, and selling retail items, marketing, establishing fees, using revenue-generating tie-ins, and record keeping and time management.

The institute offers job placement assistance, and, for the grooming entrepreneur, a current list of grooming businesses for sale.

How long it takes: 5 months

What it costs: $5,800

Installment plans and private loans are available.

Baltimore School of Dog Grooming
1007 West 41st Street
Baltimore, MD 21211
(410) 889-9070

The school offers two training programs: a Dog Groomer's Assistant program and a Professional All-Breed Dog Groomer program.

The Dog Groomer's Assistant program prepares students to assist professional dog groomers. Topics include bathing, ear cleaning, fluff drying, nail manicuring, coat conditioning, canine geriatrics, and sanitation.

The Professional All-Breed Dog Groomer program prepares students to own and operate their own business or to find employment at a grooming salon. In addition to all the courses offered in the assistant program, the professional program teaches pattern placement and styling, straight scissoring techniques, genetics and breeding, boarding kennel management, equipment maintenance, advertising, bookkeeping, shop operation, and customer relations.

How long it takes: Dog Groomer's Assistant—10 weeks
                     Professional All-Breed Dog Groomer—10 weeks

What it costs: Dog Groomer's Assistant—$1,200
                     Professional All-Breed Dog Groomer—$4,900

Payment plans are available.

Maryland School of Dog Grooming
8025 13th Street
Silver Spring, MD 20910
(800) 543-3228
(301) 585-4311
Fax: (301) 585-7683

The school offers three training programs: Poodle Grooming, All-Breed Dog Grooming, and Grooming Shop and Kennel Management. The Poodle Grooming course is the basic training, teaching clipping, brushing, combing, fluff drying, and bathing. It also teaches how to scissor a poodle—a most difficult but rewarding skill.

The All-Breed Dog Grooming course continues the training with classes on short-legged terriers, long-legged terriers, soft-coated terriers, Bouvier des Flandres, Old English sheepdogs, sporting dogs, long-haired dogs, short-haired dogs, and cats.

Students who want to operate or manage a grooming shop or kennel take the Grooming Shop and Kennel Management course, which covers first aid, business practices, kennel design, computer knowledge, obedience training, show grooming and handling, and building a clientele. The All-Breed Dog Grooming course is a prerequisite for Grooming Shop and Kennel Management.

How long it takes: Poodle Grooming—7 weeks
All-Breed Dog Grooming—14 weeks
Grooming Shop and Kennel Management—
12 weeks

What it costs: Poodle Grooming—$3,100
All-Breed Dog Grooming—$4,150
Grooming Shop and Kennel Management—$2,700

Payment plans are available and credit cards are accepted.

The Missouri School of Dog Grooming
9611 Olive Boulevard
St. Louis, MO 63132
(314) 567-3647

The Missouri School offers two training courses: a Groomer's Assistant course and a Professional Career course. The Groomer's Assistant course prepares students for employment as skin and coat technicians in a grooming shop. It teaches how to thoroughly groom over fifty dog breeds and assist a stylist in preparation of all breeds of dogs and cats.

The Professional Career course offers students a solid foundation for owning or running a grooming business, and teaches how to groom all 138 AKC recognized breeds. In addition to grooming, students learn practical business skills, including customer relations, bookkeeping, budgeting, and business plan development. Students also get a chance to work in local grooming salons to gain practical experience.

How long it takes: Groomer's Assistant—6 weeks
                                Professional Career—14 weeks

What it costs: Groomer's Assistant—$1,500
                                Professional Career—$2,800

North Jersey School of Dog Grooming
William Pitt Townsquare
11 Roosevelt Avenue
Chatham, NJ 07928
(201) 635-0101

The school offers training in professional dog and cat grooming. Students learn fashionable and practical grooming techniques for all breeds of cats and dogs through daily hands-on practice grooming dogs in the school's professional grooming salon. The school also provides classes on the business aspects of running a grooming salon, such as setting up shop, retail merchandising, mobile grooming vans, equipment and maintenance, record keeping, advertising, and insurance.

How long it takes: 12 weeks

What it costs: $4,880

A payment plan is available.

Jersey Shore School of Dog 'N' Cat Grooming
465 B Route 9
Waretown, NJ 08758
(609) 971-7000

The school offers a Professional Pet Groomer course. Students learn dog and cat grooming, basic hygiene, creative hand scissoring, pet anatomy, proper handling techniques, professional equipment care and maintenance, and basic customer relations.

How long it takes: 1 month

What it costs: $3,500

Payment plans are available.

Rochester Institute of Dog Grooming
2070 East Henrietta Road
Rochester, NY 14623
(716) 359-9710

The institute offers a course in All-Breed Dog Grooming and Shop Management. Students learn basic combing, brushing, dematting, bathing, drying, nail clipping, and ear-cleaning skills. Other courses include working with poodles, sporting breeds, long-coated breeds, terriers, and cats, shop sanitation, nutrition, anatomy, first aid, and eye care. Skills taught include clipping and scissoring of various styles and patterns, using thinning shears, coat care, and handling. The school also teaches shop management and marketing techniques.

How long it takes: 450 hours in 15 or 29 weeks

What it costs: $4,600

Payment plans are available.

Tara Lara Academy of K-9 Hair Design
16037 Southeast McLoughlin Boulevard
Portland, OR 97267
(503) 653-7134

The academy offers three levels of basic training: Pet Grooming, Pet Stylist, and Pet Care Specialist. The Pet Grooming program prepares students for employment in a grooming salon. Instruction includes equipment use and care, anatomy, handling and control, grooming short-hair and undercoated breeds, ear and gland care, clipping toenails, poodle clipping, dematting coats, and clipping and scissor finishing.

The Pet Stylist program also prepares students for employment in a grooming salon, but includes more advanced techniques, such as hand scissoring longer clips, cat grooming, hand stripping coarse-coated terriers and other breeds with wire coats, mastering scissoring, and mixing shampoos.

The Pet Care Specialist program enables students to manage or own their own styling salon. In addition to all the skills taught in the first two courses, this course teaches massage techniques, shop management, retailing, and admitting and releasing pets.

Two advanced courses—Pet Care Professional training, which is for salon owners only, and the Instructor Program, which requires two years of pet-styling experience—are also offered.

How long it takes: Pet Groomer—10 weeks
　　　　　　　　　　Pet Stylist—16 weeks
　　　　　　　　　　Pet Care Specialist—20 weeks

What it costs: Pet Groomer—$3,075
　　　　　　　　Pet Stylist—$4,383
　　　　　　　　Pet Care Specialist—$5,755

Students can house their own cat or dog for $15 per week.

Pennsylvania Academy of Pet Grooming
2860 Route 422 West
Indiana, PA 15701
(724) 463-6101
Fax: (724) 349-0237

The Pennsylvania Academy offers three training programs: Bather/Brusher Grooming, Basic Professional All-Breed Grooming, and Master All-Breed Grooming. The Bather/Brusher Grooming program prepares the student for employment as a bather/brusher in a professional grooming establishment. It includes study of first aid, internal and external parasites, skin disorders, anatomy, types of coats, clarifying texture, dematting, introduction to grooming, and feline and canine bathing.

　　The Basic Professional All-Breed Grooming program prepares the student to work as a professional pet groomer. Courses include all of the above plus lessons in grooming cats, toy dogs, nonsporting dogs, herding dogs, sporting dogs, hound dogs, terriers, and working dogs.

　　The Master All-Breed Grooming program prepares students to work as professional groomers, salon managers, or salon owners. It gives them the opportunity to refine scissoring skills, increase speed, and learn advanced grooming techniques and covers client-groomer relations, groomer-veterinarian relations, telephone business techniques, record keeping, advertising, retail merchandising, and professionalism.

How long it takes: Bather/Brusher—2 weeks
　　　　　　　　　　Basic Professional—8 weeks
　　　　　　　　　　Master All-Breed—15 weeks

What it costs: Bather/Brusher—$1,450
                  Basic Professional—$4,425
                  Master All-Breed—$6,755

The Pampered Pet School of Dog Grooming
DeWalt Professional Building
109 DeWalt Avenue
Pittsburgh, PA 15227
(412) 881-9545
(412) 881-4744

The Pampered Pet offers two training programs: Basic Training and Management Training. The Basic Training program is designed to give students hands-on experience working in a grooming shop. The curriculum includes handling and bathing, shampoos, skin treatments, parasites, nails and ears, tools and equipment, combing, brushing, dematting, clipping, scissoring, cat grooming, basic shop keeping, and on-the-job training.

The Management Training program includes all the information presented in the Basic Training program plus advanced grooming techniques and business management skills. Courses include customer relations, suppliers, extra-income tactics, handling competition, record keeping, telephone strategies, and retail merchandising.

How long it takes: Basic Training—10 weeks
                    Management Training—15 weeks

What it costs: Basic Training—$4,000
                  Management Training—$5,300

The Southern Institute of Pet Grooming
510 West Main Street
P.O. Box 313
Central, SC 29630
(864) 639-6872

The institute offers an All-Breed Career Specialist course, which prepares students for employment in pet salons, kennels, and mobile grooming businesses. Students are also taught how to start, operate, and manage their own grooming businesses. The curriculum includes the basics of grooming and equipment, sequence directional styling, scissoring skills and exercises, AKC breeds, anatomy, handling problem animals, skin problems and parasites, first aid, record keeping, retail sales, shop management, and all-breed styling. The institute also offers labs in feline grooming, hand-stripping techniques, and pet tattoos for identification.

How long it takes: 12 weeks

What it costs: $3,300

South Carolina School of Dog Grooming
P.O. Box 1353
Irmo, SC 29063
(803) 781-6598

The South Carolina School of Dog Grooming offers three training courses: Preparatory Grooming, Extensive Grooming, and Extensive Grooming Plus. The Preparatory Grooming course trains students for entry-level grooming positions. The curriculum includes bathing, dipping, fluff and cage drying, clipping nails, basic anatomy, and clipper operation.

The Extensive Grooming course trains students to work as certified professional groomers. It covers all 136 breeds, anatomy, nutrition, breeding, dog talk, blade sharpening, health care, hand scissoring, and grooming.

The Extensive Grooming Plus course is for students who want to start their own grooming businesses. Students learn to improve technique, quality, and speed—by the end of the course they are able to groom six dogs a day.

How long it takes: Preparatory Grooming—6 weeks
                     Extensive Grooming—10 weeks
                     Extensive Grooming Plus—13 weeks

What it costs: Preparatory Grooming—$2,000
                     Extensive Grooming—$3,475
                     Extensive Grooming Plus—$4,500

Credit cards are accepted.

Texas Allbreed Grooming School
1003 Enterprise Place, Suite 100
Arlington, TX 76001
(817) 472-7054

Texas Allbreed offers a dog-grooming training course that consists of six sections: Dog Grooming Equipment, Dog Psychology, Dog Grooming Biology, Dog Breed Recognition, Client Relations, and Dog Grooming. Dog Grooming Equipment trains students to use clippers, brushes, combs, rakes, mat splitters, shampoos, dips, rinses, and oils. Dog Psychology teaches how to create a safe environment, recognize potentially dangerous dogs, communicate with dogs, and introduce puppies to grooming. Dog Grooming Biology covers anatomy, skeletal system, exterior confirmation points, respiratory complications, allergies, heartworm diseases, and ear problems. Dog Breed Recognition introduces students to dogs in the AKC's Toy Group, Sporting Group, Terrier Group, Working Group, Herding Group, Non-Sporting Group, and Hound Group. Client Relations teaches students how to keep clients informed, interpret grooming instructions, suggest appropriate types of grooming, and use proper record keeping and phone techniques. And Dog Grooming, which constitutes 90 percent of the program, teaches roughing, bathing, drying, brushing, dematting, clipping, skimming and thinning, hand stripping, grooming patterns, and perfecting scissoring skills.

How long it takes: 12 weeks

What it costs: $4,500

Texas Institute of Pet Design
8617 North New Braunfels
San Antonio, TX 78217
(210) 822-9355

The institute offers three basic training programs: Apprentice Pet Stylist, DermaTech Specialist, and Petcare Hygienist. The Apprentice Pet Stylist program is the most comprehensive program, teaching about pet styling equipment, the mechanics and art of pet styling, speed trimming techniques, and shop management and human relations. The program also includes the entire curriculum of the DermaTech program, which focuses on bathing, drying, and topical conditioning of canine and feline skin and coats. Courses include breed identification, anatomy and health, ectoparasites, and finishing techniques. The Petcare Hygienist program prepares students for a supervised position in a grooming salon, providing bathing, drying, and finishing services to dogs and cats.

How long it takes: Apprentice Pet Stylist—9 weeks
DermaTech Specialist—4 weeks
Petcare Hygienist—4 weeks

What it costs: Apprentice Pet Stylist—$2,770
DermaTech Specialist—$1,606
Petcare Hygienist—$962

Canine Clippers School of Pet Grooming
264 South Fraley Boulevard
P.O. Box 207
Dumfries, VA 22026
(703) 221-3647
(703) 221-2107

Canine Clippers offers a professional training in pet grooming. Subjects taught include AKC breed information, dog terminology, first aid, equipment selection, diseases, parasites and sanitation, grooming skills, shop management, dog psychology, anatomy, skin disorders, nutrition, public relations, brushing, combing, dematting, and cat grooming. Specific instruction includes how to use a Clipper Vac System, eliminate internal and external parasites, clean ears, eyes, teeth, and feet, and use kennel management software. Students also learn management principles for operating their own grooming business.

How long it takes: 15 weeks

What it costs: $5,900

Credit cards are accepted.

Maser's Academy of Fine Grooming
P.O. Box 82344
Kenmore, WA 98028
(425) 486-1299
(425) 334-2309
Denise425@juno.com

The academy offers a Professional Pet Groomer course designed to prepare students for employment in the field of dog and cat grooming. The training focuses on teaching the practical skills needed to work on all the popular breeds that regularly visit pet salons. The curriculum includes bathing, drying, nail trimming, general health problems, scissoring, thinning and stripping, and breed studies. Maser's Academy also offers an extended learning course for groomers already working in the field who feel they need additional or advanced training.

How long it takes: 70 days

What it costs: $2,750

Wisconsin School of Professional Pet Grooming
P.O. Box 175
Okauchee, WI 53069
(414) 569-9492
Fax: (414) 569-1842

The Wisconsin School offers two courses that train Assistant Stylists and Professional Stylists. The Assistant Stylist course includes classes in sanitation, anatomy, breed identification, behavior and handling, parasites, diseases, nutrition, first aid and CPR, scissored grooming, reproduction and reproductive problems, immunization, and grooming patterns. Upon completion of the program, each student will have groomed approximately sixty dogs, including a minimum of ten brushable breeds and ten mixed and modified breeds.

   The Professional Stylist program includes all of the above plus geriatric care, cat grooming, advanced scissoring, and business skills such as client relations, retailing, record keeping, and pricing. In the Professional program, students groom approximately 125 dogs, including a minimum of twenty brushable breeds, twenty mixed and modified breeds, twenty scissored breeds, twenty spaniels, and twenty terriers. The school also offers workshops in business start-ups, creating a business plan, preparing cash-flow statements, and strategic marketing techniques.

How long it takes: Assistant Stylist—8 weeks
                    Professional Stylist—16 weeks

What it costs: Assistant Stylist—$3,100
                    Professional Stylist—$5,700

The school offers financial advice about funding your education.

Therapeutic Riding Instruction ◆ ◆ ◆

Therapeutic riding instructors offer hippotherapy—also known as equine therapy—services to clients with autism, Down syndrome, spinal bifida, and many other physical, emotional, and developmental disabilities. Instructors help clients experience the benefits of horseback riding. These benefits are both physical and emotional: clients may develop improved posture and balance, increase strength, overcome fear, build self-esteem, and deepen cognitive and social skills. All of these programs are approved by the North American Riding for the Handicapped Association (NARHA) and prepare students for the registered instructor exam—for more information about therapeutic riding, contact NARHA at (800) 369-7433 or P.O. Box 33150, Denver, CO, 80233.

Fran Joswick Therapeutic Riding Center
26284 Oso Road
San Juan Capistrano, CA 92675
(714) 240-8441

The center trains Therapeutic Riding Instructors. The training begins with instruction in human anatomy, physiology, kinesiology, psychology, growth, and development. Students then study disability definitions, characteristics, and management, precautions and contraindications, lesson plans and structure, teaching techniques, and student assessment and documentation. Students also learn mounting and dismounting techniques, exercises, games and activities, therapy horse selection, volunteer training and management, riding center administration, safe operating procedures, and fund-raising and public relations. Participants are given the opportunity to teach riders with physical, cognitive, sensory, psychosocial, and speech/language impairments.

How long it takes: 5 weeks

What it costs: $1,700

Cost includes housing.

High Hopes Therapeutic Riding
36 Town Woods Road
P.O. Box 254
Old Lyme, CT 06371
(860) 434-1974
Fax: (860) 434-3723

High Hopes offers a Therapeutic Riding Instructor Training course designed to prepare students to plan and implement safe and effective therapeutic riding classes. The curriculum includes equine movement analysis, anatomy of the rider, postural alignment and corrections, medical terminology, body mechanics of mounting and dismounting, rider assessment, precautions and contraindications, physical disabilities, neurological impairments, and orthopedic impairments. Students also learn therapy horse selection and evaluation, tack and equipment management, teaching techniques and strategies, lesson planning, and how to work with people with psychosocial issues, visual, and speech/language impairments. And that's only the first half of the training—the other half is spent in an individually designed practicum project. Prerequisites for this program include current CPR and first aid certification, previous riding experience, and a minimum of ten hours' experience teaching riding skills.

How long it takes: 6 months

What it costs: $1,300

Equest Center for Therapeutic Riding
3800 Troy Road
Wylie, TX 75098
(972) 412-1099

Equest offers a Therapeutic Riding Instructor Training course. The curriculum includes human anatomy and kinesiology, human psychology, teaching skills and approaches, disabilities, mounting and dismounting procedures, equipment selection and adaptation, volunteer management, selecting and handling therapy horses, hippotherapy, practice teaching, and augmentative communication. Prerequisites include some knowledge of stable management, good riding skills, and current first aid/CPR certification (in which students can be trained on campus).

How long it takes: 5 weeks

What it costs: $1,695

Cost includes housing.

Miscellaneous Animals ◆ ◆ ◆

There are three careers in this section: animal communication, pet sitting, and exotic animal management. The animal communication program teaches telepathic communication and healing both to help animals recover quickly from pain, illness, and surgery, and also to help them express the unmet needs that may be resulting in problem behaviors. The pet-sitting programs offer training, support, and certification to people interested in becoming professional pet sitters. And the exotic animal management program teaches students to work with exotic animals—handling, feeding, and caring for them—in zoos. If you're interested in a degree program in zookeeping, call or write the American Association of Zoo Keepers, Inc., at 635 Southwest Gage Boulevard, Topeka, KS 66606 or (800) 468-1966.

Exotic Animal Training and Management Program
America's Teaching Zoo
Moorpark College
7075 Campus Road
Moorpark, CA 93021
(805) 378-1400

America's Teaching Zoo offers a certificate program in Exotic Animal Training and Management, which prepares students to work in zoos. The program combines lectures and classes with daily hands-on work at America's Teaching Zoo. Students are responsible for cleaning cages, feeding animals, preparing diets, checking on the animal collection, and killing rodents, pigeons, and rabbits to provide fresh meat for some of the animals. Students also build and repair cages, night boxes, fences, equipment, and training props. Because of the potential of some of the animals to do serious injury, discipline in the program is strict. During the first year of study, students are not allowed to interact with the animals without specific instructions from a supervisor. Many of the animals are being trained, and outside contact can hinder the training process. In addition to working at America's Teaching Zoo, students are offered opportunities to work at the Los Angeles and Santa Barbara zoos.

How long it takes: 2 years

What it costs: California residents—$10,000
                Out-of-state students—$14,000

Financial aid is available.

Paws and Claws
614 Rudd Road
Vista, CA 92084
(760) 630-0777

Paws and Claws offers a training program in interspecies communication. The program consists of two courses—a Basic Workshop and Advanced Training—which teach students how to get in touch with the soul or spirit of animals, their thoughts, values, perceptions, and understanding. In the Basic Workshop, students learn meditation techniques and exercises to help increase their awareness and understanding of animals and become more receptive to telepathic communication. In the Advanced Training, students hone their skills and learn to overcome the inhibitions that block communication with animals. They study the use of shamanic journeying for power animal guidance, the use of mantric sounds of the Mayan language, and they are introduced to the use of color and light therapy in healing ethereal subtle bodies.

Graduates of the Advanced Training can offer their services as animal communications specialists, helping pets and their owners cope with problem behaviors that are often the result of unmet needs or physical or emotional trauma.

How long it takes: Basic Workshop—2 days
                    Advanced Training—3 days

What it costs: Basic Workshop—$150
                Advanced Training—$400

National Association of Professional Pet Sitters
1200 G Street, N.W., Suite 760
Washington, DC 20005
(202) 393-3317
Fax: (202) 393-0336
www.petsitters.org

The association offers a correspondence certification program in Pet Sitting. The training includes a course of study in business management, animal care, and health issues. It also includes viewing the video *Pet Sitting: Getting Started,* and reading the *Cat Owner's Home Veterinary Handbook* and the *Dog Owner's Home Veterinary Handbook.* Pet sitters certified through NAPPS benefit from a referral network (including a nationwide 800 number), a Mentor Program for novice sitters, and the availability of liability and bonding insurance.

How long it takes: 90 days

What it costs: $205

Credit cards are accepted.

Pet Sitters International
418 East King Street
King, NC 27021-9163
(910) 983-9222
Fax: (910) 983-3755
petsitin@ols.net

Pet Sitters International offers three correspondence training courses in pet sitting: Pet Sitting Technician, Advanced Pet Sitting Technician, and Pet Sitting Professional. The Pet Sitting Technician course includes basic psychological principles of animal intelligence and behavior, proper handling and restraint techniques, animal first aid (including bandaging and dressing wounds), sanitation, flea control, care of older animals, and information about dog, cat, and horse breeds.

The Advanced Pet Sitting Technician course offers additional training in nutrition, emergency veterinary care, and advanced animal assisting (which includes maternal care, vaccinations, labor and delivery, and newborn animal care). Students also learn to recognize common signs of disease in cats, dogs, horses, cattle, sheep, goats, swine, and birds.

The Pet Sitting Professional course emphasizes practical business information, helping pet sitters sharpen their knowledge, skills, and competitive edge. Membership in Pet Sitters International is a prerequisite for all of the courses.

How long it takes:　Pet Sitting Technician—3 to 6 months
　　　　　　　　　　Advanced Pet Sitting Technician—1 to 3 months
　　　　　　　　　　Pet Sitting Professional—6 months to 2 years

What it costs:　　Membership fee—$75
　　　　　　　　　Pet Sitting Technician—$399
　　　　　　　　　Advanced Pet Sitting Technician—$179
　　　　　　　　　Pet Sitting Professional—Varies

Credit cards are accepted.

Chapter 5

✦ ✦ ✦ ✦

Art and Design

A lthough all the training programs in this chapter center on aesthetics, they cover a wide range of careers. Some programs focus on hands-on design, some on creating visual art, some on the spiritual and health aspects of design, and some on art objects and history. Whether you're interested in art and design careers that involve *things*—antiques, fine or folk art objects, or anything else you might find in a museum—or *actions*—sketching, designing, arranging—this chapter is a good place to start your search. It covers floral design, museum studies, art appraisal, Feng Shui, fabric and pattern design, garden design. Other chapters that include programs with important components of art and design are the Craft chapter, which covers design of many objects such as jewelry and furniture, and the Media chapter, which includes animation and filmmaking.

If you're interested in training to become a fine artist, we recommend you check out *The Art Student's College Guide* (ARCO, 1996). And if you're interested in becoming a graphic artist or multimedia designer, check out *The Directory of Technical Schools, Colleges, and Universities Offering Courses in Graphic Communications* (an annual directory published by the National Scholarship Trust Fund of the Graphic Arts, 200 Deer Run Road, Sewickley, PA 15143, [412] 741-6860, nstf@gatf.lm.com) and *The Complete Guide to Animation and Computer Graphic Schools* (Ernest Pintoff, Watson-Guptill Publications, 1995).

Floral Design ✦ ✦ ✦

Flowers are big business: retail florists alone generate over $6 billion a year. And although entry-level employees tend to be less than lavishly paid, experienced florists—especially those who own their own shops—can do quite well. The schools below don't just teach floral arranging: they teach specialized floral skills for weddings, funerals, and other events, the business aspects of buying wholesale flowers and using wire orders, and marketing and sales issues. Floral design can be a great career if you love flowers, have a keen eye for design, and work well with people and events.

Southern California School of Floral Design
843 South State College Boulevard
Anaheim, CA 92806
(714) 776-7445
Fax: (714) 776-7485

The school offers basic career training in floral design—the Floral Designer and Flower Shop Operator program, which consists of six parts: Fundamentals of Floral Design, Floral Arrangements, Sympathy Design, Wedding and Personal Flowers, Shop Operations, and Fieldtrip. Subjects covered include understanding the color wheel, material usage, decorative foliage treatment, basic design shapes, European planters and decorative treatments, casket pieces, easel sprays, corsages, wedding work, special presentations, pricing, merchandising, buying, advertising, and wire service information.

The school also offers three advanced training programs: Advanced Floral Designer, Advanced Wedding Designer, and Special Events/Decor Designer. These courses cover European styles and techniques, abstract and geometric designs, using tropicals and exotics, hand-tied and Biedermeier bouquets, high-style treatments, creating floral props and pool floats, and planning and coordinating special events.

How long it takes: Floral Designer and Flower Shop Operator—
2 weeks
Advanced Floral Designer—1 week
Advanced Wedding Designer—2 days
Special Events/Decor Designer—3 days

What it costs: Floral Designer and Flower Shop Operator—$1,443
Advanced Floral Designer—$550
Advanced Wedding Designer—$295
Special Events/Decor Designer—$500

The Academy of Floral Design
837 Acoma Street
Denver, CO 80204
(303) 623-8855

The academy offers a Floral Design and Management program that consists of three parts: Design, Marketing/Merchandising, and Management. The Design classes teach the principles and elements of design, how to design with dried and silk materials, fresh flowers, and blooming and foliage plants, and how to work with wholesalers. The Design course also includes a short internship in which students work at a floral shop or wholesale house. The Marketing/Merchandising classes cover sales skills, customer relations, wire orders, and product knowledge. And the Management classes include instruction in running a profitable shop, writing a business plan, merchandising, buying, pricing, bookkeeping, and advertising.

How long it takes: 3 months

What it costs: $2,644

Payment plans are available and credit cards are accepted.

American Floral Art School
529 South Wabash Avenue, Suite 600
Chicago, IL 60605
(312) 922-9328

The school provides training in the Basics of Modern Floral Design. The curriculum includes seven core courses: Fundamentals of Artistic Design, General Instruction, Sympathy Designs, Container Arrangements, "Silk" and Dried Arrangements, Fashion Flowers, and Wedding Work. The Fundamentals course covers five types of floral designs, four shapes of flowers, four ways to arrange stems, proper proportions, and harmony of elements. The General Instruction course covers the use of all standard commercial flowers and foliages, new and unusual flowers and foliages, exotics, dried botanicals, and basic techniques of designing. Sympathy Designs covers working with funeral wreaths, pillows, and casket decorations. Container Arrangements covers the mechanics of anchoring flowers. "Silk" and Dried Arrangments covers the special art and techniques of using artificial flowers. Fashion Flowers covers corsages, wristlets, hair decorations, prom nosegays, and boutonnieres. And Wedding Work covers bouquets—from colonials to clusters to cascades—and wedding business procedures such as selling, pricing, and additional sales.

How long it takes: 3 weeks

What it costs: $690

American International Academy of Floral Design Chicago, Ltd.
8 South Michigan Avenue, Suite 210
Chicago, IL 60603
(312) 345-1600
Fax: (312) 345-1603

The academy offers a training program in Commercial Floral Design. The curriculum includes such topics as Western Floral Design History, A Study of Dimensions—Line, Shape, and Volume, Flower and Foliage Identification and Characteristics, Symmetrical and Asymmetrical Designs, Sprays and Corsages, Traditional and Modern Sympathy Designs, Party Decorations, Wreaths for All Occasions, Vase Designs, European Hand-tied Bouquets, and Wedding Bouquets and Decorations.

How long it takes: 2 weeks

What it costs: $695

Kansas School of Floral Design
836 Iowa Street
Lawrence, KS 66044
(913) 843-1400
(785) 843-1400

The school offers a four-part diploma course in floral design. The first part covers tools and materials, flower identification and care, wire orders, the principles of flower arranging, and purchasing florist supplies. It also teaches students to design vases, bowls, and baskets, use wire and tape, and tie bows, including satin and velvet roses. The second part covers corsages (including glamellias and composite corsages), novelty containers, terrarium and dish gardens, and purchasing and selling commercial varieties of green and blooming plants. The third part covers flower shop management, wedding flowers (including colonial, cascade, and crescent bouquets), dried and silk flowers, and salesmanship. And the fourth part covers selling and handling, funeral flowers, designing easel and casket sprays, wreaths and pillows, and pricing, markup, and profit. The school also organizes field trips to greenhouses and retail florists.

How long it takes: 4 weeks

What it costs: $700

Rittners School of Floral Design
345 Marlborough Street
Boston, MA 02115
(617) 267-3824
www.tiac.net/users/stevrt/index.html
Stevrt@tiac.net

Rittners offers two floral design training courses: Floral Design and Business Practices, and Floral Design. The Floral Design and Business Practices course covers wedding designs, vase arrangements, sympathy designs, Christmas decorations, flowers to wear, floriculture, business management, and merchandising. Students learn approximately one hundred designs, including Holgarth and inverted vase styles, door badge and wreath arrangements, headpieces and wrist designs, and novelty designs such as the flower poodle. The course also covers floral business practices such as shop layout, visual merchandising, home-based floral businesses, pricing, telephone sales, marketing and promotion, and how to sell a wedding.

The Floral Design course covers wedding designs, vase arrangements, sympathy designs, holiday designs, flowers to wear, and party designs and centerpieces. The Floral Design course is offered both as a regular evening course and an intensive day course.

How long it takes: Floral Design—12 weeks (part-time), 5 weeks (full-time)

Floral Design and Business Practices—500 hours

What it costs: Floral Design—$1,500

Floral Design and Business Practices—$3,554

Credit cards are accepted and a payment plan is available.

Stuppy Mid-America School of Floral Design
120 East 12th Avenue
North Kansas City, MO 64116
(800) 877-5025
(816) 842-6796

The school offers two courses in floral design and management: Basic Design and Advanced Design. Basic Design covers design, product knowledge, salesmanship, and management. Students learn basic technical skills such as wiring, taping, and gluing, and then move on to more difficult designs including asymmetrical, round, horizontal, natural, and European arrangements. Basic Design also prepares students to design sympathy and wedding arrangements, and includes classes on color theory, high-style designs, product knowledge, marketing, and special skills for selling wedding, sympathy, seasonal, and special occasion flowers.

Advanced Design builds on skills taught in the Basic Design course and focuses on advanced elements of design and advanced wedding designs. Students learn the technical skills and artistic concepts needed to create unusual and creative designs and settings.

How long it takes: Basic Design—2 weeks

Advanced Design—2 days

What it costs: Basic Design—$795

Advanced Design—$245

Creative Design Institute
4530 Route 9 South
Howell, NJ 07731
(800) 877-4785
(908) 367-2104

The institute offers three levels of floral design training: Floral Designer, Comprehensive Floristry, and Floriculture. The Floral Designer training prepares students for entry-level positions in the retail florist industry. It includes a flower-arranging lab, in which students learn to prepare floral arrangements for retail, weddings, and funerals, a business management course that covers salesmanship, merchandising, and displays, a special uses course that teaches students to develop commercial accounts and prepare for holidays, and a marketing course that covers marketing and wholesaling.

The Comprehensive Floristry training includes additional classes in weddings, funerals, high style, and plants and other materials. It covers bouquet styles, pricing, color use, developing relationships with funeral directors, and principles of European and French gardens.

And the Floriculture training prepares students for positions as floral designers or managers, or to start up their own shops. In addition to the classes above and an internship, it includes coursework in floriculture, identification, merchandising, photography, promotion, personnel management, and bookkeeping.

How long it takes: Floral Design (full-time)—4 weeks
Floral Design (part-time)—12 weeks
Comprehensive Floristry (full-time)—8 weeks
Comprehensive Floristry (part-time)—24 weeks
Floriculture—28 weeks

What it costs: Floral Design (full-time)—$900
Floral Design (part-time)—$400
Comprehensive Floristry—$800
Comprehensive Floristry—$1,800
Floriculture—$5,400

Credit cards are accepted and a payment plan is available.

Queen Bee Floral Design School
3342 South Sandhill Road
Las Vegas, NV 89121
(702) 451-4022

The school offers a floral design course. The curriculum covers shop knowledge, flower care and handling, corsages and boutonnieres, complete weddings and funerals, home and hospital arrangements, dried and silk designs, dish gardens and plants, special-occasion and novelty designs, and high-style designing. The course also includes exposure to the business operations of a successful flower shop and a field trip to a flower wholesaler.

How long it takes: 6 weeks

What it costs: $1,100

Credit cards are accepted.

Parsons School of Design
Office of Continuing Education
66 Fifth Avenue
New York, NY 10011
(800) 252-0852
(212) 229-8910
Fax: (212) 229-8975
parsadm@newschool.edu
www.parsons.edu

Parsons offers a certificate program in professional floral design that combines required and elective coursework. The required coursework covers fresh floral design, color theory, indoor plants, floral design for weddings, ikebana, and floral business practices. Electives include Silk Flower Design, Table Arrangements, Topiaries, Wreaths and Wall Hangings, Designing Floral Sympathy Tributes, Floral Arrangements for Caterers and Restaurants, Wedding Arch/Chuppa Design, and Creative Design Mechanics. Students are also required to work twenty-five hours in a floral shop and twenty-five hours with a freelance floral designer.

How long it takes: 1 year

What it costs: Approximately $4,000

Credit cards are accepted.

Floral Design Institute
2701 Northwest Vaughn Street, Suite 429
Portland, OR 97210
(800) 819-8089
(503) 223-8089

911 Western Avenue, Suite 575
Seattle, WA 98104
(800) 261-0184
(206) 749-9464
www.FloralDesignInstitute.com

The institute offers Basic and Advanced Floral Design training. The Basic course is designed to prepare students for entry-level positions. The curriculum includes courses in the care and handling of fresh flowers, floral identification and pricing, the elements of design, bow tying, floral trends, color theory and application, asymmetrical bouquets, newborn baby bouquets, hospital arrangements, balloon design, slumber room bouquets, and wire orders. The training also covers funerals and weddings: students learn funeral flowers, design, sales, and service (including full casket pieces, funeral sprays, wreaths and crosses, and funeral orders), and how to sell, package, and service wedding flowers (including bridal bouquets, corsages and boutonnieres, wristlets, halos, and cake flowers, pew bows, ribbon wrapping, and pricing a complete wedding). Other designs taught include hand-tied European bouquets, parallel and vertical design, Asian-influenced design, dressing potted plants, and creating dish gardens. Finally, students learn about floral career opportunities, starting their own businesses, marketing flowers, and worldwide floral growing and distribution.

The Advanced Floral/Design course provides additional training in bridal bouquets, wiring techniques, wedding sales and consultation, purchasing flowers, contemporary wall decor, advanced design principles and forms, working with wedding planners and caterers, and interpretive design. Students of the Advanced course also learn grouping, binding, framing, parallelism, clustering, basing, and terracing.

How long it takes: Basic Floral Design—3 weeks
Advanced Floral Design—1 week

What it costs: Basic Floral Design—$1,375
Advanced Floral Design—$575

Credit cards are accepted.

Shelton White School of Floral Design
2011 Union Avenue East
Memphis, TN 38104
(800) 748-9613
(901)274-6123
Fax: (901) 276-4001

The school offers a training program in floral design that combines lectures, demonstrations, and student practice. The curriculum includes identification of flowers and greenery, flower care, the elements and principles of design, salesmanship, potted plants, flower arranging, sympathy and wedding work, corsages, shop management, and new flower shop start-up. Shelton White also provides advanced instruction in creative sympathy design, selling sympathy work, selling, pricing, and servicing weddings, rose and church arrangements, florist shop layout, training employees, buying and selling a floral shop, and selection of a shop location.

How long it takes: 2 weeks

What it costs: $635

Credit cards are accepted.

Museum Studies and Art Appraisal ◆ ◆ ◆

This section focuses on beautiful, valuable, unique, antique, and otherwise exceptional objects. But it includes much more than art appreciation—professionals in the fields taught by schools in this section also evaluate, appraise, research, teach, manage, direct, explain, and engage in any number of other art-related tasks. The museum studies programs teach everything from curatorial research to exhibit planning and installation to working in a living museum. And the appraisal and connoisseurship courses train students to evaluate fine, decorative, and folk art, antiques, and objects as varied as Chinese porcelain, rare books, jewelry, and French furniture. If you have a critical eye and an aesthetic soul, you may have found your field.

Arizona State University
College of Liberal Arts and Sciences, Department of Anthropology
P.O. Box 872402
Tempe, AZ 85287
(602) 965-5266
Fax: (602) 965-7671
Ann.Hedlund@ASU.edu

The Anthropology Department at Arizona State offers a certificate program in Museum Studies. Although the classes are also part of the master's degree in Museum Studies, the certificate program is a non-degree preprofessional program that prepares students for museum work. Curriculum includes topics such as Museum Collection Management, Exhibit Planning and Design, Museum Interpretation, and Principles of Conservation. Students are also required to complete an internship.

How long it takes: 1 year

What it costs: State residents—$1,890
                     Nonresidents—$6,210

California State University, Chico
Department of Anthropology
Chico, CA 95929
(916) 898-5397

Chico State offers a certificate in Museology. The program consists of interdisciplinary courses emphasizing curatorial research, design and installation of exhibits, and museum management. Other topics of study include graphic communications, public relations, data collection, and conservation. The Anthropology Museum at Chico State serves as a learning center for this program, and students profit from hands-on experience while interning in the museum; past exhibits have included ancient Egypt, Polynesia, historic Chico, and women's history.

How long it takes: 2 years

What it costs: $2,000

California State University, Long Beach
6300 State University Drive, Suite 104
Long Beach, CA 90815
(800) 963-2250
(562) 985-5561
Fax: (562) 985-5823
www.uces.csulb.edu/registration.html

Cal State Long Beach offers a certificate program in Appraising Antiques and Collectibles. Students learn to identify styles and construction of furniture from antiquity to the present, to identify styles, stones, and metals used in jewelry from the Victorian era to the present, and to identify types of glass, pottery, metals, primitives, and collectibles. Specific skills taught include using instruments such as the refractrometer and polariscope to identify diamonds and colored stones, identifying ninety-five types of glass including French cameo, Burmese, and milk glass, dating and evaluating neoclassical, Victorian, and art nouveau furniture, and reading "maker's marks" to determine the identity of pottery and porcelain objects. The course also covers legal matters and ethical standards of appraising.

How long it takes: 1 to 2 years

What it costs: $2,200

Credit cards are accepted.

Center for Career Education
The George Washington University
2029 K Street, N.W., Suite 600
Washington, DC 20006
(202) 973-1175
(202) 973-1150
Fax: (202) 973-1165
cce@www.gwu.edu
www.gwu.edu/~cce

The center offers a certificate program in Appraisal Studies in Fine and Decorative Arts, which offers students technical expertise and an understanding of art objects in the context of history, aesthetics, and business principles. Students are required to take four core courses:

Personal Property Valuation, Research and Analysis, Report Writing, and Appraisal Practice and Standards. They then choose seven electives from a Fine and Decorative Arts Curriculum. Electives include Eighteenth and Nineteenth Century French Furniture, Oriental Ivory, Glass, and Hardstones, Jewelry of the Twentieth Century, Old Master Paintings, Chinese and English Ceramics of the Eighteenth Century: Authentic or Fake?, Appraising Books, Manuscripts, and Ephemera, and Tribal and Village Rugs of the Persian Revival Period.

How long it takes: 6 months

What it costs: $2,000 to $3000 (depending on electives chosen)

Credit cards are accepted.

Museum Studies Certificate Program
Professional and Continuing Studies
Tufts University
112 Packard Avenue
Medford, MA 02155
(617) 627-3562
Fax: (617) 627-3017
pcs@infonet.tufts.edu

The university offers a certificate program in Museum Studies, with concentrations in Art History, History, or Education. The Art History concentration prepares students for positions in administration, development, and collection care. The History concentration prepares them to pursue careers in historic settings or in living history museums. And the Education concentration is for students who want to design educational programming for museums. All students begin by taking a Foundation Course that covers the administrative operations of a contemporary museum, mission statements, public perceptions, planning, and the philosophical, ethical, and legal issues of museum administration. Students then take concentration-specific courses in collection care and preservation, historical interpretation, museum history, exhibition planning, museum education, and fund-raising. Finally, there is a required internship, which gives students firsthand experience in museum work.

How long it takes: Approximately 1 year

What it costs: $4,400

Financial aid is available.

Museum of American Folk Art
61 West 62nd Street
New York, NY 10023
(212) 977-7170
Fax: (212) 977-8134

The museum offers a certificate program in American Folk Art Studies. The program is a combination of classwork, independent research, museum internships (either at the Museum of American Folk Art or at another museum, gallery, or auction house), and hands-on experience working with the museum's collection and exhibitions. Required classes include Art of the Western World, American Art, Folk Art in American Life, American Folk Painting, American Folk Sculpture, and Twentieth Century Folk Art. Specific topics include sculpture, textiles, ceramics, furniture, portraits, landscapes, seascapes, gravestones, cigarstore Indians, the differences between academic and folk art traditions, and new manifestations of folk art. Electives include Architecture, Decorative Folk Art and the Home, Pottery, Needlework, Religion, Traditional and Communal Expression in Folk Art, Contemporary Expressions in Folk Art, Sources and Documentation, Care, Conservation and Restoration, Furniture, Folk Art Market, and Museum Studies.

How long it takes: 2 years

What it costs: $3,600

Sotheby's Institute
1334 York Avenue
New York, NY 10021
(212) 606-7822
Fax: (212) 606-7949

Sotheby's offers a professional training program in American Arts. As one of the leading auction houses in the world, Sotheby's offers a unique experience to students, giving them access to studios, galleries, workshops, libraries, and collections not available to the general public. The curriculum covers fine and decorative arts of America from the seventeenth century to the present, and consists of four core courses: Fine Arts, Decorative Arts, Methodology, and Style Studies and Object Connoisseurship. The Fine Arts course includes all major periods, from Colonial, Federal, and Romantic through American Impressionism, Modernism, and Conceptual Art. Specific courses include Thomas Cole and the Hudson River School, Trompe L'Oeil Painting, Mary Cassatt, the Ashcan School, Pop Art, Fluxus, and the Development of Photography. The Decorative Arts curriculum includes courses in regional development, wood identification, cabinetmakers and carvers, innovative production techniques, art nouveau, contemporary furniture makers, and ceramics, glass, and metal. The Methodology course helps students develop visual analysis skills and become familiar with bibliographic investigations, cataloging techniques, and library resources. The Style Studies and Object Connoisseurship course develops students' knowledge of style, condition, quality, and values as they examine objects—from paintings to snuffboxes to ink pots—from Ancient Greece to Regency England. The course also contains sessions on career opportunities, which include introductions to art world professionals.

How long it takes: 9 months

What it costs: $23,400

Financial aid is available.

Appraisal Studies Certificate
Division of Arts, Sciences, and Humanities
New York University School of Continuing Education
48 Cooper Square, Room 203
New York, NY 10003
(212) 998-7130
sceinfo@nyu.edu
www.sce.nyu.edu

NYU offers a certificate in Appraisal Studies in Fine and Decorative Arts. Students are required to complete four core courses and four electives. The core courses teach ethics, legal guidelines, appraisal of fine and decorative arts, appraisal research methods, and appraisal writing.

Electives include subjects such as case studies in damage and loss, uniform standards of professional appraisal, the business of antiques, Chinese porcelain, textiles auctions, interiors from the sixteenth to the twentieth centuries, French and English furniture, Oriental rugs, and appraising contemporary art. Students can also elect to do an internship with a practicing appraiser of fine and decorative arts. In conjunction with the internship, students complete a written research project. This program is affiliated with the Appraisers Association of America.

How long it takes: 2 years (part-time) or 4 weeks (intensive)

What it costs: $2,840

Parsons School of Design
Office of Continuing Education
66 Fifth Avenue
New York, NY 10011
(800) 252-0852
(212) 229-8910
Fax: (212) 229-8975
parsadm@newschool.edu
www.parsons.edu

Parsons offers a professional certificate program in Antiques Connoisseurship. The program requires coursework in decorative arts from the 1800s to the present, the antique marketplace, fakes and forgeries, connoisseurship, and techniques of furniture construction. Students then choose among electives such as Antique American Furniture, Italian Architecture and Furniture, Decorative Arts of the Victorian Era, Oriental Rugs and Kilims, Auction Houses for Fun and Profit, and Illustrations and Posters as Art and Collectibles.

How long it takes: 1 year

What it costs: Approximately $4,000

Credit cards are accepted.

International Society of Appraisers
Riverview Plaza Office Park
16040 Christensen Road, Suite 320
Seattle, WA 98188

(206) 241-0359
Fax: (206) 241-0436
ISA_HQ@compuserve.com
www.isa-appraisers.org

The society offers certification training in Personal Property Appraising. Three required core courses cover markets and values, basic appraisal techniques, ethics, identification and authentication, laws, taxes, and appraisal report writing. Students learn to work with clients, market a business, determine fair market value, use three approaches to determine value, and complete insurance appraisals. The organization also offers specialty studies courses in a variety of subjects including gemstones, antiques and residential contents, fine art, and period jewelry.

How long it takes: Courses generally run about 5 days.

What it costs: 3 required core courses—$1,350
Specialty studies courses—$500 to $850 per course

Students who join the organization can take all 3 core courses for $800. Credit cards are accepted.

Feng Shui • • •

Feng Shui is the traditional Chinese art of placement and design. Practitioners determine if buildings—homes, offices, and shops—are supportive of health, harmony, love, and prosperity by evaluating the flow of energy and the placement of rooms, furniture, and architectural features. If they discover energy blockages or other problems, practitioners suggest various cures, using techniques and suggestions ranging from color theory to the location of stairways and the placement of beds. Feng Shui combines a sense of design, awareness of the effects of energy, and the ability to offer helpful feedback and consultation in an alternative career that is steadily gaining recognition.

Another method of evaluating the effects of buildings on health is bau-biologie, which can be found in the section on Miscellaneous Consulting.

Feng Shui Designs
P.O. Box 399
Nevada City, CA 95959
(800) 551-2482
Fax: (800) 551-2482
fengshui@oro.net
www.cwo.com/~ashlin/fengshui.html

Feng Shui Designs offers an intensive practitioner training course designed to help students set up a professional Feng Shui practice. It focuses on advanced techniques of Chi flow enhancement and the diagnosis and solution of a multitude of design problems. Courses include instruction in diagnosing floor plans using the Ba-Gua, adjusting energy flow with the Nine Cures, Five Element Theory, I-Ching divination, field diagnosis, secret cures, making indoor water fountains, and setting up a professional practice.

How long it takes: 6 days

What it costs: $918

Credit cards are accepted.

Feng Shui Warehouse
P.O. Box 6689
San Diego, CA 92106
(800) 399-1599
(619) 523-2158

The Feng Shui Warehouse offers beginning and intermediate Feng Shui classes for students not necessarily interested in becoming practitioners, and a Practitioner Intensive Training for those interested in practicing Feng Shui professionally. The beginning courses cover basic cures, proper positioning, use of the ba-gua, and site evaluation. The Intensive, which is only open to students who have either taken the foundation classes or studied elsewhere, includes instruction in the essential elements of Feng Shui analysis. Students learn to identify and evaluate the key factors affecting location, design, and arrangement using the most advanced techniques, cures, and secret solutions. The Intensive also covers residential and commercial field experiences, and teaches students how to perform major and minor adjustments, work with clients, and develop a successful consulting practice.

How long it takes: Beginning/Intermediate Classes—1 to 3 evenings
Practitioner Intensive Training—5 days

What it costs: Beginning/Intermediate Classes—$33 per class
Practitioner Intensive Training—$975

Credit cards are accepted.

Geomancy/Feng Shui Education Organization (GEO)
2939 Ulloa Street
San Francisco, CA 94116
(415) 753-6408
Fax: (415) 753-1186
joe1080@aol.com
Fngshuigeo@aol.com
www.lapage.com/geo

GEO offers a practitioner certification training program in Black Sect Feng Shui, the art/science of the constant, mutual, interactive communication and conditioning between the chi of place or environment and the chi of individuals. This form of Feng Shui synthesizes Tibetan and Chinese Buddhist, Taoist, and folk wisdom with modern psychology and design principles. The certification program is divided into three sections.

The first section teaches Black Sect methods, lotus trigram meditation, basic methods of consulting practice, Feng Shui solutions and remedies, and Client Chi/Site Chi. Students are introduced to Chinese astrology, blessing rituals, Chi Kung, cosmology, and adjusting chi. Four field trips and two site assessments are also included.

The second section includes topics such as the Nine Stars, the Eight Doors, working with architects and designers, human face diagnosis, universal ideas in geomancy, multicultural traditions, and new developments in psychology, proxemics, and therapy. Five supervised consultations are also required.

The third section covers specialized topics, individual research projects, assistant teaching, and urban planning. Students at this level work jointly on five consulting projects with professional Feng Shui practitioners.

How long it takes: 3 years

What it costs: $10,200

Payment plans are available.

The Metropolitan Institute of Interior Design
13 Newtown Road
Plainview, NY 11803
(516) 845-4033
Fax: (516) 845-8787
fengshui@met-design.com
www.met-design.com

The institute offers a certificate program in Feng Shui Consulting. The program focuses on teaching students to design and create environments that are not only comfortable, but also support the goals, good health, and prosperity of the occupants. Subjects taught include five element theory, testing for electromagnetic fields, reading blueprints and floor plans, advanced transcendental cures, using the ba gua and lo pan, making home and office visits, and working with clients. Classes include Interior and Exterior Design Factors, Bau-Biology, Chi Kung, Color Theory and Interior Design, Creating a Sacred Space, Earth Design, Feng Shui for Business, and Chinese Astrology. Each student is assigned to a mentor who will provide personalized technical and spiritual guidance throughout the course.

How long it takes: 1 year, or 1 month intensive

What it costs: $3,400

Miscellaneous Art and Design • • •

The schools in this section teach pattern and surface design and garden design. Surface and pattern design is the design of repetitive patterns for surfaces—such as wallpaper, gift wrap, napkins, and textiles—that usually are produced in industrial quantities. What we call garden design is an alternative version of the more common and conventional landscape design. Instead of (or in addition to) focusing on lawn care and maintenance, the trainings focus on aesthetics and the design of one-of-a-kind gardens and botanical wonders. For more traditional programs in garden or landscape design, check out *Careers for Plant Lovers and Other Green Thumb Types* (Blythe Camenson, VGM Career Horizons, 1995).

California School of Professional Fabric Design
2331 Acton Street
Berkeley, CA 94702
(510) 549-3051

The school offers training in Industrial Fabric Design. Students learn to create drapery, rugs, wallpaper, pillowcases, lingerie, children's clothing, gift wrap, paper plates, and other fabric products. Industrial fabric designers primarily design for companies that print mass-produced products rather than small amounts of hand-printed yardage. Since they will be designing for six thousand yards of fabric or more, students are taught to understand the limitations of mass production printing methods, the requirements of manufacturers and sales personnel, production deadlines, and consumer demands.

The course consists of six levels of training. Level I includes classes in stylized drawing procedures, industrial practices, creative principles, design aesthetics, and the fabric design field. Level II covers watercolor painting techniques, designing for apparel fabrics, converting designs to fabric, the repeat, and major printing processes. Level III teaches professional crayon techniques, rug and carpet design, home furnishing fabrics, contracts, and trade customs. Level IV helps students develop an eye-catching portfolio. Level V offers advanced portfolio development, plus discussion of manufacturers' requirements, job positions, advanced apparel design, designing bath products, and professional issues. And Level VI includes portfolio completion, designing for paper products, wallpaper design, speculation work, color for interior fabrics, and the role of the computer in fabric design.

How long it takes: 18 months

What it costs: $2,310

Surface Pattern Design
Kathi Alice Saks
1328 Sixth Street
Berkeley, CA 94710
(510) 526-6097

Kathi Saks offers training classes in surface design intended for design students who need additional instruction and people interested in exploring surface design as a career. The training program focuses on creating repeated patterns for commercial printing and specific products and emphasizes trend analysis, markets, color use, and forecasting for the various industries in the surface design field.

The program includes four classes: Professional Surface Pattern Design, Product Development, Color: Understanding It and Using It Well, and Advanced Surface Pattern Design. Professional Surface Pattern Design introduces the fine art and technical aspects required for employment in the field. Product Development covers commercial printing processes, two- and three-dimensional design, and developing products such as towels, ceramic accessories, paper plates and napkins, and dinnerware. In Color: Understanding It and Using It Well, students learn about analyzing color, mixing gouache, the effects of color, color trends, and colorways for repeat pattern. And Advanced Surface Pattern Design prepares students for job hunting, getting freelance work, working with reps and agents, understanding contracts, operating their own studios, and promoting their services.

How long it takes: 106 hours

What it costs: $1,600

School of Pattern and Design
Image West Design Studio
P.O Box 613
San Anselmo, CA 94979
(415) 492-8736
Fax: (415) 472-7672
imagewest@aol.com

The School of Pattern and Design offers professional training in Surface Pattern Design. Students learn to design and paint in a variety of media, acquire the skills necessary to create portfolio-quality work, develop essential computer skills, learn professional trade practices, and create a personal career strategy. The courses include three broad subjects: Pattern and Design, which includes color, rendering, surface pattern design, and presentation; Computer Art Training, which includes Photoshop, Fractal Design Painter, and Textile Design on the Mac; and Business and Marketing in the Arts, which includes professional practices, marketing, and career strategies.

Specific classes include: a Manufacturer's Insights into Production and Marketing, Color Design Workshop, Color and the Phenomenon of Light, Designing for the Paper Products Industry, Repeat Patterns Using Fractal Design Painter, and Individual Computer Training.

The director of the School of Pattern and Design also operates Image West Design Studio, which was created to represent and market beginning commercial designers. Many of the school's students experience their first professional success while represented by Image West.

How long it takes: Variable (2 years is the average for students without a thorough background in the graphic arts).

What it costs: $2,000 to $4,000

School of Professional Horticulture
The New York Botanical Garden
200th Street and Southern Boulevard
Bronx, NY 10458
(718) 817-8797
Fax: (718) 220-8666
cdewilde@nybg.org

The school offers a training program in Ornamental Horticulture. The program is divided into two parts: academic courses and a hands-on practicum. The academic portion of the training includes courses in botany, commercial horticulture, and landscape design. Classes include Morphology of Flowering Plants, Entomology, Soil Science, Ornamental Woody Plants, Insect Pests of Ornamental Plants, Weed Control, Nursery Management, and Site Analysis and Schematic Design.

The practicum begins with assignments in the following areas: arboriculture, forest management, greenhouse and conservatory maintenance, grounds maintenance, native plant cultivation, perennials, plant production, plant records, rock gardening, and display gardening. Students finish the practicum with an internship at the New York Botanical Garden, with which the school is affiliated. Possible internships include working in the rose garden, rock garden, display gardens, native plant garden, border gardens, and arboretum.

Prerequisites for this program include some horticultural experience and at least two years of college credit. Students who lack sufficient experience can seek placement assistance from the school before starting the program.

How long it takes: 2 years

What it costs:　　$10,150

Payment plans and some scholarships are available.

Oxford College of Garden Design
San Francisco, CA
(530) 878-1776

5 Kit Lane
Checkendon-near-Reading
Oxon, RG9 0TY
England
International telephone: (011-44) 1491-682-3222

The college offers a Garden Design training program in San Francisco and England. The course consists of eight modules: The Site and Its Setting, Garden History, Site Assessment, Design Principles, Hard Landscape Portfolio, Construction and Costing, Planting Design, and Running a Design Practice. The Site and Its Setting covers site evaluation, the function of the garden, allocation of space, and climatic, geographical, and historical influences. Garden History teaches the evolution of the modern landscape from the eighteenth to the twentieth century. Site Assessment covers measurement of the site, recording the measurements, site analysis, levels, and plotting the site to scale. The Design Principles module includes classes in basic drafting skills and techniques, design tools, design theory, division of the site, the design brief, landscape graphics, principles of style, scale and proportion, axonometric drawing and cross-sections, and garden design as an art form. Hard Landscape Portfolio covers furnishing the garden and hard landscape detailing. Construction and Costing includes classes in hard and soft landscape specifications, ergonomic considerations, contouring, costing, and scheduling. Planting Design covers color theory, plant forms, trees and arboriculture, planting style, and maintenance. And the Running a Design Practice course includes office practices, marketing, meeting the client, presenting a portfolio, design fees, and business planning for a prosperous future.

How long it takes: 1 year

What it costs: $4,500

Inchbald School of Design
Garden Design Department
32 Eccleston Square
London SW1V 1PB
England
International telephone: (011-44) 171-630-9011/2/3
Fax: (011-44) 171-976-5979
design@inchbald.demon.co.uk
www.inchbald.demon.co.uk

This school is included despite its location because it's one of few schools that offer nondegree courses in garden design and it's very open to American students. The school offers a diploma course and three levels of certification in garden design. The diploma course includes classes in commercial and domestic design, site analysis and appraisal, visual communication, surveying, garden history, plant associations, business practices, costing and quantifying, and computer-aided design. The course also includes research and design projects, ranging from analysis of design detail to a site survey to client proposals. A comprehensive final project enables students to learn commercial and large-scale private design—incorporating elements such as swimming pools, water gardens, and wild gardens, fee structuring, project cost determination, and specification writing. The three certification courses—Garden and Landscape Design Principles, Intermediate Garden Design, and Advanced Garden Design—include instruction in basic design principles, surveying and drawing, client liaison, planting design, nursery practice, pests and diseases, commercial design, specialist design, business practice, and presentation skills.

How long it takes: Diploma course—1 year
                     Certificate courses—10 weeks each

What it costs: Diploma course—$19,600 (£12,250)
                     Certificate courses—$6,860 (£4,287)

Cost is approximate and will vary according to the exchange rate.

Chapter 6

✷ ✷ ✷ ✷

Bodywork and Physical Health

This chapter covers bodywork, movement training, and body-oriented alternative healing—any health technique that is primarily physical instead of medicinal, psychotherapeutic, or energetic. Bodywork is straightforward. If you want to work hands-on with clients, kneading, stretching, poking, prodding, rocking, or cradling them, you're interested in bodywork. That doesn't mean you're just interested in conventional Swedish or sports massage, though. You might be looking for something more therapeutic or spiritual or structural—if so, take heart. There are many, many bodywork methods that begin where traditional massage ends.

Movement training is also fairly straightforward. You learn to help clients feel more at home in their bodies—moving, standing, breathing, and so on. Although many of the movement therapies can have profound emotional or psychological effects, the programs in this chapter focus on the physical: if you're interested in a more emotional or psychological emphasis, check out the movement and dance programs in the Therapy chapter.

Finally, this chapter includes colon hydrotherapy and natural vision correction training programs, as they deal with specific physical ailments and treatments. Colon hydrotherapy is, well, colon hydrotherapy. High colonics. Colon irrigation. You know. Do we have to spell it out? And the natural vision correction programs teach practitioners to train clients to improve their eyesight without using glasses or surgery.

Bodywork ◆ ◆ ◆

The most common alternative careers are health careers, and the most common of those are massage and bodywork. In fact, they're so common that there are too many to list in this book—this section contains, instead of individual training programs, organizations affiliated with the various types of bodywork. So if you're interested in a specific type of training, you can call the association to get a list of training programs. If you don't find what you're looking for here, we suggest that you call the two associations in the General Massage section, below. Also check out *Massage: A Career at Your Fingertips, 2nd ed.* (Martin Ashley, Enterprise Publishing, 1995) and *Planning Your Career in Alternative Medicine* (Dianne J. B. Lyons, Avery Publishing Group, 1997).

General Massage

American Massage Therapy Association
820 Davis Street, Suite 100
Evanston, IL 60201
(847) 864-0123
Fax: (847) 864-1178
www.amtamassage.org
info@amtamassage.org

Associated Bodywork and Massage Professionals
28677 Buffalo Park Road
Evergreen, CO 80439
(800) 458-2267
(303) 674-8478
Fax: (303) 674-0859
expectmore@abmp.com
www.abmp.com

These associations both maintain lists of massage schools. If you're interested in sports or Swedish massage, can't find your favorite body-work method among those listed below, or just want more exhaustive information, they are perfect places to start.

Acro-Sage

Marantz School of Acro-Sage
331 Mirada Road
Half Moon Bay, CA 94019
(415) 458-3282
acrosage@aol.com

Acro-Sage combines inverted partner Yoga postures with Shiatsu massage. In inverted partner Yoga, practitioners lie face up on the floor and use their legs to hold the client in the air above them, in a variety of possible positions. Then, with their hands, they do the Shiatsu massage. This technique aids gravitational alignment of the spinal column, strengthens the immune and nervous systems, improves digestion, circulation, and complexion, detoxifies the lymph and adrenal glands, and reverses aging and the damaging effects of gravity.

Acupressure

American Oriental Bodywork Therapy Association
Laurel Oak Corporate Center, Suite 408
1010 Haddonfield-Berlin Road
Voorhees, NJ 08043
(609) 782-1616
Fax: (609) 782-1653
AOBTA@Prodigy.net
www.healthy.net/AOBTA

Acupressure is a healing art in which finger pressure is applied to specific points on the client's skin to restore the balance of chi (energy), release stress and tension, increase circulation, reduce pain, and foster vibrant health. Acupressure training courses tend to include classes in specific point locations and interrelations, organ meridians, pulse reading, the five elements, pressure techniques, point combining, and basic anatomy and physiology.

Craniosacral Therapy

The Upledger Institute
11211 Prosperity Farms Road, #D325
Palm Beach Gardens, FL 33410
(800) 233-5880
(407) 622-4334
(407) 622-4771

Craniosacral Therapy is the use of gentle manipulation to correct distortions in and enhance the function of the craniosacral system (which includes the brain, spinal cord, and the vertebral column). Practitioners use very light touch to allow free movement of the cerebrospinal fluid and encourage the body to heal itself, improving the function of the central nervous system, relieving stress, and enhancing health. Instruction includes evaluation of the craniosacral system, craniomandibular work, using breath and movement, anatomy and physiology of the craniosacral system, developing and refining light-touch palpation skills, and using a ten-step protocol to evaluate and help clients.

Hakomi Therapy and Hakomi Integrative Somatics

Hakomi Institute
P.O. Box 19438
Boulder, CO 80308
(303) 447-3290
Fax: (303) 402-0862

Hakomi Therapy and Hakomi Integrative Somatics are both body-centered approaches to healing, but while Hakomi Therapy is a body-centered psychotherapy, using touch and body awareness to access psychological information, Hakomi Integrative Somatics focuses on using bodywork and movement to resolve developmental issues and traumatic wounds in the body itself. The trainings include classes on body awareness and sensation, hands-on bodywork, strategies for resolving trauma, body reading, framing, working with memory, and integration techniques.

Hellerwork

Hellerwork International
406 Berry Street
Mt. Shasta, CA 96067
(800) 392-3900
(916) 926-2500
Fax: (916) 926-6839

Hellerwork is a healing system that combines movement education, structural bodywork, and dialogue to free clients of limiting mental and physical patterns, enhance their ability to easily adapt to life's changes, and realign the body using connective tissue reorganization techniques. Hellerwork training includes classwork in anatomy and physiology, myofascial anatomy, body systems, deep tissue bodywork, movement, psychological inquiry, and ergonomics.

Manual Lymph Drainage

North American Vodder Association
Dr. Vodder School–North America
P.O. Box 5701
Victoria, BC V8R 658
Canada
(250) 598-9862

U.S. Chapter
(440) 729-3258
Fax: (440) 729-2648

Manual Lymph Drainage is a gentle massage technique designed to stimulate the lymphatic system, thus cleansing the connective tissues, enhancing the activity of the immune system, and facilitating the healing of injuries, surgical trauma, and chronic conditions. Training courses teach anatomy and physiology, the five basic movements of Manual Lymph Drainage, therapeutic movements for the head, abdomen, and joints, and Manual Lymph Drainage theory.

Ortho-Bionomy

Society of Ortho-Bionomy International
P.O. Box 869
Madison, WI 53701
(800) 743-4890
(608) 257-8782

Ortho-Bionomy combines gentle movements, comfortable positions, dialogue, and energy work to reeducate and realign the body and stimulate the self-healing mechanism. Classes cover postural assessment, anatomy and physiology, neurolymphatic reflexes, isometric exercises, joint mobilization, and working with the energetic field.

Reposturing Dynamics

Phyziquest
111 St Matthews Avenue, Suite 3
San Mateo, CA 94401-2851
(888) 784-8257
Fax: (415) 344-7783
Vitality7@aol.com
www.Vitality7.com

Reposturing Dynamics is a system of breathing, stretching, and massage techniques that not only restores balance and flexibility to the body, but also provides natural body shaping and posture enhancement. Reposturing Dynamics Practitioner Certification programs include training sessions in anatomy, body balancing, and the full array of Reposturing

Dynamics techniques, geared toward reducing or eliminating sunken chests, sagging breasts, swayback, potbellies, saddlebags, pain, discomfort, and stress.

Polarity Therapy

American Polarity Therapy Association
2888 Bluff Street, #149
Boulder, CO 80301
(303) 545-2080
Fax: (303) 545-2161
Satrahq@aol.com

Polarity Therapy releases emotional and physical tension and pain by balancing the flow of energy in the body. Polarity practitioners use light touch, rhythmic motions, and deep pressure to resolve the energy blockages and imbalances that cause disease and discomfort. Classes cover such subjects as five element theory, core energy release, subtle energy balancing, polarity nutrition, anatomy and physiology, palpation skills and bodywork techniques, and breathing and energy exercises.

Reflexology

American Reflexology Certification Board
P.O. Box 620607
Littleton, CO 80162
(303) 933-6921
Fax: (303) 904-0460

Reflexology Association of America
4012 South Rainbow Boulevard, K-585
Las Vegas, NV 89103
(702) 871-9522
Fax: (702) 871-9522

Reflexology is the stimulation of reflex areas in the feet and hands that correspond to the organs, glands, and tissues of the body. This accelerates the body's healing ability, relieves stress, increases energy and circulation, and restores the free flow of energy. Reflexologist training courses include instruction in anatomy and physiology, the locations of reflex areas and points and their relationship to various body systems, using therapeutic Reflexology techniques, energy flow, and relaxation skills.

Reiki

American Reiki Masters Association
P.O. Box 130
Lake City, FL 32056
(904) 755-9638
Fax: (904) 755-9638

Reiki Alliance
East 33135 Canyon Road
P.O. Box 41
Cataldo, ID 83810
(208) 682-3535
Fax: (208) 682-4848
ReikiAlliance@compuserve.com

Reiki is a healing technique in which a practitioner gently places her or his hands on the client in a variety of specific areas, channeling spiritual energy to the client that reduces stress, promotes relaxation, and facilitates healing. Reiki training can include instruction in hand positions, symbol use, distance healing, giving attunements, harmonizing the energy of the chakras, removing negative energy, meditation, and several styles of healing.

Rolfing

The Guild for Structural Integration
P.O. Box 1559
1800 30th Street, Suite 310
Boulder, CO 80301
(800) 447-0150
(303) 447-0122
Fax: (303) 447-0108

Rolfing is a process of body reeducation that releases patterns of stress and impaired function through a deep-tissue massage technique. This results in improved posture, greater flexibility and balance, increased energy and breathing capacity, and a feeling of lightness and fluidity. Rolfing practitioner training programs include instruction in anatomy, kinesiology, physiology, analysis of human structure and movement, recognizing structural patterns, and mastering the ten-session series of Rolfing.

Rosen Method

Rosen Method Professional Association
(510) 644-4166

The Rosen Method combines bodywork and movement education to relax muscle tension and chronic holding, increase flexibility and vitality, and encourage physical and emotional awareness and personal growth. The bodywork technique uses gentle, direct touch to relax the client, which promotes the emergence of unconcious feeling, attitudes, and memories. The practitioner then uses words and touch to allow the client to release habitual tensions and old patterns. Rosen Method Movement consists of easy, unhurried movements that prevent physical difficulties before they arise and help clients feel better and age gracefully. Classes cover using the power of touch to loosen rigid postures, using breath to understand tension and inner barriers, and beginning and advanced bodywork and movement skills.

SHEN Therapy

International SHEN Therapy Association
3213 West Wheeler Street, #202
Seattle, WA 98199
(206) 298-9468
Fax: (206) 283-1256

SHEN Therapy is a noninvasive energy-based therapy that helps clients access, experience, and then release trapped negative emotions. SHEN is applied with a gentle touch, while working with the Biofield (chi energy), which moves through the body in specific patterns. SHEN training includes instruction in hand scanning, biofield sweeps, chronic pain evaluations, intrinsic motional techniques, and dealing with such emotional issues as depression, anxiety attacks, blocked grief, and post-traumatic stress disorders.

Shiatsu

Shiatsu Therapeutic Association of America
1314 South King Street, #601
Honolulu, HI 96814

American Oriental Bodywork Therapy Association
Laurel Oak Corporate Center, Suite 408
1010 Haddonfield-Berlin Road
Voorhees, NJ 08043
(609) 782-1616
Fax: (609) 782-1653
AOBTA@Prodigy.net
www.healthy.net/AOBTA

Shiatsu is a method of activating and balancing the flow of chi in which practitioners use their fingers, thumbs, palms, elbows, and knees to apply pressure to the client's acupuncture points. Shiatsu relieves muscle soreness, aids digestion and the nervous system, increases mental alertness, and harmonizes the body, mind, and spirit. Shiatsu training program includes classes that cover such topics as meridian theory, how to apply pressure, anatomy and physiology, surface reflex zones, abdominal massage, Hara diagnosis, and five element theory.

Soma Neuromuscular Integration

Soma Neuromuscular Integration Association
730 Klink Road
Buckley, WA 98321
(360) 829-1025
Fax: (360) 829-2805
www.Soma-Institute.com

Soma Neuromuscular Integration is a bodywork system that improves posture, joint, and nervous system function, and body alignment through physical manipulation of the muscular and connective tissues. Practitioners offer a ten-session series that includes, in addition to the deep bodywork, movement training and somatic education. Trainings include classes in anatomy and physiology, psychology for the bodyworker, pathophysiology, clinical applications of soma principles, and structural and anatomical assessment.

Trager Psychophysical Integration

Trager Institute
21 Locust Avenue
Mill Valley, CA 94941
(415) 388-2688
(415) 388-2710
tragerd@trager.com

Trager Psychophysical Integration is a system of movement reeducation that uses gentle and nonintrusive movements to release deep-seated physical and mental patterns and increase physical mobility and mental clarity. Practitioners use gentle rocking, cradling, and shaking movements to help clients change physically restrictive patterns, and then teach clients a system of simple movement sequences that maintain and enhance the benefits of the bodywork. Trager training includes classes in tablework, Mentastics, neuropatterning, anatomy and physiology, and hands-on practice sessions.

Trigger Point Myotherapy

National Association for Trigger Point Myotherapy
P.O. Box 68
Warmouth Port, MA 02675
(800) 845-3454
www.frontiernet.net/~painrel

Trigger Point Myotherapy combines trigger point compression (not unlike acupressure), massage, stretching, and exercise to relax muscles, relieve pain, and increase motion and strength. Trigger Point training includes courses in point location, anatomy, kinesiology, myofascial bodywork, corrective and therapeutic exercise.

Watsu

Worldwide Aquatic Bodywork Association
P.O. Box 889
Middletown, CA 95461
(707) 987-3801

Watsu is a form of water massage in which practitioners use the stretches and principles of Shiatsu on clients floating in 96-degree water, which relaxes the client, increases flexibility, and takes weight off the vertebrae allowing the spine to be moved in ways unavailable out of water. Watsu instruction teaches students Watsu's major positions, such as the Water Breath Dance and the Simple Transition Flow, detailed bodywork, and specific points, moves, and stretches.

Zero Balancing

Zero Balancing Association
P.O. Box 1727
Capitola, CA 95010
(408) 476-0665
zbaoffice@aol.com
www.zerobalancing.com

Zero Balancing is a method of aligning body energy with the body's physical structure that integrates Eastern and Western systems of touch therapy. Zero Balancing practitioners evaluate client's energy fields and balance their skeletal structure by focusing on the client's mind, body, or spirit to remove energy blockages. Zero Balancing training includes coursework on touch techniques that organize vibratory fields in the body, relieve stress, and promote a sense of wholeness and well-being.

Colon Hydrotherapy ◆ ◆ ◆

Colon hydrotherapy, or colonic irrigation, is the therapeutic introduction of water, sometimes combined with healing herbs, into the colon. This cleanses the body, removing accumulated impurities and waste and preventing toxins trapped in the colon from being released into the bloodstream. Colon hydrotherapy is often used to promote general health and purity, or to complement another alternative healing modality such as naturopathy or acupuncture.

Internal Environment Institute
11739 Washington Boulevard
Los Angeles, CA 90066
(310) 572-6223
Fax: (310) 572-6217

The institute trains professional colon hydrotherapists. The curriculum includes classwork on the history, purpose, and benefits of colon hydrotherapy, the anatomy, physiology, pathologies, and parasites of the colon, and how meridian lines and acupressure points relate to bowel function and stimulation. Students also learn how the various systems of the body (circulation, digestion, respiration) relate to colon hydrotherapy, and the proper procedure for administering a colonic, including instruments, sanitation, sterilization, room presentation, and supplies. Students gain much hands-on experience: there are between two and four hours of class participation every day, and each student gives and receives one colonic per day. The institute also offers classes in related areas, teaching the benefits of fasting, skin brushing, deep breathing, internal detox methods, food combining, supplements, laxatives, and business ethics.

How long it takes: 16 days

What it costs: $1,495

Credit cards are accepted.

ReNew Life School of Colon Therapy
1007 North MacDill Avenue
Tampa, FL 33607
(800) 690-9988
(813) 871-3200

The school offers a professional training course in colon hydrotherapy that consists of a correspondence course and classroom-based classwork. The training includes instruction in anatomy and physiology, nutrition, parasites, equipment and supplies, sanitation and hygiene, ethics, practitioner/client relationships, and business. Students learn the basics while completing the correspondence course, and then participate in lectures and hands-on work to gain proficiency.

How long it takes: Correspondence course—students work at their
own pace.
Classroom-based course—9 days

What it costs: $1,550

Visa and Mastercard are accepted.

DoveStar Institute
50 Whitehall Road
Hooksett, NH 03106-2104
(603) 669-5104
(603) 669-9497
Fax: (603) 625-1919

120 Court Street
Plymouth, MA 02360
(508) 830-0068
Fax: (508) 830-0288

39 Main Street
Attleboro, MA 02703
(508) 222-1683
Fax: (508) 222-3691

4C Northridge Drive
Hilton Head Island, SC 29928
(803) 342-3361
Fax: (803) 342-3639

The institute offers a Colon Hydrotherapy practitioner course that trains students to give colonics using the Toxygen Colon Therapy Machine. Students learn to help clients eliminate toxins, purify the liver, blood, and organs of elimination, and strengthen the lymph and digestive systems. Classes include Detox Hydrotherapy, Colon Hydrotherapy, and the Digestive System.

The institute also offers training programs in hypnotherapy and breathwork. See the appropriate sections for more information.

How long it takes: 2 months

What it costs: $885

The institute accepts credit cards, and there are some work-study positions available.

Colon Therapeutics Research Institute
2909 Main Avenue
Groves, TX 77619
(409) 963-0300
Fax: (409) 962-2251

The institute offers a training program that certifies colonic hygiene technicians. Coursework includes anatomy and physiology, colon irrigation procedures, disinfection procedures, pathology of the digestive system, food combining, psychophysiological responses to colon irrigation, business practices, and professional ethics. There is also hands-on training; students participate in administration of twenty to forty colon irrigations, including the student's solo administration of between ten and twenty irrigations. The trainee will also receive four colon irrigations personally to gain an understanding of the client's experience of the process.

How long it takes: 100 hours

What it costs: $750

Mind Body Naturopathic Institute
10911 West Avenue
San Antonio, TX 78213
(210) 308-8888
Fax: (210) 349-5679

The institute offers colon hydrotherapy certification workshops. Courses include health and hygiene, anatomy and physiology, sanitation procedures, colon hydrotherapy procedures, breath and energy techniques, Neuro-Linguistics for the Colon Hydrotherapist, and how to build a successful business. The workshop also includes hands-on sessions with real clients, giving students the opportunity to document up to twenty-five client colon hydrotherapy sessions. The Institute will offer a class in your area if you can provide ten students.

How long it takes: 8 days

What it costs: $1,100

Credit cards are accepted.

Movement Training ◆ ◆ ◆

Movement training, although it's not as common as bodywork, is a large and growing field. And this section, like the bodywork section, primarily includes associations that represent a variety of movement training systems. What all the methods have in common, though, is a focus on movement education in which the client relearns to move, stand, and breathe, in a way that supports and enhances health, grace, balance, relaxation, and physical—and often psychological—growth.

Many of the programs also include some elements of hands-on body-work.

Alexander Technique

North American Society of Teachers of the Alexander Technique
(800) 473-0620
Fax: (612) 822-7224
nastat@ix.netcom.com

The Alexander Technique is an educational process in which practitioners teach students (clients) to identify and change the faulty habit patterns that interfere with their natural design for movement and expression. Practitioners use hands-on guidance and verbal and visual instruction to teach efficient ways of moving that improve posture, balance, poise, and coordination, and relieve tension and pain. The curriculum of Alexander Technique training courses focuses on hands-on study, and also includes instruction in anatomy and physiology and the writings of F. M. Alexander, the originator of the technique.

Aston-Patterning

Aston-Patterning
P.O. Box 3568
Incline Village, NV 89450
(702) 831-8228
Fax: (702) 831-8955
AstonPat@aol.com

Aston-Patterning is comprised of four forms of work: movement coaching, bodywork, ergonomic work, and fitness training. Movement coaching teaches clients to move with ease and efficiency, decreasing tension and stress. Bodywork releases structural and functional holding patterns. Ergonomic work focuses on achieving optimal alignment, functionality, and integrity. And fitness training includes loosening, toning, stretching, and cardiovascular fitness. Training programs include classes in movement education, soft tissue work, facial toning, and using ergonomic products.

Dynamic Movement

Dynamic Health and Fitness Institute
P.O. Box 355
Corte Madera, CA 94976
(415) 924-4013
Fax: (415) 924-5342
dynamic@well.com

The institute offers certified instructor training in Dynamic Movement, a system of movement education that helps people relieve their chronic musculoskeletal pain, exercise with more comfort, feel more graceful in their bodies, and minimize the effects of aging. Certified Dynamic Movement Instructors teach clients how to elongate their bodies, strengthen neglected postural muscles, improve flexibility, move in a pain-free fashion, maximize muscle recruitment to get better workouts, and breathe more deeply and rhythmically.

There are three levels of training: Level I covers Dynamic Walking, focusing on developing correct technique and flexibility. Level II trains students to teach Dynamic Pace and Dynamic Speed, and focuses on aerobic conditioning. Level III trains students to teach Dynamic Hiking, Dynamic Power Walking, and Dynamic Running, and focuses on building strength. Students can begin teaching on the day they complete the first level of training, and can use the designation of Dynamic Walking Instructor after completing this level. They become Dynamic Walking Trainers after completion of the third level. The institute provides marketing materials to help graduates build a clientele.

How long it takes: Each of the 3 levels—7 to 8 days

What it costs: Each of the 3 levels—$1,300

A prepayment discount is available.

Feldenkrais Method

Feldenkrais Guild
P.O. Box 489
Albany, OR 97321
(800) 775-2118
(541) 926-0981
(541) 926-0572
feldngld@peak.org
www.Feldenkrais.com

The Feldenkrais Method combines movement awareness and functional integration into a system that increases body awareness, aids physical rehabilitation, reduces pain, and improves balance and coordination. In movement awareness, practitioners teach students improved ways to move their bodies, and in functional integration they use gentle hands-on manipulation to address the students' breathing and body alignment. The training program includes instruction in large actions of the entire body, fine movements of the hands, feet, mouth, and eyes, developmental movements of infants, movement sequences, functional anatomy, skeletal contact points, nonverbal communication skills, and using subtle movement and mental imagery.

Rubenfeld Synergy Method

Rubenfeld Synergy Center
115 Waverly Place
New York, NY 10011
(212) 254-5100
(212) 254-1174
Rubenfeld@aol.com

Rubenfeld Synergy combines elements of the Alexander Technique and the Feldenkrais Method with Gestalt theory and Eriksonian hypnotherapy. Practitioners use verbal expression, movement, breathing patterns, body posture, kinesthetic awareness, imagination, sound, and bodywork to access the emotions and memories that often result in energy blocks, tensions, and imbalances. They then help clients integrate the emerging feelings with the present experience. Instruction includes where, how, and when to use therapeutic touch, how conscious control affects movement, the use of words and images, kinesthetic awareness, integrating polarities, appropriate use of timing in verbal and nonverbal interventions, reading the client's coding patterns, developing intuitional capacities, and listening to process as well as content.

Yoga Instruction and Therapy

International Association of Yoga Therapists
20 Sunnyside Avenue, Suite A-243
Mill Valley, CA 94941
(415) 332-2478

Yoga Journal (magazine)

Each year, *Yoga Journal* publishes a national list of Yoga teacher training programs in their July/August Issue.

The many systems of Yoga are based on the ancient Indian teachings of physical, mental, and spiritual development. Yoga instructors teach postures, breathing, and some elements of meditation to help clients address back pain or other specific medical conditions, work toward optimal posture and alignment of the body, and achieve spiritual enlightenment and access to higher consciousness. Yoga therapy practitioners combine Yoga postures and breathing with therapeutic verbal dialogue to help clients address mental and physical problems and achieve a fuller spiritual life.

Natural Vision Correction ◆ ◆ ◆

Most of the natural vision correction programs are based on the Bates Method of Vision Re-Education, a system of mental and physical exercises designed to improve vision in a natural, holistic way. The idea is that most poor vision is caused by weak or stressed eye muscles, so strengthening and relaxing those muscles leads to improved eyesight. Although this career is in the Bodywork and Physical Health chapter, practitioners do not usually touch clients—instead, they teach them the principles of vision re-education (with various refinements depending on the school) to naturally correct their own eyesight. Some common techniques used by vision improvement practitioners are physical and mental exercises, meditation, and visualization.

The Natural Vision Center of San Francisco
P.O. Box 16403
San Francisco, CA 94116
(415) 665-2010
Fax: (415) 664-2121
relrn2see@aol.com
www.nvcsf.com

The center trains Certified Natural Vision Teachers, who help clients use the Bates Method of Natural Eyesight Re-Education to improve their eyesight and relearn the correct habits of natural seeing. The program includes classes on the Bates principles of natural vision, anatomy and physiology of the eye, fusion principles and techniques, color awareness and 3-D perception, physiological aspects of visual blur, and methods for building a clientele. Other subjects include theories of visual distortion, effects of nutrition and herbs on eyesight, teaching individuals, groups, infants, children, and the elderly, and the legal status of natural vision teachers. The training also includes an apprenticeship and practice teaching opportunities.

How long it takes: 2 months

What it costs: $2,200

Credit cards are accepted.

School for Self-Healing
1718 Taraval Street
San Francisco, CA 94116
(415) 665-9574
Fax: (415) 665-1318
school@self-healing.org
www.self-healing.org

The school offers a Teacher of Vision Improvement training program. Students must first complete the Meir Schneider Self-Healing Method practitioner/educator course, which teachs them to use movement, massage, and other tools to support weak organs and organ systems, reverse degenerative conditions, increase movement and mobility, and improve general health. Students then take the Vision Improvement training program, which covers the Schneider Vision Improvement Method. It includes classes in biofeedback and cranial massage for vision improvement, Yoga for the eyes, supervised client sessions, and supervised teaching of a vision support group.

How long it takes: Self-Healing Practitioner/Educator Training—260 hours
Teacher of Vision Improvement Training—72 hours

What it costs: Self-Healing Practitioner/Educator Training—$4,400
Teacher of Vision Improvement Training—$700

Students may repeat courses for one-third the initial tuition. Payment plans are available.

Khalsa School of Good Vision
8925 Keith Avenue
West Hollywood, CA 90069
(310) 550-7203

The Khalsa School combines the Bates Method of vision improvement with training in the use of herbs, minerals, meditation, eye exercises, and psychic protection information to provide clients with better vision and relief from eye strain. The school offers teacher training on an individual basis.

How long it takes: 28 hours

What it costs: $1,120

Vision Training Institute
1351 Gibson Highlands
El Cajon, CA 92021
(619) 440-5224
Fax: (619) 440-5224
eyerobics@aol.com
http://members.aol.com/eyerobics/welcome/htm

The institute offers a Bates Method teacher training program. Students learn a natural method of visual education that uses relaxation, movement, imagery, and an understanding of the visual process to help clients improve their vision. The curriculum covers the history and development of the Bates Method, the structure and function of the eye, the causes of defective vision, the mental side of seeing, the psychology of attention, memory, and imagination, the autonomic nervous system, and breathing and body posture. The training includes practice applications for conditions such as myopia, presbyopia, glaucoma, strabismus, and astigmatism. Business-related topics such as creative teaching methods, the legal status of the Bates Method, setting up a vision studio, and methods of building a practice are also covered.

How long it takes: 3 months (intensive) or 6 to 12 months (part-time). One hundred hours of practice teaching are also required.

What it costs: $5,000

Beyond 20/20 Vision
RR#5 S26 C39
Gibsons, B.C. VON 1VO
Canada
(604) 885-7118
Fax: (604) 885-0608
beyond_20/20@sunshine.net
www.sunshine.net/www/0/sn0011/what.htm

Beyond 20/20 Vision offers Professional Vision Educator certification training programs in Canada and the United States. The training teaches students a holistic approach of well-being, clearer eyesight, and deeper vision. Vision Educators help clients go to the root causes of vision distortion, clarify life vision and purpose, and improve eyesight. The training includes coursework in assessing vision fitness, designing a program of vision fitness activities, mastering therapeutic processes based on information gleaned from the iris and from lens prescriptions, understanding the connection between food, light, color, and well-being, and designing compensating and therapeutic lens prescriptions.

How long it takes: 21 days

What it costs: $3,300

Credit cards are accepted.

Chapter 7

✹ ✹ ✹ ✹

Consulting and Counseling

This chapter includes careers that require one-on-one consultation with clients. Consultants and counselors offer expertise, information, and support for specific goals, issues, and questions. These careers differ from therapy careers in that their main focus is not aiding psychological or spiritual transformation but providing useful information. However, there is some overlap—if your primary interest is counseling, be sure to also read the Therapy chapter.

The categories included in this chapter are Birth, Pregnancy, and Labor Support, Coaching and Life Guidance, Genealogy, Graphology, and Health-Related Consulting. If you're interested in gathering and disseminating information and offering educated advice—whether you want to work with pregnant women, professionals, businesses, families, people with health concerns, couples, or other groups—check out the following careers. Just because you've always offered your wise advice for free doesn't mean that, with a little training, it's not a salable commodity.

Birth, Pregnancy, and Labor Support ◆ ◆ ◆

Most of the programs in this section train labor or birth assistants, also known as doulas. Doulas offer emotional and physical support to a pregnant woman and her family during pregnancy, labor, and the postpartum period. They provide explanations of medical procedures, exercise and positioning suggestions, massage and other pain relief measures, and many other services. In fact, the presence of a doula reduces the likelihood of cesarean section by half, the length of labor by a quarter, and the use of narcotics by about a third. If you're interested in advocating for and assisting a birthing woman or couple, birth, pregnancy, and labor support can be an exciting and extremely fulfilling career. Other programs in this section offer training in other baby-related fields such as breast-feeding consulting and infant massage.

Doulas of North America (DONA) is a national organization that certifies doulas and provides a list of doula training courses in North America. If you're interested in a career as a professional doula, call them first (you can find their information below—they offer their own classes in addition to acting as a referral source).

Not included in this section is midwifery, as it requires a nursing or master's degree. If you're interested in midwifery, contact the American College of Nurse-Midwives Education Department at 818 Connecticut Avenue, N.W., Suite 900, Washington, D.C. 20006, (202) 728-9860, for a list of training programs.

The Chapman Family Center
1151 25th Street
Santa Monica, CA 90403
(310) 453-5144

The center offers a Birth Assistant training course that combines lectures, texts, role-play, and hands-on practice to develop theoretical knowledge and build practical skills. The course assumes that students are familiar with the basics (such as anatomy of the reproductive system, physiology of pregnancy, common procedures and tests, and so on). If they aren't, the center provides a reading list and suggests that prospective students attend a childbirth education class. The coursework itself covers the prenatal experience, the role of the doula, interpartum and postpartum support, and the scope of a doula's practice.

The center also offers a Postpartum Doula course, which trains doulas to provide support with breast-feeding and newborn care and health, and even help new mothers eat right for the first few weeks after giving birth.

How long it takes: Birth Assistant—3 days
                        Postpartum Doula—3 days

What it costs: Birth Assistant—$395
                   Postpartum Doula—$395

Academy of Certified Birth Educators
2001 East Prairie Circle, Suite 1
Olathe, KS 66062
(800) 444-8223
(913) 782-5116
Fax: (913) 397-0933

The academy offers two programs: Professional Labor Support (Doula) and Childbirth Educator. The Labor Support program begins with a course designed to teach students anatomy, physiology, and terminology, and to review the labor and birth process. A more in-depth course follows, which prepares students to become qualified labor support professionals. This course covers the emotional and psychological aspects of labor and birth, how to deal with difficult labors and births, and how to empower the woman and her partner to cope with complications. Classes include Prenatal Contact, Intrapartum Support, Comfort Measures, Pain Relief, Labor and Birth for Teens, Caesarean Birth, Breast-Feeding, and Marketing.

The Childbirth Educator training and certification is based on the academy's Birth and Beginnings Education (BABE) course. The BABE training includes coursework on birth positions, nutrition, fetal development, breathing, pain theory, breast-feeding, teen pregnancy, group dynamics, communication skills, and adult learning principles. It also discusses how to set up and market your own childbirth education classes, and it provides students with a teacher's manual.

How long it takes: Labor Support—3 days
                      Childbirth Educator—3 days

What it costs: Labor Support—$275
                    Childbirth Educator—$350

Association of Labor Assistants and Childbirth Educators

P.O. Box 382724
Cambridge, MA 02238
(617) 441-2500
Fax: (617) 441-3157
alacehq@aol.com
www.alace.org

The association offers two certification training programs: Certified Labor Assistant and Certified Childbirth Educator. Certified Labor Assistants learn to help women avoid unnecessary interventions and cesareans, provide practical suggestions for working with contractions and pain, reinforce women's confidence in their own ability to birth normally, act as advocates for the woman within the birth team of care providers, and offer follow-through during the postpartum period. The certification process includes attending a workshop, receiving infant CPR certification, successful completion of a written exam, self-evaluations of six births at which the Labor Assistant has attended, and three written evaluations from mothers, midwives, doctors, or nurses.

Certified Childbirth Educators educate and empower parents to choose the best birthing options for themselves, teach skills and tools to help women reclaim the process of birth, encourage holistic, woman-centered care, and help women experience birth's transforming power with respect, dignity, safety, and confidence. Educators are encouraged to develop their own teaching styles and curriculum to suit the needs of their community. Recommended classes include Pregnancy—Growth and Decision Making, The Process of Birth, When Giving Birth Is Difficult, and The Newborn, Postpartum, and the Family. The provisional certification process requires that the student complete the home-study learning modules and pass the final exam. Full certification requires that the student receive positive evaluations from six women or couples who have attended classes.

How long it takes: Labor Assistant—3-day workshop plus approximately 12 months for the other requirements
                     Childbirth Educator—2 to 12 months

What it costs: Labor Assistant certification—$385
Tuition for Childbirth Educator certification—
$695

Payment plans are available, and credit cards are accepted.

MotherLove
20 Ash Street
Westwood, NJ 07675
(201) 358-2703
Fax: (201) 664-4405

MotherLove offers labor support doula and postpartum doula training. The labor support doula training includes coursework on female reproductive anatomy and terminology, fetal development, the stages of labor, problem labors, common interventions (such as induction, pain medication, forceps, vacuum extraction, and cesarean section), breathing patterns, and bearing-down techniques. Students also learn about prenatal contact between the doula and the client, how to provide emotional support and physical comfort measures during labor, how to support a client during a difficult labor, breast-feeding skills, and, finally, business practices.

Postpartum doulas provide information and experience about baby care, such as bathing, diapering, circumcision and umbilical cord care, sleeping, coping with crying babies, and so on. They also help with postpartum adjustment of the woman and her family, postpartum depression, and breast-feeding. The postpartum doula training covers home visit protocol, working with fathers, offering comfort measures, and evaluating warning signs (such as perineal tears, lochia, afterbirth contractions, and uterine infections).

Postpartum doula students are also required to get certified in infant/child CPR and first aid. MotherLove offers a one-day certification class to fill this requirement.

How long it takes: Labor Support Doula—3 days
Postpartum Doula—4 days (including CPR certification)

What it costs: Labor Support Doula—$350
Postpartum Doula—$540

International Association of Infant Massage—US Chapter
1720 Willow Creek Circle, Suite 516
Eugene, OR 97402
(800) 248-5432
(541) 431-6280
Fax: (541) 485-7372

The association offers a Certified Infant Massage Instructor training program, in which students are taught to encourage caregivers to interact with their babies using loving and appropriate touch. As a result, caregivers learn to recognize their babies' body language and cries and to provide relief techniques for gas and colic. Instructors teach a series of classes for caregivers on the benefits and methods of interactive infant massage. The classes include information on strengthening and regulating the digestive, respiratory, and circulatory systems, enhancing the caregiver's ability to deal with fussy, sick, or special-needs babies, relieving discomfort and promoting relaxation and loving communication.

The training program is offered nationwide by IAIM-certified trainers. Call the association for specific locations.

How long it takes: 4 days

What it costs: $550

Breastfeeding Support Consultants
228 Park Lane
Chalfont, PA 18914
(215) 822-1281
Fax: (215) 997-7879
bsccenter@aol.com

BSC trains lactation consultants to care for breast-feeding mothers and infants in a variety of settings. Consultants educate and counsel breast-feeding mothers, handle special breast-feeding problems, develop support programs and plans of care, train health care providers, and work with primary care providers. The training includes classes in breast milk production and synthesis, counseling and communication skills, immunology and allergy protection, cultural issues in nutrition, dietary advice to low-income women, infant growth and development, dehydration and hypernatremia, supplemental foods and weaning, devices and techniques to assist feeding, postpartum depression, maternal and infant health conditions, professional development, and employment considerations.

Students have the option of taking the BSC training either through home study or through a combination of home study and classroom instruction.

To qualify for the certification exam, students need to complete 2,500 hours of hands-on, professional breast-feeding counseling. Five hundred hours are awarded for completion of the course. Additional hours can be obtained through a formal mentor program or traineeship in a hospital-based lactation clinic.

How long it takes: Home study—24 to 36 months
Classroom/home study—6 days of classroom
instruction, plus 6 to 12 months of home study

What it costs: Home study—$2,125
Classroom/home study—$1,970

Payment plans are available, and credit cards are accepted.

Doulas of North America
1100-23rd Avenue East
Seattle, WA 98112
(206) 324-5440
AskDONA@aol.com
www.dona.com

Doulas of North America, in addition to being a national doula information center, offers doula training classes. The courses prepare students to offer emotional and physical support to pregnant women during pregnancy, labor, birth, and the postpartum period. The classes train students to explain medical procedures, offer advice during pregnancy, suggest exercise and physical modifications to increase the comfort of the pregnant woman, help with preparation of a birth plan, offer massage and other nonpharmacological pain-relief measures, and make positioning suggestions during labor and birth. Students also learn to support the woman's partner, help avoid unnecessary interventions, and help with breast-feeding preparation.

For certification, DONA requires that prospective doulas complete an approved doula training course, complete a reading list, provide labor support to at least three clients after taking the training, provide evaluations from at least three clients and at least three nurses, doctors, or midwives, and meet several other requirements.

How long it takes: 2 to 3 days

What it costs: $125 to $300

Coaching and Life Guidance ◆ ◆ ◆

You're reading this book because you're trying to figure out what to do with your life. If you're also interested in helping other people figure out what to do with their lives—or, if they already know *what*, helping them figure out and achieve *how*—you've come to the right section. Life purpose consulting and professional coaching schools train students to meet with individuals—and sometimes couples, families, groups, and businesses—to help them define and achieve their goals, especially (but not exclusively) their vocational and financial goals. This section also includes holistic coaching and a color-based counseling system—if you're interested in coaching, healing, and a touch of therapy, pay particular attention to them. If you're interested in a more standard counseling career, focus on the life purpose and professional coaching programs.

The Coaching Exchange
1527 Veteran Avenue, Suite 7
Los Angeles, CA 90024
(310) 479-3519
Fax: (310) 478-9892
cex@pacificnet.net

The Coaching Exchange offers a professional coaching training program that combines group training courses and personal coaching with business and training manuals, workbooks, tapes, tool kits, and software. Students are trained to establish, build, and manage their own coaching company through three courses in an Evolutionary Transitions Course Series: Foundations, Conversations, and Intentions. The Foundations course helps students confront their patterns of ineffectiveness, discover their most fundamental commitments, and learn a technology for generating more personal greatness on a daily basis. The Conversations course teaches students how to reshape their entire reality through conversation, whether it be related to personal well-being, relationship, family, or business. And the Intentions course shows students how to harness the power of their intention to manifest their goals with ease, grace, and power. By the completion of the first course, students will know if they should pursue coaching professionally. By the completion of the second course, they'll begin practicing coaching participants in a concurrent Foundations course. And by the end of the third course, they will fully launch their business and establish their own clientele. The Coaching Exchange also offers an Advanced Coaching Program and an Executive Coaching Program.

How long it takes: 1 year

What it costs: $12,500

Occasional scholarships and fee deferment options are available.

Life Purpose Institute
5755 Oberlin Drive, Suite 208
San Diego, CA 92121
(619) 552-2575
Fax: (619) 452-7303

The institute trains Life Purpose and Career Consultants, who use a career and life clarification process to help clients discover their life purpose and find the work they love. Consultants guide clients through a self-exploration process, help them design and select a career, develop a plan, overcome obstacles, and find a job or start a business. Students learn career counseling theory and techniques, as well as how to facilitate the Life Purpose Process, provide ongoing business and personal coaching, and use unique exercises to help clients discover exciting career options. They also learn how to create a customized marketing program and build their own private practice.

The institute will come to your area if you gather eight or more people interested in taking its course.

How long it takes: New Facilitator Training—4 days
                            Advanced Training and Certification—4 days

What it costs: New Facilitator Training—$1,500
                            Advanced Training and Certification—$1,000

Credit cards are accepted.

Professional Coaching Training
The Hudson Institute of Santa Barbara
3463 State Street, Suite 520
Santa Barbara, CA 93105
(800) 582-4401
(805) 682-3883
Fax: (805) 569-0025
Hudson@silcom.com

The Hudson Institute offers professional certification in Individual and Organizational Coaching. The certification course is an advanced learning process that trains qualified professional coaches in both core skills and specialized fields of coaching. Students learn how to form the coaching relationship, use change as a resource, tap emerging purpose and passion, link inner purpose with outer work, find bridges to the future, and inspire and guide new scenarios through mentoring, training, planning, and networking. Specialized areas of training include coaching nonprofits, young adults, organizations in transition, couples, and executives.

Completion of a LifeLaunch Seminar and a Coaching Seminar are prerequisites for entrance into the Certification Program. The LifeLaunch Seminar helps students define a meaningful purpose, identify significant priorities for the next few years, connect their beliefs to their daily schedules, link personal goals to opportunities and resources, and write a specific plan with strategies to address their concerns and obstacles. The Coaching Seminar then presents the basic skills and concepts of professional coaching and allows students to practice coaching skills and receive feedback in small supervised groups. And, finally, the Certification Program follows up on what students learned at the Coaching Seminar with supervised field experience. Trainees receive support and supervision from the institute's coaching faculty through intensive coaching training sessions and written, telephone, and E-mail contacts. Successful completion of the Certification Program is based on the demonstration and application of coaching skills and knowledge.

How long it takes: LifeLaunch Seminar—4 days
Coaching Seminar—3 days
Certification Program—4 4-day intensives (which generally take 1 year to complete)

What it costs: LifeLaunch—$1,495
Coaching Seminar—$1,150
Certification Program—$6,950

Credit cards are accepted.

The Coaches Training Institute
1879 Second Street
San Rafael, CA 94901
(800) 691-6008
(415) 451-6000
Fax: (415) 460-6878
CoachTrain@aol.com
www.thecoaches.com

CTI trains professional coaches. The training program focuses on encouraging students to develop their own personal coaching style as they help clients set and prioritize goals, move through obstacles, and realize fulfillment and balance in their lives. The institute offers three levels of training: the Professional Coaching Course, the Advanced Curriculum, and the Certification Program.

The Professional Coaching Course teaches students coaching and communication skills, how to respond to the most common coaching situations, how to help clients set and prioritize goals, how to move clients through fears and concerns, and how to lay the foundations of a coaching practice. The Advanced Curriculum includes topics such as conducting values clarification, identifying self-defeating behavior, integrating fulfillment, balance, and process coaching, and designing and implementing a life plan. The Certification Program is for students who are committed to becoming Certified Professional Personal Coaches. It consists of hands-on coaching and supervision of coaching appointments, and provides structure and support for students to build a thriving coaching practice. Certification also requires being a client in a professional coaching relationship, participating in weekly group calls, and completing one hundred billable coaching hours.

How long it takes: Professional Coaching—3 days
Advanced Curriculum—3 days
Certification Program—7 months (primarily via telephone)

What it costs: Professional Coaching—$575
Advanced Curriculum—$425
Certification Program—$2,475

Credit cards are accepted.

Journeys of Wisdom
4889 Sinclair Road, #202
Columbus, OH 43229
(800) 889-1976
(614) 888-1240
Fax: (614) 848-4342
Iamwisdom@ibm.net
www.Iam-wisdom.com

Journeys of Wisdom offers a series of ten workshops that lead to certification as a Holistic Coach. After the first workshop, Level I, students
can choose to take Levels II through IX in any order they choose, finishing with Level X.

Level I, Harmonizing Mind, Body, and Spirit, explores how energy
created from the conscious, subconscious, and unconscious affects the
body, mind, and spirit. Level II, Advanced Healing Techniques, builds
on the healing techniques introduced in Level I and introduces NLP,
hypnotherapy, gestalt, meridian and chakra balancing, and creating
healthy relationship patterns. Level III, Awakening the True Self, shows
how to use Holistic Kinesiology to uncover the patterns or "armor" used
to numb emotional, physical, mental, or spiritual pain. Level IV,
Mind/Body Kinesiology Integration Technique, teaches how to use
muscle-testing techniques to locate and release unbalanced energy in
the body. Level V, Piercing Illusions, explains how to transform illusions
in order to heal and grow. Level VI, the 37 Universal Laws, offers students a clear understanding of the laws that govern existence and how
they affect daily living. Level VII, Creating Clear Light Healing Energy,
trains students to scan for, experience, and balance body energy. Level
VIII, Expanding the Dominion and Domain of Our Influence, explores
the limits created by the ego and human control dramas that drain
energy and teaches how to manifest new possibilities. Level IX,
Conscious Creation toward the Divine Order of Life, prepares and conditions the mind to feel harmony with all life experiences. And Level
X, Holistic Coaching, ties it all together and addresses the responsibil-

ities and opportunities of professional Holistic Coaching, including how to develop a mission statement and attract prosperity.

How long it takes: Each workshop—3 days

Entire series—approximately 9 months

What it costs: $190 per workshop

Scholarships are available and credit cards are accepted.

Aura-Soma USA
P.O. Box 1688
Canyon Lake, TX 78130
(830) 935-2355
Fax: (830) 935-2508

Aura-Soma USA offers Aura-Soma Practitioner training courses, and serves as a national information clearinghouse, referring prospective students to practitioner training programs nationwide.

Aura-Soma is a color system that combines the energies of color with essential oils, herbs, and crystals, to help people discover their special gifts, the purpose of their life journey, and the personality issues and challenges in their lives. A client begins an Aura-Soma session by selecting four balance bottles—glass bottles filled with two layers of colored liquid containing herbal extracts, essential oils, gems, and crystals. These bottles reveal the client's life purpose, the challenges on her or his path, how the purpose and challenges are incorporated and integrated, and the future the client is creating for himself or herself. The Aura-Soma practitioner then does a color reading to determine which frequencies the client most needs, and applies them in a healing session.

Aura-Soma practitioner training consists of three courses—Foundation, Intermediate, and Advanced. The Foundation course teaches color theory, sympathetic resonance, interpretation of color selections, consultation procedures, the principles of Aura-Soma as a noninvasive soul system, and offers practical experience with a hand massage technique and aura and subtle energy work.

The Intermediate Course introduces the connection between Aura-Soma and Buddhism, numerology, astrology, and homeopathy. It teaches the symbolism of color, Aura-Soma and the Yogic view of subtle energies, diagnostic interpretation at the chakra and subtle energy levels, and the use of gems. It also includes an introduction to color correspondence with astrology, color in clothing and decor, and the primary colors in relation to Buddhist metaphysics.

The Advanced Course enables students to use their intuition to connect with the essence of the training. It covers color theory in relation to consciousness evolution, balance in relation to the Tree of Life, the Tarot, and the Kabballah, subtle anatomy, and a deepening of consultation skills.

Finally, two ten-thousand-word papers, sixty hours of consultation, and a basic anatomy and physiology course must be completed in order to be certified and receive a license to practice.

How long it takes: 6 days per course

What it costs: $550 per course

Genealogy ◆ ◆ ◆

Professional genealogists offer a wide range of services, including teaching and lecturing, documenting Native American lineages, preparing lineage applications, and helping clients discover their family history. And they must develop a basic knowledge of the principles, resources, and research methodologies of many fields, including history, geography, law, and paleography. If you find the prospect of such varied work with so many subjects intriguing, you're halfway home—if you also enjoy delving into archives, rooting out records, and performing meticulous research, you are definitely genealogist material.

This is one field in which we recommend certification—contact the Board for Certification of Genealogists (P.O. Box 14291, Washington, D.C. 20004) for more information.

If you're interested in becoming a professional genealogist, you may want to combine two of the followings trainings, particularly the National Genealogical Society's correspondence course and the Samford Institute's specialized courses, to get both a basic grounding and hands-on experience in the field.

Institute of Genealogy and Historical Research
Samford University
Birmingham, AL 35229
(205) 870-2198

Fax: (205) 870-2642
www.samford.edu/schools/ighr/ighr.html
mbthomas@samford.edu

The institute offers intensive genealogical training courses for beginning and advanced genealogists. Classes include Techniques and Technology, Library and Archival Resources, Advanced Methodology and
Evidence Analysis, Writing and Publishing for Genealogists, and Finding English Roots: Colonial Times to the Industrial Age. Instruction
covers topics such as probate records, county courthouse research, military and pension records, ship passenger lists, psychological frameworks
for tracking men and women, tax rolls, electoral rolls, and parish
records. Other areas of study include computer use for professional
genealogists, genetic research, lecturing and instructing, commercial
publishng, using law libraries, preparing a client report, and designing
a professional genealogy business. The institute also offers training
trips to England and Scotland for students specializing in British
research.

How long it takes: 1 week

What it costs: $425

Credit cards are accepted.

Brigham Young University
Department of Independent Study
206 Harman Building
P.O. Box 21514
Provo, UT 84602
(800) 298-8792
(801) 378-2868
Fax: (801) 378-5817
indstudy@byu.edu
http://coned.byu.edu/is/

Brigham Young offers a correspondence certificate program in Family
History that provides a solid background in genealogical research principles and specialized training in either North American or British family history. All students must take the Family and Law in American
History, and English Language Paleography. Students focusing on

North America then take courses such as Northeastern States and Canada, Midwestern States, Hispanic Family History, Writing Family Histories, and Oral History Interviewing and Processing. Students who concentrate on British family history take classes such as England and Wales from 1700, Scotland and Ireland, German for Family Historians and Genealogists, the Family in Europe, Latin for Genealogists, and Writing Family Histories. Certificate students must also attend a week-long Genealogy and Family History Seminar on campus, or complete an independent study.

How long it takes: Correspondence course—students work at their own pace.

What it costs: $1,458

Scholarships and grants are available.

National Genealogical Society
Education Department
4527 17th Street, North
Arlington, VA 22207
(703) 525-0050
Fax: (703) 525-0052
76702.2417@compuserve.com

The society offers a home study course in American genealogy. Subjects of study include family records, interviews and correspondence, secondary sources, census records, vital records, land and tax records, military and veterans records, church and cemetary records, migration routes and maps, and intepreting and evaluating evidence. Students learn which records may contain the information they need, where to find them, how to understand them, how to write citations for them, and how to maintain them. Coursework includes research at local libraries and courthouses. Some professionals recommend that students combine the society's home study course with the Samford Institute's hands-on training.

How long it takes: 18 months

What it costs: $375

Payment plans are available and credit cards are accepted.

Graphology ◆ ◆ ◆

Graphology, or handwriting analysis, is the study and interpretation of handwriting as an indicator of personality. Professional graphologists offer four primary services: graphology classes to hobbyists, personality profiles to help individuals increase their self-knowledge and potential for change, personnel screening and consultation for employers, and questioned document examination, or forensic graphology, to identify forged handwriting and documents for legal purposes. The following training programs can lead to a career if you're interested in providing one of the above graphology services to individuals, businesses, or the legal system—but it'll be more profitable if you provide several of them to a variety of clients.

The Academy of Handwriting Sciences
11481 Caminito Garcia
San Diego, CA 92131
(619) 586-1511
Fax: (619) 695-8526
Hapiwriter@aol.com

The academy offers a home study professional graphologist training program that consists of four courses: the Write Slant, Personal Worth, Personality Evaluation, and Vocational Evaluation. The Write Slant is an introductory course that covers spacing, size, zones, connectives, slant, pressure, traits, gestalt graphology, and basic psychology. Personal Worth trains students to generate a personality profile by measuring, scoring, and charting forty writing factors to graphically illustrate such traits as intellect, self-image, social awareness, vitality, and inhibitions. Personality Evaluation teaches students to use the Personal Worth chart to measure emotional maturity, leadership, social maturity, communication skills, money sense, and physical and sexual drives, and introduces Jungian psychological interpretations. Finally, Vocational Evaluation covers the professional use of graphology in the business field. Students learn to evaluate vocational skills in Strong/Campbell categories such as realistic, investigative, artistic, social, enterprising, and conventional. The academy also offers a software package designed to calculate and score the Personal Worth chart and transfer the scores to the personality and vocational charts. Guidance in specialty areas such as criminal writing, document examination, behavior profiling, and children's writing is also available.

How long it takes: 2 years

What it costs: $1,735

Credit cards are accepted.

American Association of Handwriting Analysts
P.O. Box 95
Southfield, MI 48037
(248) 746-0740
Fax: (248) 746-0756
aahaoffice@aol.com
hwateacher@aol.com
www.handwriting.org/aaha/aahamain.htm

The association offers a course in handwriting analysis that consists of three parts. The first part covers the background of handwriting analysis, the space and movement of script, and how to do a beginning analysis. Specific topics include margins, baselines, measuring, size and space, the ductus, slant, pressure, speed, rhythm, regularity/irregularity, expansion/contraction, and evaluation of major and minor traits exhibited in a script. The second part teaches a gestalt approach to analysis of movement, space, and form. Topics include stroke, legibility/expressive freedom, letter formation, connection/disconnection, and connectives (including garland, arcade, angle, and thread connectives). The second part also includes sections on signatures, printing, envelopes, the personal pronoun, and capital letters. The third part covers analysis by trait stroke, and discusses various personality traits, defense mechanisms, psychological typologies, and advanced handwriting features (such as directional pressure and counterdominants). The association also offers advanced courses in questioned document and forensic handwriting analysis.

How long it takes: 12 to 18 months

What it costs: $1,650

Credit cards are accepted and a payment plan is available.

National Society for Graphology
250 West 57th Street
Room 1228A
New York, NY 10107
(212) 265-1148
Fax: (212) 307-5671

The society offers a correspondence course in graphology. The course is composed of three levels: Elementary, Intermediate, and Advanced. The Elementary course covers zones and connections, regularity and pressure, margins and space, style evaluation, slant and size, and simplification and directional pressure. The Intermediate course includes lessons in left-handed writing, advanced connections, the pictures of movement, form, and color, insincerity and dishonesty, printed writing, how to find the "guiding image" or gestalt in the writing, and extremes in handwriting. The Advanced course includes lessons in vocational guidance, personnel selection, and the psychological theories of Freud, Jung, Adler, Fromm, and Wittlich. In addition, students learn about major psychological theories as they reveal a writer's developmental stages, where problems originated, how well the ego is able to distribute the energies of the id, and other psychological indicators as seen in handwriting.

How long it takes: Correspondence course—students work at their own pace. In general, students complete all three levels in 18 months.

What it costs: Elementary Level—$600
Intermediate Level—$600
Advanced Level—$750

A payment plan is available.

International Graphology Association
Stonedge
Dunkerton
Bath BA2 8AS
England
International telephone: (011-44) 1761-437809
Fax: (011-44) 1761-432572
ljw@graphology.org.uk

The association offers a correspondence course that trains graphology practitioners. The program covers many aspects of personality, including emotions, thinking, communication, energy level and lifestyle, self-image, fears, work attitude, creativity, diplomacy, enthusiasm, pessimism, reticence, persistence, imagination, loyalty, and timidity. Some specific classes are Allport's Trait Theory, Spatial Arrangement, Content Analysis, Global Factors, Factor Analytic Theory, Eysenck's Typology, Report Production, Personality Assessment and Psychometrics, Word Spacing, Vocational Guidance, and Setting Up a Business. Personal tutors—all of whom are professional graphologists certified by the association—work one-on-one with students as they complete the course, offering advice and assistance as needed.

How long it takes: 18 months

What it costs:　　$2,000 (£1,200)

Cost is approximate and will vary according to the exchange rate.

Credit cards are accepted and payment options are available.

The Institute of Graphological Science
3530 Forest Lane, #30
Dallas, TX 75234
(800) 960-1034
(214) 351-3668
Fax: (214) 351-5412

The institute trains and certifies students as Graphologists, Master Graphologists, Specialized Graphologists, and Questioned Document Examiners. The Graphologist training includes lessons in basic stroke formation, spacing, baselines and line slopes, emotional slant measurement, personality characteristics, zones, pressure, size, personal philography, stems and crossings, subconscious fears, and mental processing.

The Master Graphologist training includes instruction in harmonious versus inharmonious writing, margins, connectives, the personal pronoun, printing, rhythm, upslant and downslant, pressure, graphotherapy, and becoming a professional graphologist.

The Specialized Graphologist training includes seminars in chemical abuse, sexuality, codependency, graphotherapy/recovery, children's handwriting, graphology in the corporate world, and graphological potpourri (which includes subconscious games, introvert/extrovert, and extreme right and left slants).

The Questioned Document Examiner training teaches students to apply scientific techniques to expose fraudulent documents and authenticate genuine ones. Courses include the Physiology of Writing, Ink and Writing Instruments, Forgery and Other Types of Fraud, Disguised Writing, Typewriter Cases, Desktop Forgery, Checks and Credit Cards, and Wills and Contracts. Upon completion of the course, students begin an apprenticeship in which a professional mentor guides them through their first five cases.

How long it takes: 6 to 12 months per Course

What it costs: Graphologist—$985

                   Master Graphologist—$825

                   Specialized Graphologist—$500

                   Questioned Document Examiner—$1,285

Payment plans are available and credit cards are accepted.

Miscellaneous Consulting and Counseling ◆ ◆ ◆

This section includes careers in bau-biologie, health education, couples counseling, firewalk instruction, and music for healing and transition. Bau-biologie involves the evaluation of the effect of buildings—from their location to construction materials to electrical systems to water supply—on health, and the implementation of corrective systems and technology when necessary. If you were interested in Feng Shui, but wanted a more left-brained, scientific approach, check out bau-biologie. Health Educators help clients understand their bodies and illnesses, and the health care system, to become informed consumers and make intelligent health choices. The couples counseling course trains student to facilitate couples workshops. Firewalk Instructors conduct firewalks, demonstrating the power of the human mind and helping clients build leadership skills and self-confidence. And the Music for Healing and Transition Program trains Music Practitioners, who provide live music in hospitals and other medical settings for the benefit of patients, fam-

ilies, and health care practitioners, all of whom can gain from the sooth-
ing, humanizing effect of live music.

Mars Venus Institute
20 Sunnyside Avenue, A-130
Mill Valley, CA 94941
(888) 463-6684
(415) 389-6857
Fax: (415) 389-1597
bmb4@ix.netcom.com
www.mars-venus-institute.com

The institute trains Mars-Venus Facilitators, whose work is based on
John Gray's best-selling book *Men Are from Mars, Women Are from
Venus*. Facilitators present Mars-Venus Workshops, which help married
couples improve their marriages, and anyone else, married or single,
improve their relationships with the opposite sex. The workshops are
usually presented in four two-hour segments, for a total of eight hours.
The segments can all be presented in one day, or can be spread out over
a month. Each segment includes an introduction by the facilitator, a
short video of John Gray discussing the topic, and a group exercise.

Although facilitators definitely benefit from being associated with
the *Men Are from Mars* "brand name," the institute cautions that facilitating workshops may not provide sufficient living and recommends
that students have another source of income (perhaps another consulting career). Students are expected to be familiar with the Mars-Venus
approach before beginning the training—reading several of Gray's
books should do it.

How long it takes: 3 days

What it costs: Training per individual—$1,000
                      Training per couple—$1,750
                      Annual retraining fee—$500
Credit cards are accepted.

SUNDOOR Foundation for Transpersonal Education
Box 669
Twain Harte, CA 95383
(800) 755-1701
(209) 928-1700
Fax: (209) 928-4800

The foundation offers a firewalk instructor certification training. Before enrolling in the certification course, students must attend SUNDOOR's Fire Initiation Training—a course in leadership, personal development, and spiritual expansion that helps students eliminate past negative patterns, regain a sense of purpose, and connect with a universal energy source for guidance and direction.

The firewalk instructor certification program teaches students to lead their own dynamic firewalks, demonstrating the potential of the human mind and inspiring clients to reach for success in every aspect of their lives. It provides an in-depth study of leadership methods, healing practices, and all the details of the firewalk—from building and preparing the fire to developing the presentation skills needed to make a firewalk a truly transformative experience.

The foundation also offers Breathwork Practitioner training. See Breathwork for information.

How long it takes: Fire Initiation Training—7 days
Firewalk Instructor Training—5 days

What it costs: Fire Initiation Training—$995
Firewalk Instructor Training—$995

Credit cards are accepted and payment plans are available.

International Institute for Bau-biologie and Ecology
P.O. Box 387
Clearwater, FL 33757
(813) 461-4371
Fax: (813) 441-4373
baubiologie@earthlink.net
www.bau-biologieusa.com

Bau-biologie is the study of the impact of buildings on human health and the application of that knowledge in the construction or modification of homes and workplaces. The institute trains Bau-biologie Environmental Inspectors to consult with homeowners and businesses, helping them develop healthy living spaces. The training consists of two levels.

The first level requires the completion of the bau-biologic correspondence course, which covers ecology, building sites, biologically sound building materials, heating and insulation, furnishings and interior design, acoustics, home inspection, and electrical and sanitary installations, among many other topics. The correspondence course consists of twenty-three course packs, totaling about nine hundred pages.

The second level of training involves the completion of three seminars. The Electrobiology Seminar discusses electrical and magnetic fields and teaches students to measure and reduce the effects of EMFs. In the Indoor Air, Water, and Chemicals Seminar students learn about indoor air and water pollution and chemical issues, and formaldehyde, biological contaminants, asbestos, carbon monoxide, and other nasties are discussed. The Review, Update, and Case Study Seminar is a practicum, wherein students spend three days doing hands-on home inspection with professional Bau-biologie Environmental Inspectors.

How long it takes: Correspondence course—6 months
Seminars—5 days per seminar

What it costs: Correspondence course—$1,089
Per seminar—$975

The institute offers a price reduction if the total tuition is paid in advance. Credit cards are accepted.

New England School of Whole Health Education
636 Beacon Street, Suite 405
Boston, MA 02215
(617) 267-0516
Fax: (617) 247-0896

The school trains Whole Health Educators to work with clients who are functioning but have chronic conditions that adversely affect their lives. The conditions that Educators deal with are largely caused by habit and lifestyle, and can be best addressed by changes in behavior. Educators help clients make these behavioral changes by teaching how the body systems interact, how the mind and body communicate, how stress adaptation functions in health and disease, and by giving clients the most current scientific information available. The goal is to help clients understand the cause and effect of their condition, to provide them with the tools to speak with their health care providers, and to empower them to have greater control over their well-being.

The curriculum of the foundational courses includes classes in nutrition, anatomy and physiology, understanding alternative treatments, medical terminology, cell metabolism, and exercise physiology.

The advanced courses teach how to educate and counsel individuals with a wide variety of health-related issues and concerns. Additionally, an internship and a counseling supervision class are required.

How long it takes: Bimonthly classes for 2 years. Internships are a minimum of 130 hours.

What it costs: $6,300

The Music for Healing and Transition Program
P.O. Box 249
Vashon, WA 98070
(206) 463-6449
mhtp@seanet.com
www.vashonisland.com/mhtp

The Music for Healing and Transition Program certifies Music Practitioners, who employ the therapeutic value of music to enhance the healing process of the chronically ill or to ease the life to death transition of those with terminal diseases. Music Practitioners provide live music to patients in hospitals, connecting with the patients (even those who can't interact), providing a pleasant atmosphere for the hospital staff and patients' families, calming and caring for all present, and providing a humane element in a sterile environment. Recent scientific studies have shown many benefits of listening to music: premature babies gain weight faster, migraine sufferers experience fewer headaches, and surgical patients require fewer anesthesia and pain relievers.

The curriculum includes classes on philosophies of healing, how music heals, music as a language, repertoire development, anatomy/physiology overview, understanding hospital equipment and procedures, diseases and pharmacology, etiquette, understanding current medical issues, the profession of music practitionership, and care of the dying. Requirements for graduation include music practice and lessons (for those not yet proficient), creating a ninety-minute repertoire, practicing a daily form of self-nurturing (meditation, running, journaling, etc.), and completing a twenty-hour internship in a hospital or hospice setting by playing music for patients. Classes for the program are held in different parts of the country, with students working closely with a mentor/coordinator in their area.

How long it takes: Students work at their own pace.

What it costs: $1,080

Chapter 8

✳ ✳✳ ✳

Craft and Trade

This section includes careers that involve using your hands to create functional and beautiful objects—and using your head for research, evaluation, customization, planning, and design. The careers covered in this chapter are boatbuilding, yacht design, horseshoeing, jewelry making and design, watchmaking and repair, piano tuning and repair, musical instrument repair, violin and guitar making and repair, furniture making, woodworking, glassblowing, neon tube bending, sign painting, jade and wood carving, saddlemaking, blacksmithing and bladesmithing, and bookbinding. We also included some certificate programs that train students to make a living as artisan craftspeople in fields such as fiber, ceramic, and metal.

Boatbuilding and Yacht Design ● ● ●

Boatbuilding and yacht design are really two careers, but they're so closely related we thought they should share a section. If you're interested in hands-on work, physically fabricating a boat from a blueprint and a bunch of assorted parts, focus on the boatbuilding programs. If you like the idea of designing a boat—which involves math, physics, and engineering—focus on yacht design. The two are not mutually exclusive, though; many boatbuilding programs teach boat design and proficient yacht designers must also understand construction.

The Arques School of Traditional Boatbuilding
P.O. Box 2010
Sausalito, CA 94966
(415) 331-7134
Fax: (415) 331-7134
arqueschl@aol.com

The school offers an apprenticeship program in traditional boatbuilding. Students learn history, design, lofting, hand tool use, wood technology, bronze casting, rigging, and sailing. Specific skills taught include marlinspike seamanship, scale model making, boat and sail repair, framing, caulking, joining, and wood harvesting and drying. The program also includes the construction of four boats: two historic boats, one carvel, and one lapstrake. (For the 1998 class, the boats were a Providence River Boat, a Pacific Gill-Net Boat, an Old Sailing Peapod, and a Bush Island Double-Ender.) Short-term classes are also available at the school, and apprentices have full access to all of the school's classes as well as the school's shop.

How long it takes: 1 year

What it costs: $4,600

Westlawn Institute of Marine Technology
School of Yacht Design
733 Summer Street
Stamford, CT 06901
(203) 359-0500

Westlawn offers a home study course in Yacht Design. The program is divided into four modules: Principles of Small Craft Naval Architecture, Boat and Yacht Design, Boat and Yacht Instruction, and Marine Systems Engineering. Principles of Small Craft Naval Architecture includes classes in basic math, hydrostatics, principles of resistance, marine drafting, and line drawing. Students learn fluid dynamics, flow characteristics, transverse stability, how to describe boat hulls by orthographic projection, and how to prepare a finished set of hull lines and offset tables based on the preliminary workup.

Boat and Yacht Design covers exterior and interior design, high-speed powerboat design, sailboat design, and multihull design. Specific topics include the interrelationship of hull and superstructure elements, ergonomic principles, selecting hull design parameters, problem solving, and how to prepare a set of hydrostatic calculations and a performance prediction.

Boat and Yacht Instruction includes lessons in wood boat construction, fiberglass boat construction, fiberglass production methods, aluminum yacht design and construction, and computer-aided yacht design. Students learn deck and interior joinery, spray molding, laminate design, scantlings for welded and riveted boats, and computer-aided boat design hardware and software.

And Marine Systems Engineering covers propulsion systems, electrical systems, specifications, and professional practice. It includes lessons on marine engine performance curves, propeller anatomy, wiring and circuit protection, bilge pumping and drainage, and how to set up and operate a private yacht design practice.

How long it takes: 2 to 4 years

What it costs: $4,000

Payment plans are available, and credit cards are accepted.

The Landing School of Boatbuilding and Design
P.O. Box 1490
Kennebunkport, ME 04046
(207) 985-7976
Fax: (207) 985-7942

The Landing School offers two vocational training programs: Boatbuilding and Boat Design. The Boatbuilding course begins with a class in naval architecture for boatbuilders, which introduces students to the fundamentals of yacht design and engineering theory. Students then concentrate on either small boat or cruising boat construction. The small boat course covers construction of dories and daysailers, including classes on lofting, planking, finishing, sailmaking, spars and rigging, frames, deck and beams, carlins, coaming, and rudder and tiller. In the cruising boats portion of the course, students learn all

aspects of construction, including lofting, interior joinery, engine installation, plumbing, wiring, finishing, casting patterns, and deck hardware.

The Boat Design program teaches the principles of naval architecture, marine engineering, and drafting. Courses cover computational
methods, sail plans, stress calculations, hydrostatics, propeller calculations, lofting, curved raked transom development, composite engineering, engine room layout, and tank testing. The course also includes
instruction in computer-aided yacht design: students learn to use Auto-
CAD, AutoYACHT, and other yacht design applications that calculate
such things as the wind velocity in knots required to heel a boat a given
number of degrees.

How long it takes: Boatbuilding—10 months
Boat Design—10 months

What it costs: Boatbuilding—$9,350
Boat Design—$9,150

Financial aid, scholarships, and payment plans are available.

International Yacht Restoration School
449 Thames Street
Newport, RI 02840
(401) 848-5777
Fax: (401) 842-0669
info@iyrs.com

The school offers a full-time yacht restoration training program that
combines theoretical and hands-on work to teach students the skills,
history, and related sciences involved in the construction, restoration,
and maintenance of classic yachts. Subjects include surveying yacht
condition, reading line and construction drawings, half-hull modeling,
developing deck cambers, plank fastening, laying decks, interior joinery, rig construction, installing electrical and mechanical systems, and
yacht finishing. Among the skills taught are using and maintaining
hand and power tools, lofting, joinery and finishing techniques, performing historical research, oar and paddle building, boat handling, and
navigation and seamanship.

The school offers training at three levels: Apprentice, Journeyman,
and Master. Depending on prior experience, students can enroll and
train at any of the levels.

How long it takes: Apprentice—1 to 3 years

Journeyman—2 years

Master—2 years

What it costs: $6,000 per year

Financial aid is available and credit cards are accepted.

Northwest School of Wooden Boatbuilding
251 Otto Street
Port Townsend, WA 98368
(360) 385-4948
Fax: (360) 385-5089

The Northwest School offers a training course that teaches the traditional skills of wooden boatbuilding. The program emphasizes the use of hand tools and joinery, and teaches everything from working with angles, bevels, and twists to transferring designers' plans into a full-size working drawing on the loft floor. The course guides students through an intensive program that enables them to tackle fairly complex new construction and repairs, either for their own building projects or in the boatbuilding industry. The heart of the program is the time spent on the shop floor and involved in the actual construction of project boats—which include cruising yachts, commercial fishing boats, historical replicas, and small skiffs and yacht tenders.

How long it takes: 6 months

What it costs: $5,600

Bookbinding and Book Arts ◆ ◆ ◆

Bookbinders repair old books, bind new ones, perform a variety of restoration and conservation procedures, and use many ornamental and decorative techniques. The following programs prepare students for employment as hand binders in custom, production, and institutional (including private, public, academic, and research libraries) binderies, as well as for self-employment. Consider bookbinding and the book arts if you're interested in making something new—with embossing, gold tooling, and other artistic and productive skills—or maintaining something old—with restoration, conservation, and other preservative skills.

Waterleaf Mill & Bindery

Pequeño Press
P.O. Box 1711
Bisbee, AZ 85603
(520) 432-5924
Fax: (520) 432-3065
patbooks@primenet.com

Waterleaf offers an apprenticeship program for those interested in learning papermaking, marbling, and bookbinding. Apprentices assist with all shop projects, including box making, binding limited-edition books (particularly miniatures), book design, working with the marbling chemical mixer, making paper, and, primarily, bookbinding. Some topics introduced in the apprenticeship are paper casting techniques, traditional, experimental, and Suminagashi marbling, traditional fine binding, and contemporary eccentric binding.

Apprentices are responsible for some of the more mundane tasks in the shop, such as assisting with promotional mailings and advertising, but when they are not busy, they may use the studio equipment and machinery to create their own projects.

How long it takes: 2 to 6 months

What it costs: This is a no-fee apprenticeship program.

Capricornus School of Bookbinding & Restoration

P.O. Box 98
Berkeley, CA 94701
(510) 658-7930

Capricornus offers training in bookbinding. Instruction begins with pulling, repairing, and the construction of flat-backed casebound notebooks and half- and full-cloth hollow-back bindings. Once students demonstrate competence with the above, they are taught quarter- and full-leather bindings, including various forms of decoration, headbands, and gilt edges. Other skills taught include various methods of cloth and paper decoration, making portfolios, photo albums, and boxes, and using handle letters and decorative tools. Advanced students are also taught rebacking, mildew control, cleaning, washing and sizing, and deacidification. The school offers both an apprenticeship program and ongoing classes that students are free to take until they feel they have achieve sufficient expertise.

How long it takes: Apprenticeship—6 months to 1 year (usually requires 3 months of regular classes as a prerequisite)
Regular classes—3 to 21 hours per week

What it costs: Apprenticeship program—$5,000 per year
Regular classes—$75 to 495 per month

American Academy of Bookbinding
P.O. Box 1590
Telluride, CO 81435
(970) 728-3886
Fax: (970) 728-9709

The academy offers a diploma program in Fine Leather Bookbinding, consisting of in-class and at-home work and study. Required courses include French Style Leather Binding, Chemise and Slipcase, and Gilding and Onlay. Other courses include Tooling and Execution of Design and The Logic of German Fine Binding. Students learn such skills as edge decoration, headband sewing, gold tooling, embossing, leather molding, and making suede doublures. Students are expected to complete ten bindings while they are attending workshops and ten while working on their own. Other independent study requirements include completion of various styles of case bindings, a millimeter binding, a half-leather binding, and a full-leather binding with design, chemise, and slipcase. Students may take individual courses without being enrolled in the diploma course.

How long it takes: 5 years; meets 1 month per year

What it costs: $10,000

Credit cards are accepted.

Garage Annex School for Book Arts
One Cottage Street, #5
Easthampton, MA 01027

(413) 527-8044
Fax: (413) 529-0071
Foliotrope@aol.com

The Garage Annex offers professional-level training classes in Book Arts. Classes include The Book Restructured: Wire-Edge Hinging, Paper Casting and Mold Making, Box Design and Construction, Full Metal Binding, Leather Onlay and Inlay, and Leather Bookbinding. Students learn to use wire-edge configurations for books, enclosures, and articulated sculptures, create 3-D surfaces for book covers, boxes, and artwork using mold making and paper casting techniques, bind paper with unique metal structures, prepare paste and leather for onlay/inlay application, and construct full-leather bindings with both French and English methods. Individual educational internships are also available.

How long it takes: 2 or 5 days per class

What it costs: 2 days—$165
                          5 days—$375

North Bennet Street School
39 North Bennet Street
Boston, MA 02113
(617) 227-0155
Fax: (617) 227-9292

North Bennet offers an apprenticeship-type program in Bookbinding. The course teaches students to bind and repair nineteenth- and twentieth-century books, construct protective boxes, perform simple conservation procedures, bind books in leather, and do blind tooling and gold lettering. Students also learn folding, gathering, sewing, tilting, and casing-in.

The school also offers training programs in Cabinet and Furniture Making, Preservation Carpentry, Jewelry Making and Repair, Piano Technology, and Violin Making and Restoration. See the appropriate section for more information.

How long it takes: 2 years

What it costs: $17,700

Financial aid and payment plans are available.

Horseshoeing ◆ ◆ ◆

Horseshoeing involves much more than using blacksmithing skills to create horseshoes. Skilled horseshoers, also known as farriers, evaluate horses' individual needs and, when necessary, provide corrective or therapeutic shoes to improve faults of gait and compensate for physical limitations. If you like working with your hands, enjoy the company of horses and horse people, and are interested in horse anatomy, physiology, and health . . . well, you know what they say—if the shoe fits.

Western's School of Horseshoeing
2801 West Maryland Avenue
Phoenix, AZ 85017
(602) 242-2560

The school trains professional horseshoers. The curriculum at Western's includes forge work, anatomy and physiology, shoeing and trimming, and veterinary lectures. The course begins at the forge, teaching blacksmithing skills for the farrier. After students learn to make shoes from steel bar stock, they study hand tools, trimming, and corrective trimming, ultimately learning to make all types of corrective horeshoes. Having mastered trimming, students learn to level and balance the foot, turn heel calks, pull clips, square toes, and forge weld bar shoes.

How long it takes: 8 weeks

What it costs: $2,800

Credit cards are accepted.

Sierra Horseshoeing School
Route 2, Box 22B
Bishop, CA 93514
(800) 211-4493
(619) 872-1279

Sierra offers a Professional Farrier Science course that includes instruction in six major subjects: Anatomy and Physiology, Conformation, Problems and Causes, Correctional Horseshoeing, Blacksmithing, and Business Practices. The Anatomy and Physiology course covers terminology, muscles, bones, joints, ligaments, elastic structures, and dissections. The Conformation class discusses conformation types such as base wide, splayfoot, cow hocked, narrow hips, buck kneed, standing under, straight behind, and camped behind. The Problems and Causes course covers stride alignment, physiological movement of the hoof, winging in, winging out, forging, scalping, cross-firing, bowed tendons, and ring bone. The Correctional Horseshoeing course teaches students about proper shoeing, trimming, braces and trusses, medications, padding, hoof preparations, orthopedic shoes, and hoof gauges. The Blacksmithing course covers shearing, drawing, upsetting, shaping, punching, welding, and brazing. And the Business Practices course teaches students about public relations, bookkeeping, advertising, taxes, scheduling, and dealing with veterinarians, trainers, and owners. Other classes cover equine psychology, fitting, nailing, and specialized shoeing.

How long it takes: 8 weeks

What it costs: $2,900

Credit cards are accepted.

Pacific Coast Horseshoeing School
9625 Florin Road
Sacramento, CA 95829
(916) 366-6064
Fax: (916) 366-6618
pchs@inreach.com

Pacific Coast offers professional farrier training with three areas of study: classroom work, forge work, and horse work. The classroom work includes hoof construction and function, basic anatomy and physiology, conformation evaluations, lameness (including angular foot deformities, bog spavin, bowed tendon, and bursitis), and how to trim and shoe for many problems (such as toed-in, toed-out, bowlegged, knock-kneed, slopping pastern, cow hocked, sickle hocked, and camped behind). Forge work includes making a forepunch, pritchel, rolled toe shoe, toe clip shoe, keg shoe, and egg bar, and working aluminum. And horse work includes handling, pulling shoes and trimming feet, and applying shoes.

How long it takes: 10 weeks

What it costs: $3,350

Credit cards are accepted.

Colorado School of Trades
1575 Hoyt Street
Lakewood, CO 80215
(800) 234-4594
(303) 233-4697
Fax: (303) 233-4723

The school offers a Farrier Science certificate program. The program consists of two sections: Hoof Care, and Blacksmithing. The Hoof Care section includes instruction in horse handling, equine anatomy, corrective shoeing, hoof problems, hoof trimming, and customer relations. The Blacksmithing section teaches hammer blows, use of a forge, heat color, making tools, turning a shoe, forge welding a bar shoe, and applications of handmade shoes. The school also offers classes in corrective and pathological shoeing, modifying keg shoes, and diagnosing leg and hoof disorders. Instruction in entrepreneurial aspects of farrier science, such as determining start-up costs, approaching investors, and preparing a business plan, is also available.

How long it takes: 4 months

What it costs: $5,350

Financial aid is available.

Casey and Sons Horseshoeing School and Clinic
14013 East Highway 136
LaFayette, GA 30728
(706) 397-8909

Casey and Sons offers two levels of Professional Farrier training. The beginning course trains students to address problems caused by poor leg and hoof conformation or previous improper shoeing, to recognize, prevent, and correct lameness, and to balance and shoe all breeds and types of horses. It also teaches handling of difficult and spoiled horses, basic horse psychology, and how to set up a farrier business. The advanced course further prepares students to become professional farriers. It teaches them to perfect their techniques, use the arc welder to make corrective shoes, and use advanced techniques for shoeing, hoof repair, and leg braces. The school also shows students how to use high-speed video cameras to observe and analyze gait problems and apply solutions.

How long it takes: Beginning—6 weeks
              Advanced—12 weeks

What it costs: Beginning—$2,450
              Advanced—$3,600

Midwest Horseshoeing School
2312 South Maple Avenue
Macomb, IL 61455
(309) 833-4063

The school offers professional horseshoer training. The curriculum includes anatomy, diagnosis of faulty gaits, conformation problems, iron work, forge work, hoof repair and trimming, corrective shoeing, and custom shoeing. Lectures cover leg and foot conformation, flight patterns, interference, brushing, stumbling, overreaching, forging, scalping, pathological shoeing, diagnosing lameness (including suspensory sprain, windpuff, quittor, seedy-toe, founder, and navicular disease), repairing cracks, and business management. Shop classes include clipping heels, making bevel edge, concave, and square toes, forge welding jar calks, forge brazing jar calks and grabs, working with full swedges and half rounds, and electric and torch welding.

How long it takes: 12 weeks

What it costs: $2,000

Shur Shod Horseshoeing School
P.O. Box 119
Cimarron, KS 67835
(316) 855-2303

Shur Shod trains professional horseshoers. The training program includes demonstrations, lectures, and hands-on work. Students learn to make basic, corrective, and special breed shoes. Other subjects covered are horsemanship, lameness, gaits, anatomy and physiology, operation of a horseshoeing business, and public relations.

How long it takes: 1 month

What it costs: $1,250

Cost includes housing.

Heartland Horseshoeing School
327 Southwest 1st Lane
Lamar, MO 64759
(417) 682-6896

The school offers four Farrier courses: Introductory, Intermediate, Comprehensive, and National Certification. The Introductory course is designed to give students a foundation in horseshoeing skills. It covers anatomy, basic corrective shoeing theory, and common problems, and gives students the opportunity to shoe a minimum of ten horses.

The Intermediate course includes classes in correcting faults of gait, therapeutic shoeing techniques, tool and handmade horseshoe forging, and running a successful business. Students work on a minimum of fifty horses in the Intermediate course, and after completing this level, they may consider working professionally as farriers.

The Comprehensive Farrier course is much more complete. It includes thirty-three projects, all aspects of corrective and therapeutic shoeing, and teaches the ability to shoe for virtually any type of problem in the horse world. In the comprehensive course, students work on a minimum of one hundred horses.

The National Certification course is designed to help students pass the American Farrier's Association tests to become a Certified Farrier. The course includes book work, bar shoes and shoe boards, and shoeing the horse to AFA standards in the time allotted. Heartland helps place students in apprenticeship programs, but the majority of students start their own businesses.

How long it takes: Introductory—2 weeks
Intermediate—6 weeks
Comprehensive—12 weeks
National Certification—1 week

What it costs: Introductory—$750
Intermediate—$1,800
Comprehensive—$3,200
National Certification—$400

Oklahoma Farrier's College
Route 2, Box 88
Sperry, OK 74073
(800) 331-4061
(918) 288-7221
Fax: (918) 288-2757

Oklahoma Farrier's College offers eight levels of farrier training. The program starts with an introductory course that covers fieldwork, forge work, trimming, and shoeing the hoof. The second course, Primary Horseshoeing, introduces the basic techniques of horseshoeing, such as starting fires, bending and shaping shoes, and punching nail holes in the shoe. The third course, Undergraduate Farrier, completes the study of farrier fundamentals, including anatomy, corrective shoeing, and hand-making several types of shoes. The fourth course, Achievement Farrier, introduces advanced techniques and covers handmaking fourteen shoe types. The fifth course, Master Farrier, provides study of braces and artificial limbs, and specialized training for working with trotters, pacers, gaited walkers, and racehorses. The sixth course, Advanced Master Farrier, covers more advanced techniques, emphasizes increasing speed of horseshoeing, and requires that students handmake nineteen types of shoe. The seventh course, Superior Master Farrier, offers specialized training in aluminum, welding the egg bar shoe, and corrective shoeing, and prepares students for the highest level of employment. And the eighth course, Supreme Master Farrier, is designed to teach the ultimate level of knowledge for working with all types of horses. Instruction includes farriery, anatomy, physiology, horsemanship, business management, and communications.

How long it takes: Introductory—2 weeks
Primary—4 weeks
Undergraduate—8 weeks
Achievement—14 weeks
Master—20 weeks
Advanced Master—32 weeks
Superior Master—44 weeks
Supreme Master—56 weeks

What it costs: Introductory—$660
Primary—$1,080
Undergraduate—$1,700

Achievement—$2,940
Master—$3,900
Advanced Master—$4,888
Superior Master—$8,056
Supreme Master—$10,000

Federal assistance programs are available for veterans and students who are at least one quarter American Indian.

Jewelry Design and Watchmaking ♦ ♦ ♦

Jewelry and watch careers range from the extremely artistic to the exclusively utilitarian. The training programs teach everything from how to design and fabricate art jewelry to how to cut diamonds and other precious stones to how to repair cuckoo clocks and digital watches. These careers demand much attention to detail—you're not working with your hands so much as your fingers. There are many excellent career possibilities designing, making, and repairing jewelry, watches, and clocks for people who enjoy small-scale work and are drawn to aesthetic or mechanical projects and problems.

Gemological Institute of America
World Headquarters and Campus
5345 Armada Drive
Carlsbad, CA 92008
(800) 421-7250
(760) 603-4000
Fax: (760) 603-4080
www.gia.edu

580 Fifth Avenue
New York, NY 10036
(212) 944-5900
Fax: (212) 719-9563

GIA offers four professional jeweler training programs: Graduate Jeweler, Graduate Jeweler Gemologist, Graduate Jeweler with Design and Wax, and Graduate Jeweler Gemologist with Design and Wax. The Graduate Jeweler program teaches basic and advanced metalworking, jewelry repair, basic and advanced stone setting, fabrication, counter sketching, and gold and precious metals. Skills taught include making and modifying tools, retipping and repronging, repairing hinges, using flush, channel, gypsy, and star settings, making bezels, and developing drawing techniques.

The Graduate Jeweler Gemologist program includes all the coursework of the Graduate Jeweler program, plus gemology courses such as proportion grading, judging finish details, handling diamonds, displaying diamonds and colored stones, and how and when to plan recutting.

Students who choose to add Design and Wax classes to either of the above programs learn comprehensive wax techniques and jewelry design. The wax techniques class includes instruction in creating designs in wax, hollowing models in preparation for casting, creating mirror-image pieces, carving jewelry, working with injected wax models, carving relief images, spruing and casting, and marketing. The design class teaches students how to use drafting tools, illustrate shape and form of metal, adapt textures, use watercolor to create professional renderings, design jewelry for women and men, and keep design ideas flowing.

The institute has additional campuses in Hong Kong, Italy, Japan, Korea, Taiwan, and Thailand.

How long it takes: Graduate Jeweler—6 months
Graduate Jeweler Gemologist—12 months on campus or 6 months on campus plus home study
Design and Wax Certification—additional 14 weeks

What it costs: Graduate Jeweler—$10,700
Graduate Jeweler Gemologist—$20,000
Graduate Jeweler with Design and Wax—$16,000
Graduate Jeweler Gemologist with Design and Wax—$26,000

Credit cards are accepted, and payment plans are available.

California Institute of Jewelry Training
4020 El Camino
Sacramento, CA 95821
(916) 487-1122
Fax: (916) 487-1189
aura@calweb.com

The institute offers a jewelry training program that consists of three modules: Basic Jewelry Repair, Advanced Repair and Fabrication, and Advanced Stone Setting, Wax Carving, and Casting. Basic Jewelry Repair covers soldering, piercing, ingots and drawing wire, ring sizing, chain repair, repronging, basic stone setting, bezel and oval setting, and tools and equipment. Advanced Repair and Fabrication refines the skills taught in the basic course and introduces basic casting, advanced fabrication, and ten methods of stone setting and finishing. And Advanced Stone Setting, Wax Carving, and Casting teaches advanced marquise and pear setting, baguettes and cluster setting, wax carving and casting, mold making, spruing, and wax injecting. The institute offers additional courses in Sales and Merchandising, Design, and Gem Identification.

How long it takes: 6 months

What it costs: $8,800

Credit cards are accepted.

Revere Academy of Jewelry Arts
760 Market Street, Suite 900
San Francisco, CA 94102
(415) 391-4179
Fax: (415) 391-7570
www.RevereAcademy.com

The academy trains and certifies Jewelry Technicians and Graduate Jewelers. The Jewelry Technician course includes classes in casting, fabrication, polishing and finishing, repair, setting, and trade practices.

The Graduate Jeweler course requires, in addition to the above, completion of classes in design, engraving, platinum fabrication, gemology, metalsmithing, mold making, rendering, and wax modeling. Some of the skills taught include carving a patterned wedding band, forging and fabricating a platinum ring and pendant, identifying gems, rendering professional-quality illustrations, grading diamonds, and marketing your jewelry. The academy also offers advanced classes such as Celtic silversmithing, goldsmithing, enameling, and gemstone carving.

How long it takes: Jewelry Technician—6 weeks
Graduate Jeweler—3 months

What it costs: Jewelry Technician—$4,310
Graduate Jeweler—$8,660

Credit cards are accepted.

American Institute of Diamond Cutting
1287 East Newport Center Drive, Suite 202
Deerfield Beach, FL 33442-7706
(800) 831-8470
(954) 574-0833

The institute offers three levels of training in diamond cutting: Beginning, Intermediate, and Advanced. The Beginning course trains students to identify crystal symmetry, axis, plane, form, and habit of diamond crystals, to use a cutter's loupe, crown and pavilion gauges, and girdle markers, to cut pavilion mains and in-between facets, and to master all the other skills necessary to cut a well-made brilliant from the rounded state to the finished product without supervision or assistance.

In the Intermediate course, students learn how to identify the grain in cleaved and whole diamonds, prepare diamonds for girdling, facet any girdle symmetrically, recut old mines and old European diamonds to modern proportions, cut irregular and knotted diamonds, appraise diamonds, use a binocular microscope, proportion scope, ultraviolet lamp, color graders, and merchandise and market diamonds.

The Advanced diamond-cutting course helps students increase proficiency in every technique of diamond manufacture and grading, teaches them to sort and buy diamonds in rough and cut states, trains them to cut fancy-shape diamonds, and helps them develop the confidence and skills necessary for self-employment.

How long it takes: Beginning—20 weeks
Intermediate—20 weeks
Advanced—20 weeks

What it costs: Beginning—$2,800
                       Intermediate—$2,800
                       Advanced—$2,800

Miami Jewelry Institute

The Bakehouse Art Complex
561 Northwest 32nd Street
Miami, FL 33127
(305) 573-5707

The institute offers two career training courses: Graduate Jeweler/Manufacturer and Graduate Jewelry Designer, each of which is offered both as a regular and a comprehensive course. The regular Jeweler/Manufacturer course includes basic and advanced repair, construction techniques, beginning and advanced stone setting, casting, designing, mold making, and production. It also includes courses in gemstone and jewelry appraisal, jewelry rendering, metallurgy, and basic watch information. The comprehensive Jeweler/Manufacturer course teaches more advanced techniques in all of the above subjects, and offers more bench, casting, construction, and repair experience. It also offers classes in enameling, hinges and catches, and computer design.

The regular Jewelry Designer course emphasizes bench skills, design, and instruction in traditional and nontraditional manufacturing techniques. Classes include stone setting, wax techniques, casting, gemology, jewelry appraisal, mold cutting, forging, and computer design. The comprehensive Jewelry Designer course includes special projects in enamel, chasing and repoussé, photo-etching design, and reactive metals.

How long it takes: Jewelry/Manufacturer—3 months
                       Jewelry/Manufacturer, Comprehensive—6 months
                       Jewelry Designer—3 months
                       Jewelry Designer, Comprehensive—6 months

What it costs: Jewelry/Manufacturer—$4,000
                       Jewelry/Manufacturer, Comprehensive—$6,300
                       Jewelry Designer—$4,000
                       Jewelry Designer, Comprehensive—$6,300

School of Horology
Gem City College
700 State Street
P.O. Box 179
Quincy, IL 62306
(217) 222-0391
Fax: (217) 222-1557

Gem City College offers three professional training programs: Watchmaking and Repair, Clock Repair, and Jewelry Design and Diamond Setting. The Watchmaking and Repair course teaches students how to use a watchmaker's lathe, set jewels into a plate, assemble and disassemble hairsprings, figure the number of teeth in a wheel, repair a hole in a mainspring, use a pallet warmer, repair jeweled watches, fix a distorted handspring, repair overcoils, clean and oil automatic watches, and repair electric watches.

The Clock Repair course includes much of the above, plus specialized instruction in clockmaking skills such as repivoting, drilling, brushing, and replacing teeth in a wheel. The course trains students to repair mantel, chime, alarm, electric, 400-day, cuckoo, and electric clocks.

The Jewelry Design program focuses on diamond setting, repairing jewelry, casting and rolling gold and silver, enameling, soldering, ring sizing, and making medals. Students learn to make tools, cast and size rings, and set stones. They also master eight basic design patterns, design and manufacture dinner rings, and design rings of three or more stones.

How long it takes: Watchmaking and Repair—15 months
Clock Repair—6 months
Jewelry Design—9 months

What it costs: Watchmaking and Repair—$7,500
Clock Repair—$3,000
Jewelry Design—$4,500

Financial aid is available.

North Bennet Street School
39 North Bennet Street
Boston, MA 02113
(617) 227-0155
Fax: (617) 227-9292

North Bennet's Jewelry Making and Repair program trains students to design and construct gold and silver jewelry, set precious stones, and finish the final product. The course includes instruction in replacing prongs, rebuilding ring shanks, casting in cuttlefish, making wax models, and setting faceted stones in a variety of settings.

The school also offers training programs in Bookbinding, Cabinet and Furniture Making, Preservation Carpentry, Piano Technology, and Violin Making and Restoration. See the appropriate section for more information.

How long it takes: 2 years

What it costs: $15,570

Financial aid and payment plans are available.

Maryland Institute College of Art
1300 Mount Royal Avenue
Baltimore, MD 21217
(410) 225-2219
Fax: (410) 225-2229
cs@mica.edu
www.mica.edu

The institute offers a certificate in jewelry that provides a foundation in traditional and contemporary jewelry making, training students to create one-of-a-kind art objects and production jewelry. Required coursework includes two- and three-dimensional design, fabrication, wax working and casting, metal forming, enameling, and art jewelry. Students are also required to complete an internship or independent jewelry project, and to enroll in an advanced studio class. Electives include courses in epoxy resins, combined metals for patterned jewelry, anodizing aluminum, electroforming as an art form, bead working, gemstones, and stone setting.

How long it takes: 2 years

What it costs: Approximately $6,000

Financial aid and scholarships are available and credit cards are accepted.

St. Paul Technical College
235 Marshall Avenue
St. Paul, MN 55102
(800) 227-6029
(612) 221-1300

The college offers three certificates in watchmaking that prepare students for various levels of employment in the watchmaking industry, and a watchmaking diploma that prepares them to open their own shops. The three certificates, Watch Repair, Watch Technician, and Watchmaking, include classes in basic, intermediate, and advanced watch repair, watch technology, and watchmaking. The diploma program includes courses in goldsmithing, clock benchwork, specialty clock repair (including repairing European antiques), clock repair lathes, Oriental movements, Westminster chimes, and small business management.

How long it takes: Watch Repair—3 months
Watch Technician—6 months
Watchmaker—9 months
Watchmaking Diploma—1 year

What it costs: Watch Repair—$1,715
Watch Technician—$3,430
Watchmaker—$5,145
Watchmaking Diploma—$6,000

Tuition for Minnesota residents is roughly half the above. Financial aid is available.

Joseph Bulova School
40-24 62nd Street
Woodside, NY 11377
(718) 424-2929
Fax: (718) 335-0545

The school offers courses in Watch Repair, Watchmaking, and Jewelry Design and Repair. Both the Watch Repair and the Watchmaking programs teach lathe skills, repair and diagnosis techniques, electronic horology, and jewelry skills such as soldering, filing, and fabrication of hinges. These programs include classes such as Balance Wheel Turning, Pivot Polishing and Poising, Blueprint Reading, Toolmaking,

Hairspring Manipulation, Truing, Vibrating, Escapement, Finishing, Applying Stems and Staffs, and Watch and Repair Sales. The Watch-making program includes, in addition to the above, extended instruction in and greater expertise with general repairs and more experience in the machine shop.

The Jewelry and Design and Repair program teaches the basics of jewelry design and fabrication: making chains and rings, setting stones, electroplating, mold making, investment casting, stone setting, polishing, and design for lost wax casting. Classes include Soldering Principles, Metals Technology, Polishing and Buffing, Piercing Techniques, Engraving Machine, Grinding Machines and Wheels, Investment Casting, and Jewelry Design Principles.

How long it takes: Watch Repair—13 months
Watchmaking—17 months
Jewelry Design—8 months

What it costs: Watch Repair—$15,750
Watchmaking—$19,250
Jewelry Design—$10,275

Scholarships are available.

The Jewelry Arts Institute
2180 Broadway
New York, NY 10024
(212) 362-8633

The institute offers training in Ancient and Classical Jewelry Making from 2500 B.C.E. to 1300 C.E. Students learn the principles and history of the art form and all the basic skills of classical jewelry making. The course emphasizes the foundations of classical jewelry making, particularly copper induction braising, or granulation, and cloisonné enamel jewelry making. The curriculum also includes Byzantine enameling, classical chain making, classical setting, granulation in silver and gold, lapidary, and other related techniques. Students graduate from the program with a collection of ancient and medieval jewelry that they've fabricated for their portfolio.

How long it takes: Most students attend for about 1 year. The institute offers 4 seasonal sessions per year (Fall, Winter, Spring, Summer), which meet once a week for 3 hours. The month of July is dedicated to intensive workshops that are 5 days of full-time instruction.

What it costs: Seasonal sessions—$425 each
                   July intensives—$550 each

Jewelry Learning Center
Studio Jewelers, Ltd.
32 East 31st Street
New York, NY 10016
(212) 686-1944

The center offers short- and long-format comprehensive jewelry training programs that cover four major areas: fundamental jewelry techniques, stone setting, wax modeling and casting, and decorative processes. Fundamental jewelry techniques taught in the short format include sawing, piercing, filing, sanding, polishing, soldering, and annealing. The short-format stone setting course includes classes on bezel, prong, and channel settings, and bead work. The short-format wax modeling and casting course teaches students about wax sheet and wire, spruing, investing, and centrifugal casting. And the short-format decorative processes course includes texturing, etching, enameling, and electroplating.

The long-format program covers all of the above plus instruction in using rolling mills and draw plates, constructing hinges, marquise, pavé, and gypsy settings, wax carving, chasing/repoussé, fusing, and marriage of metals. The studio offers additional short-term workshops in diamond setting, pearl and bead stringing, and design.

How long it takes: Short-Format—12 weeks
                     Long-Format—24 weeks

What it costs: Short-Format—$3,316
                   Long-Format—$5,167

Payment plans are available.

American Watchmakers-Clockmakers Institute
701 Enterprise Drive
Harrison, OH 45030
(513) 367-9800
Fax: (513) 367-1414
www.awi-net.org

The institute offers a career training program in watchmaking. The program is designed to prepare students with no previous watchmaking skills or knowledge for entry-level careers in the field of horology. The curriculum includes filing, sawing, hardening and tempering metals, working with the watchmaker's lathe, machine shop practices, case finishing, crystal replacements, and band repairs. It also covers watch movement, mainspring and barrel adjustments and repairs, pocket watches, automatic winding mechanisms, calendar mechanisms, chronographs, electricity, quartz watch repair, and basic jewelry and watch case repair. The institute helps students find employment.

How long it takes: 45 weeks

What it costs:　　$7,750

Scholarships are available.

Drouhard National Jeweler's School
5262 Cleveland Avenue
Columbus, OH 43231
(888) 663-9335
(614) 891-9914

The school offers three professional training programs in jewelry: Jewelry Repair and Diamond Setting, Advanced Diamond Setting, and Design, Casting, and Production. The Jewelry Repair and Diamond Setting program covers precious metals, jewelry cleaning, soldering, hand tools, ring assembly and sizing, shank repair, jewelry supplies, diamond setting and polishing, removing and tightening gemstones, prong repair, annealing, bezel setting and fabrication, chain repair, and rhodium and gold electroplating.

Advanced Diamond Setting includes classes in gemstone characteristics, setting the emerald cut, graver design, bead setting, star and block bright cutting, and cluster, bar, tiffany, channel, baguette, and many other settings.

The Design, Casting and Production Program includes instruction in lost wax casting, design and illustration, carving wax, determining metal needs, spruing, mold making, metal melting, casting, porosity, clean-up and finishing, molding for duplication, wax injecting, multiple spruing, nugget casting, commercial casting, and shop set-up.

How long it takes: Jewelry Repair and Diamond Setting—1 week
Advanced Diamond Setting—1 week
Design, Casting, and Production—1 week

What it costs: Jewelry Repair and Diamond Setting—$600
Advanced Diamond Setting—$600
Design, Casting, and Production—$600

Virginia Marti College of Fashion and Art
11724 Detroit Avenue
Lakewood, OH 44107
(800) 473-4350
(216) 221-8584
www.vmarti.com

The college offers a jewelry design and repair certificate course. Coursework includes color theory, gemology, jewelry repair, jewelry history, jewelry shop skills, wax carving and casting, diamond grading, and a jewelry design workshop. Students learn ring sizing, electroplating, polishing, design rendering, crystal buffing, wax casting, mold making, and merchandising. The course also includes an internship that gives students on-the-job training and the opportunity to work in a professional situation.

How long it takes: 9 months

What it costs: $950

Financial aid is available.

American Jewelers Institute
11904 Southeast Stark Street
Portland, OR 97216
(503) 255-4517

The institute offers a professional training course in Jewelry Arts and Manufacturing. The core courses are Tool Orientation, Material Orientation, Gemology, Fabrication, Soldering, Repairs, Diamond/Colored Stone Setting, Wax Carving, Casting, and Rubber Mold Making. Students learn to use flexible shafts, burrs, polishing tools, rolling mills, ultrasonic vacuums, and casting and vulcanizing machines. They are taught skills such as annealing, torch use, retipping, soldering jump

rings, wax modification, spruing and treeing, melting torch and quench-
ng procedures, and bezel, burnish, hammer, bead, and bright settings.
Lifetime employment placement assistance is available to students.

How long it takes: 16 weeks

What it costs: $5,360

Financing is available.

Kilgore College
1100 Broadway
Kilgore, TX 75662
(903) 983-8209
(903) 983-8220
Fax: (903) 983-8607

Kilgore offers training in jewelry making and horology. The Horology
course provides students with hands-on experience making parts on the
lathe, correcting parts with poising tools, truing calipers and staking
sets, cleaning, lubricating, and regulating the timing and beat of
mechanical timepieces, and repairing quartz watches using the Citizen
multimeter. The Jewelry program teaches how to size rings, make
shanks, use a rolling mill, set stones, make molds, do lost-wax casting,
and design jewelry.

How long it takes: Horology—1 year
                    Jewelry Making—1 year

What it costs: Horology—$2,232
                    Jewelry Making—$2,232

Financial aid is available.

Texas Institute of Jewelry Technology
2400 Clarksville Street
Paris, TX 75460
(800) 232-5804
(903) 782-0361
Fax: (903) 782-0452
fpoye@paris.cc.tx.us
www.paris.cc.tx.us/TIJT

The institute offers certificate programs in horology and jewelry technology. The horology program covers watch repair, material systems, automatics, calendars, quartz, timers, chronographs, electric watches, accutrons, digital watches, step motor quartz, lathe work, and business practices. Students learn advanced hairspring manipulation, friction jeweling, disassembly, cleaning, and repair, electrical theory as it applies to watches and timepieces, and repairing tuning fork electronic movements.

The jewelry technology program includes coursework in fabrication, repair, casting, stone setting, and precious metals. Students learn layout, piercing, hand finishing, flex-shaft techniques, wax carving, vibratory finishing, catch construction, gold and platinum fabrication, and shop practices.

The institute also offers an Applied Jewelry Practices program in which students learn about common industry practices and prepare themselves for the job market. The program includes résumé writing, job interview skills, business ethics, small business development, sales techniques, and insurance and appraisals.

How long it takes: Horology—12 months
Jewelry Technology—12 months

What it costs: Horology—$2,852
Jewelry Technology—$3,102

Texas state residents receive a discount on tuition. Financial aid is available.

Jewelry Design Institute
13354 Midlothian Turnpike
Colony Plaza, Suite 202
Midlothian, VA 23113
(800) 756-1227
(804) 794-9312

The institute offers two jewelry design career programs: Career Program One and Career Program Two. Career Program One consists of Jewelry Design and Fabrication, Jewelry Repair, Stone Setting, and Wax Modeling and Casting. The Design and Fabrication course teaches rendering designs, annealing, piercing, doming, drilling, forging, die pressing hollow forms, and several surface-embellishing techniques such as roller printing and reticulation. The Jewelry Repair class teaches students to solder, pierce, drill, and rivet metal, repair chains, size rings, replace shanks, rebuild prongs, and polish and clean jewelry. The Stone Setting course trains students to set stones in four- and six-prong Tiffany mountains, bar settings, pinpoints, and cluster settings. The Modeling and Casting course teaches students spruing, investing, vacuum casting, finishing, injecting, and cutting rubber molds.

Career Program Two covers many of the same subjects as the first training, but focuses on bringing students to a higher level of proficiency. It offers advanced classes in using the Sparkie welder, making basket heads for larger stones, sinking a bowl, and designing and fabricating rings, bracelets, neckpieces, earrings, and pins. This program focuses on encouraging students to develop their own unique style of design and fabrication.

How long it takes: Career Program One—5 weeks
Career Program Two—3 months

What it costs: Career Program One—$2,975
Career Program Two—$4,500

North Seattle Community College
9600 College Way North
Seattle, WA 98103
(206) 527-3663

The college offers a vocational certificate program in Watch and Clock Technology. Core courses include Equipment and Measurement, Making Tools and Repair Parts for Clocks, Theory and Overview, Basic Mechanisms of Clocks, Clock Repair, Watch and Clock Technology, and Jewelry Design. In the various Clock and Watch courses, students learn to use the jeweler's saw and watchmaker's lathe, temper and anneal steel, construct and repair clock movements, work with hairsprings, escapements, and jewels, replace balance staffs, and size bands. The Jewelry Design courses teach students to work with precious and semiprecious stones, cast jewelry with the lost-wax method, make rubber molds, use electroforming and enameling, set stones, and repair jewelry. The program also teaches business skills such as estimating, record keeping, ordering, and setting up a shop. Students get hands-on experience working with antique watches, modern watches, lever and pin-lever watches, quartz watches, and many different types of clocks.

How long it takes: 18 months

What it costs: $2,900

Financial aid is available.

Piano Tuning and Musical Instrument Repair ◆ ◆ ◆

You don't need to have been born with a discriminating ear to become a piano tuner—though you do need to be able to find middle C. But that, unlike perfect pitch (also not required), is teachable. And the following programs teach it, as well as how to tune, repair, and rebuild all sorts of upright, grand, and concert pianos. If you're interested in more than pianos, the music instrument repair programs teach everything from fixing oboes and kettle drums to rewiring digital music devices.

The American Institute of Piano Technology
P.O. Box 4418
Chatsworth, CA 91313
(213) 223-2010
(818) 348-1530

The institute offers two professional piano technology training programs: Rebuilding and Piano Service.

The Rebuilding program focuses on restoration. Students complete an introductory rebuilding course that covers nomenclature, documentation of projects, shop safety, and project disassembly. They then work on their own projects under the supervision of an instructor. The duration of the rebuilding class depends on the speed at which the student project is completed.

The Piano Service curriculum includes tuning, repairs, action regulation, voicing, action rebuilding, stringing, touch-up, structural repairs, and business practices.

How long it takes: Rebuilding—variable
                     Piano Service—18 weeks

194 + *You're Certifiable*

What it costs: Rebuilding—$300 per 9 weeks
Piano Service—$600

San Francisco School of Piano Tuning
657 Mission Street, Suite 507
San Francisco, CA 94105
(800) 247-0702
(415) 543-9833
Fax: (415) 896-2866

The school offers two training courses: Piano Tuning and Fundamentals of Piano Repair. The Piano Tuning course covers unisons, octaves, pitch raising, temperament, and stretching octaves. The school's training emphasizes the use of acoustical beats instead of pitch tone to tune pianos. The Piano Repair course, which is only available to graduates of the tuning course, teaches students to replace broken music wires and dampers, and to understand how a piano is regulated.

How long it takes: Piano Tuning—21 hours
Piano Repair—16 hours

What it costs: Piano Tuning—$1,100
Piano Repair—$450

Credit cards are accepted.

The Larry Crabb School of Piano Technology
4299 Hugh Howell Road
Tucker, GA 30084
(770) 491-1432
Fax: (770) 908-2331

The Larry Crabb School offers three piano technology courses: Basic Piano Tuning and Vertical Piano Technology, Advanced Piano Tuning and Grand Piano Technology, and Concert Piano Tuning and Preparation of the Performance Piano. The Basic Piano Tuning and Vertical Piano Technology course teaches students everything they need to know to get started as piano tuners/technicians. The curriculum includes piano terminology, harmonic series, inharmonicity, interval ratios and coincident partials, tuning hammer technique, electronic tuning aids, repairing key, hammers, and dampers, regulating keys and pedals, and starting a business and getting customers.

The Advanced Piano Tuning and Grand Piano Technology course teaches advanced theory, perfecting tuning hammer technique, voicing the hammers, special grand piano repairs, rebuilding grand pianos, ordering parts and supplies, developing industry contacts, and bidding for contract work.

The Concert Piano Tuning and Preparation of the Performance Piano course teaches advanced students the skills needed to prepare a grand piano for a concert performance. Classes cover the piano artist's needs, the concert hall, pin and string setting, advanced voicing techniques, and giving the piano evenness, speed, and power.

How long it takes: Basic Piano Tuning—1,150 hours
Advanced Piano Tuning—575 hours
Concert Piano Tuning—276 hours

Roughly a third of each course must be completed at the school and in the school's shop. The balance consists of required reading, practice tuning, and working on a practice piano.

What it costs: Basic Piano Tuning—$5,000
Advanced Piano Tuning—$2,500
Concert Piano Tuning—$1,250

Financing is available.

Western Iowa Tech Community College
4647 Stone Avenue
P.O. Box 5199
Sioux City, IA 51102
(712) 274-6400, ext. 1306

Western Iowa Tech offers a diploma program in Band Instrument Repair Technology. Students learn to restore brass and woodwind instruments, use buffing and dent removal equipment, and operate a machine lathe to make tools and perform special repairs. Woodwind repair coursework includes installing key pads and corks, adjusting key mechanisms, and repairing cracks. And brass instrument repair coursework includes removing dents, making parts and special fittings, repairing casings and pistons, and soft soldering of braces, tubes, and small parts. Students also gain a solid knowledge of practical business skills and customer relations.

How long it takes: 1 year

What it costs: Iowa residents—$1,770
                     Out-of-state residents—$3,540

Financial aid is available.

North Bennet Street School
39 North Bennet Street
Boston, MA 02113
(617) 227-0155
Fax: (617) 227-9292

North Bennet offers two levels of Piano Technology training: Basic and Advanced. The Basic course trains students to tune upright and grand pianos and repair and regulate their actions. The Advanced course teaches students to make major structural repairs and completely rebuild upright and grand pianos. This includes disassembly, casework and veneer repair, refinishing, soundboard repair, grand and upright plank installation, and troubleshooting.

   The school also offers training programs in Bookbinding, Cabinet and Furniture Making, Preservation Carpentry, Jewelry Making and Repair, and Violin Making and Restoration. See the appropriate section for more information.

How long it takes: Beginning Piano Technology—1 year
                      Advanced Piano Technology—1 year

What it costs: Beginning Piano Technology—$9,300
                      Advanced Piano Technology—$9,050

Financial aid and payment plans are available.

Gavin School of Piano Technology
P.O. Box 10806
White Bear Lake, MN 55110
(612) 644-3111

The school offers a Piano Technician training program. The course teaches tuning, regulating, repair, restringing, theory, and practical business skills. Students learn to hear beats per second, use a tuning hammer, correct the thirty-seven adjustments per key, replace broken and damaged parts, install a piano humidity-control system, and work with suppliers.

How long it takes: 12 weeks

What it costs: $1,750

Red Wing Technical College
308 Pioneer Road
Red Wing, MN 55066
(800) 657-4849
(612) 385-6300
Fax: (612) 385-6378

Red Wing offers three instrument repair training programs: Band Instrument Repair, Electronic Music Technology, and Musical String Instrument Repair. The Band Instrument Repair program teaches students to repair brass, percussion, and woodwind instruments. The curriculum includes acoustics, machine tool operation, shop procedures, repair labs, and independent study courses.

The Electronic Music Technology course trains students to diagnose, troubleshoot, repair, and assemble keyboards, amplifiers, synthesizers, and studio equipment. Classes include Semiconductors, DC Theory and Circuits, Digital Logic Circuits, MIDI Applications, Servicing Concepts, and Digital Music Devices.

The Musical String Instrument Repair course trains students to clean, adjust, and repair violins, violas, cellos, and acoustic and electric guitars. Classes cover fretwork, crack repair, finishing, construction, bow maintenance and repair, and small business management.

How long it takes: Band Instrument Repair—16 months
Electronic Music Technology—32 months
Musical String Instrument Repair—24 months

What it costs: Band Instrument Repair—$4,000
Electronic Music Technology—$8,000
Musical String Instrument Repair—$5,800

Minnesota residents pay approximately half the listed tuition. Financial aid is available.

Museum of the American Piano
211 West 58th Street
New York, NY 10019
(212) 246-4646

The museum offers a Piano Tuning and Technology course that consists of five parts: Tuning, Regulating, Repair, General, and Tenets. Tuning covers acoustic theory, tuning hammer techniques, temperament study, and complete tuning. Students learn about the behavior of strings and soundboards, and how to test for accuracy, set the string and pin, and raise and lower pitch. The Regulating courses cover both grand and upright pianos. They include instruction in basic action principles, action assembly and removal, keyboard construction and regulating, damper actions, and pedals and trapwork. The Repair courses cover repinning, rebushing, dealing with clicks and sticking parts, repairing and replacing broken keys, working with the hammer and shank, understanding the tonal function of the keys and the structure of the frame and pin block, scale drafting, and string and pin replacement and repair. The General courses cover evaluation, complete rebuilding, piano supply houses, piano breakdown and reassembly, and employment and self-employment options. And Tenets covers tuning by comparison of beats rather than counting, correcting malfunctions due to regulating failure, and regulating analysis of action design/geometry.

How long it takes: 100 hours

What it costs: $2,500

Emil Fries Piano Hospital and Training Center
2510 East Evergreen Boulevard
Vancouver, WA 98661
(360) 693-1511
Fax: (360) 693-6891

The mission of the training center is to preserve Piano Tuning as a viable career for blind people; however, sighted people are also accepted when space permits. The training focuses on seven subjects: tuning, regulating, repairing, reconditioning, rebuilding, theory, and business operations and personal skills. The Tuning classes teach how to use tuning hammers, mutes, and temperament strips, and how to tune unisons, pure octaves, and tempered intervals. The Regulating course covers the proper use of tools, manufacturers' specifications, action adjustment, hammer voicing, and regulation of vertical and grand pianos. The Repairing class teaches students how to replace and splice strings, repair keys, replace bridle taps, and repair soundboards, ribs, and pin-block-back separation. The Reconditioning course covers reconditioning hammers, replacing ivory key tops, and restoring tone. The Rebuilding course offers instruction in restringing, and replacing hammers, key bushings, and key bed felt. The Theory class teaches music theory, history, music appreciation, and the theory of acoustics. And the Business Operations and Personal Skills class teaches bookkeeping, advertising, telephone skills, and basic business psychology.

How long it takes: 20 months

What it costs: $10,500

Violin and Guitar Making and Repair ◆ ◆ ◆

Professional violin making, or luthiery, requires a combination of fine woodworking skills, attention to design and detail, and an understanding of—and often proficiency in—musical performance. Luthiery can be a terrific career if you enjoy detail-oriented woodworking or want to integrate your love of music with your love of crafting. And note that, despite the section heading, many luthiers focus on building and repairing cellos, violas, and other stringed instruments.

Roberto-Venn School of Luthiery
4011 South 16th Street
Phoenix, AZ 85040
(602) 243-1179

The school offers a guitar-making course that consists of practical and theoretical training in acoustic and electric guitar making. Students attend lectures and demonstrations, and construct one acoustic and one electric (or bass) guitar from scratch. Among the building styles students learn are dreadnought, jumbo, classical, folk, cutaway, hollow body, and carved top. Coursework covers milling and wood selection, guitar design, tool use and maintenance, scale and template derivation, finishing (with lacquer, oil, stain, or paint), guitar electronics, tremolo installation, and care and preservation of stringed instruments. Advanced courses include specialized repair techniques and luthiery business subjects.

How long it takes: 5 months

What it costs: $5,950

Financial aid is available.

Luthiers International Guitar Repair and Building Schools
The Fret Shop
4615 Highway 78
Lilburn, GA 30247
(770) 982-0007
(770) 469-3000

The schools offer professional training in Guitar Repair and Building. The program begins with instruction in basic setups, understanding radius, scale length, pulling frets, refretting, and crowning and leveling frets. Students then learn how to repair such problems as cracked tops and broken necks, to replace bridges and braces, and to make nuts and saddles. The training also covers neck resets, tremolo bridges, wiring, switches, pickups, and how to make tools such as neck jigs, clamps, and cauls. Students complete the course by building a finished guitar. Luthiers International also offers training in Umeå, Sweden, and Qualicum Beach, British Columbia.

How long it takes: 2 months

What it costs: $3,750

Chicago School of Violin Making
3636 Oakton Street
Skokie, IL 60076
(847) 673-9545

The Chicago School offers a Professional Violin Making training program in which students make a minimum of seven instruments, including at least three violins and one viola. The program consists of four parts. In the first part, students learn the proper use of hand tools and the sequence of steps in violin construction, and construct three violin bodies, begin mechanical drawing, and take violin lessons. In the second section, students fashion scrolls and neck sets for the three violin bodies previously built, study the theory and application of varnish, build a viola, and continue with violin lessons and mechanical drawing. The third part covers the construction of another instrument, basic and advanced repair techniques, and more violin lessons and mechanical drawing. Finally, the fourth section—the Graduation Semester—is spent preparing for the final exam, which includes building one unvarnished instrument, varnishing another, completing a written test and a technical drawing, and performing on a stringed instrument for the graduation ceremony.

How long it takes: 3½ years

What it costs: $17,220

An installment plan is available.

Leeds Guitarmakers' School
8 Easthampton Road
Northampton, MA 01060
(413) 582-0034
leeds@crocker.com
www.crocker.com/~leeds

Leeds offers a comprehensive course in Guitar Construction, Finishing, and Repair. The curriculum consists of five parts: Tool Craft, Wood Preparation, Basic Flat Top Guitar Construction, Basic Arched Top Guitar Construction, and Finishing/Repair. The Tool Craft course teaches basic hand- and power-tool setup and fabrication of basic edge tools such as the skew chisel. Wood Preparation covers the fabrication of parts for flat top, arched top, and electric guitars, and includes the use of the table saw, band saw, disc and thickness sanders, drill press, joiner, bending irons, and assorted hand tools. In Basic Flat Top Guitar Construction, students build either a classical or steel string guitar. Basic Arched Top Guitar Construction teaches students to build either an acoustic or acoustic/electric arched top guitar. And Finishing/Repair covers the use of lacquer and shellac, and the basic repair methods used for cracks, regluing loose braces, neck resetting, and various instrument adjustments. Leeds also offers beginning intensives,

202 ◆ *You're Certifiable*

private tutorials and short-term courses in finishing, polishing, and refretting.

How long it takes: 13 weeks

What it costs: $8,750

The Luthier's Workshop
99 Moody Street
Waltham, MA 02154
(781) 894-4292

The workshop offers three forms of luthiery training: a part-time course, a full-time course, and an apprenticeship program. The part-time course teaches students to care for their tools, measure and choose the proper wood, understand acoustics, and use basic woodworking skills such as operation of power tools and finishing techniques. Although this isn't a professional training course, students do learn all aspects of building a guitar. The full-time course is open-ended, offering students the run of the shop for as long as they need. The apprenticeship program includes part-time instruction plus full-time work in the shop—doing everything from sweeping up to all phases of instrument construction and repair.

How long it takes: Part-time course—9 months to 1 year to finish 1 guitar
Full-time course—variable
Apprenticeship—4 months

What it costs: Part-time course—$1,000 to $1,400
Full-time course—$50 per day
Apprenticeship—$40 per week, plus 22 to 24 hours of unpaid work per week

Credit cards are accepted.

North Bennet Street School
39 North Bennet Street
Boston, MA 02113
(617) 227-0155
Fax: (617) 227-9292

North Bennet offers an apprenticeship-type training program in Violin Making and Restoration. The program trains students to build, repair, and restore stringed instruments and bows. Students learn such skills as using hand tools, varnishing, cutting bridges, fitting sound posts, planning fingerboards, and using glues and clamps. During the program, students build six violins, a viola, and a cello. Students keep the first and last violins: the school gets the rest of the instruments in exchange for tuition credit.

The school also offers training programs in Bookbinding, Cabinet and Furniture Making, Preservation Carpentry, Jewelry Making and Repair, and Piano Technology. See the appropriate section for more information.

How long it takes: 3 years

What it costs: $24,300

Financial aid and payment plans are available.

Violin Craftsmanship Institute
University of New Hampshire
24 Rosemary Lane
Durham, NH 03824
(603) 862-1088
Fax: (603) 862-1113
learn.dce@unh.edu
www.learn.unh.edu/Violin

The institute offers a variety of programs in violin making and repair. Classes are offered only during the summer, so students who want to learn advanced skills must attend several sessions. Courses include Cello Repair, Viola Repair, Advanced Violin Repair, Bow Maintenance and Repair, Bow Rehairing, Frog and Button Making in the French Tradition, Advanced Bow Finishing, and Violin Building. The most extensive course is Violin Building, which consists of three levels. The first level teaches students to create templates and molds, place blocks, ribs, and liners, join pieces for the back and belly, and complete rough arching. At the end of the first level, students will have two complete rib assemblies, two joined and roughly arched sets of plates, and enough basic tool skills to permit home practice. The second level begins with students outlining the body, and it ends with their removing the mold

204 ● *You're Certifiable*

and closing the body. Students will have two completed violin bodies by the end of the second level. The third level trains students to carve scrolls, make fingerboards, and set necks. At the end of the third level, students will have made two complete violins.

How long it takes: Violin Building—1 to 6 weeks
Other classes—1 to 2 weeks

What it costs: Violin Building—$2,395 for 6 weeks ($595 for 1 week)
Other classes—$495 to $995

Credit cards are accepted.

The Chimney's Violin Shop
614 Lerew Road
Boiling Springs, PA 17007
(717) 258-3203
Fax: (717) 258-3201

The Violin Shop offers two courses: a journeyman program and a more comprehensive violin maker apprenticeship program. The apprenticeship program teaches students to handcraft violins using traditional methods. They learn to sharpen carving tools, create a mold for the ribs of the instrument, work within tolerances of less than one millimeter, carve and tune the top and back plates, apply and make their own varnish, and rehair and maintain bows. Other classes in the apprenticeship program include music lessons, the history of the instruments, and business practices. In the course of the program, students make approximately nine violins, two violas, and one cello. The journeyman program is a less thorough course. It covers the construction of fewer intruments, and doesn't include instruction in violin or bow restoration and repair.

How long it takes: Journeyman—4 years, 9 months per year
Apprenticeship—4 years, full-time

What it costs: Journeyman—$3,150 per year
Apprenticeship—$3,600 per year

A payment plan is available.

The Violin Making School of America
308 East 200 South
Salt Lake City, UT 84111
(800) 801-3651
(801) 364-3651
Fax: (801) 364-3652
www.prierviolins.com

The Violin Making School offers a comprehensive course in all aspects of violin making. The curriculum includes knowledge of woods and tools, constructing and playing stringed instruments, mechanical and artistic drawing, varnishing, adjustment, history and theory, acoustics, and technical repair. Requirements for graduation include presenting a written thesis, completing one unvarnished violin and one finished instrument, and a violin recital on a completed instrument.

How long it takes: 4 years

What it costs: $9,200 per year

Woodworking and Furniture Making ◆ ◆ ◆

Unlike other training programs that involve working with wood (such as boatbuilding and violin making, above), most of the programs in this section offer more generalized training. Students learn a wide range of techniques and styles, from chair making to dovetail cutting to wood turning to cabinetmaking to finishing. A few programs, though, offer advanced or specialized training (such as in wood carving and furniture restoration) that can be combined with woodworking careers or developed into a niche career. We did not include more conventional cabinetmaking, carpentry, or wood technology courses, with the exception of Maharishi University's program (which offers a fairly conventional training in a fairly unconventional setting—in addition to including meditation classes in the furniture-making curriculum, the university accepts completed projects in lieu of tuition).

The School of Classical Woodcarving
319 Dolan Avenue
Mill Valley, CA 94941
(415) 381-9474
Fax: (415) 381-9475
carving@slip.net
www.agrellandthorpe.com

The school teaches fine hand-carving skills: how to create traditional carved decoration with designs from the ancient Greeks through the Gothic, Renaissance, and Rococo periods. Classes cover carving the acanthus leaf, creating decorative moldings and panels, carving cabriole (or ball and claw) legs, working "in the round" (three-dimensionally), and carving and gilding letters. Although the program isn't exclusively for those who wish to become professional carvers, it is a good first step for a carving or sign-making career. Students who intend to use the school's training as vocational preparation tend to enroll in several sessions or return periodically to update their skills.

How long it takes: 2 weeks

What it costs: $1,200

Credit cards are accepted.

Maharishi University of Management
Fairfield, IA 52557
(515) 472-1110
Fax: (515) 472-1179
admissions@mum.edu/ffw
www.mum.edu

The university offers a certificate program in Fine Furniture and Woodworking that teaches students furniture design and construction, cabinet construction, and architectural millwork while helping them develop consciousness and creativity. The curriculum for basic certification includes courses in the fundamental elements of woodworking, furniture design and construction, joinery, cabinetmaking design and construction, cabinetmaking details, woodworking and art, and the business of woodworking. Students learn shop safety, hand and power tool usage, wood turning, carving, and finishing. The university offers advanced study for students who want to specialize in one particular area, focus on quality and craftsmanship, and master furniture design.

How long it takes: 1 year

Three additional years of advanced training are available.

What it costs: Because student woodworking projects are used to help beautify the campus, the full tuition of $8,000 per year is covered by grants and scholarships for all students.

Mark Adams School of Woodworking
5504 East, 500 North
Franklin, IN 46131
(317) 535-4013
Fax: (317) 535-1713

The school offers a master woodworker program based on seven core classes: Joinery, Finishing, Veneering and Marquetry, Carving, Chair Making, Woodturning, and Apprenticeship. The Joinery class covers dovetails, mortise and tenons, lap joints, bridal joints, compound miters, scarf and hip joints, finger joints, and decorative joints. The Finishing course covers preparing the wood, sealing, using varnish and polyurethane, two-part finishes, French polishing, understanding solvents and strippers, applying pigments, stains, and glazes, and caring for finishes. The Veneering and Marquetry class includes instruction in design techniques, flattening, star bursts, border work, cutting, edging, taping, parquetry, creating geometric shapes, and pressing odd shapes. The Carving class includes instruction in layout, transferring patterns, sharpening tools, and carving cabriole legs, grapevines, crolls, lettering, and other ornamentation. The Chair Making class teaches hip, dowel, and mortise and tenon joints, using rasps, gouges and spokeshaves, lamination, design, and ergonomics. The Woodturning class covers tool selection, application, grinding, spindle turning, faceplate work, and hollowing end grain—students get experience making furniture parts, bowls and plates, and lidded boxes, goblets, and scoops. And the Apprenticeship class offers intensive study of design and hands-on practice of many skills, including wood selection, traditional hand skills, bending and forming wood, and surface preparation.

How long it takes: 9 weeks

What it costs: $4,525

The Furniture Institute of Massachusetts
116 Water Street
Beverly, MA 01915
(978) 922-0615

The institute offers a furniture-making training program that focuses on the art of classical and contemporary furniture making. The program begins with instruction in design techniques such as orthographic and isometric drawing and making and using full-size furniture layouts. Students then learn fundamental woodworking skills, such as tool sharpening and joinery, and complete a number of projects, including a tool chest, chairs, tables, casework, and beds. During the construction process, students learn design, ornamentation, milling, staining and finishing, costing and pricing, and hardware and wood selecting skills.

How long it takes: 2 years

What it costs: $24,000

A payment plan is available.

New England School of Architectural Woodworking
One Cottage Street
Easthampton, MA 01027
(413) 527-6103
nesaw@crocker.com
www.tufts.edu/~camass/nesaw.html

The school trains woodworkers who specialize in architectural work such as corporate interiors, kitchen cabinets, aviation outfitting, custom interiors, and store fixtures, displays, and exhibits. The training program teaches basic and advanced skills—from joinery techniques to finishing to job estimating—and introduces students to blueprint reading, drafting, full-scale drawing, parts listing, and hardware specifications. Specific skills taught include rabbeting, edge jointing, finish preparation, using table saws, planers, and pneumatic nailers, veneering, and designing and constructing special jigs and templates.

Students get hands-on experience by completing projects for public and nonprofit organizations, such as the construction of computer tables, built-in cabinets, or office furniture. This also gives them a glimpse of how an architectural woodworking shop operates on a daily basis.

How long it takes: 37 weeks

What it costs: $6,500

North Bennet Street School
39 North Bennet Street
Boston, MA 02113
(617) 227-0155
Fax: (617) 227-9292

North Bennet offers an apprenticeship-type program in cabinet and furniture making. The course teaches students to estimate materials, design, draw, construct, and finish fine furniture using hand tools and power equipment for joinery and ornamentation. Students construct several small projects using planes, chisels, and a wood lathe, then make a tool chest, a table, a chair, and another piece of casework. The course also teaches carving, inlay, and veneering.

North Bennet also offers a training program in Preservation Carpentry. This program teaches students to work on pre-twentieth-century buildings and new construction of traditional styles. Students learn to select appropriate materials, preserve architectural detail, stabilize structural elements, and re-create historically accurate elements and millwork. The course also teaches how to re-create siding, door and window trim, cornices, roofing, molding, window sashes, and frame-and-panel doors.

The school also offers training programs in Bookbinding, Jewelry Making and Repair, Piano Technology, and Violin Making and Restoration. See the appropriate section for more information.

How long it takes: Cabinet and Furniture Making—2 years
Preservation Carpentry—2 years

What it costs: Cabinet and Furniture Making—$20,100
Preservation Carpentry—$20,000

Financial aid and payment plans are available.

Wm. B. Sayer, Inc.
One Cottage Street
Easthampton, MA 01027
(413) 527-0202
Fax: (413) 527-0502

William Sayer offers a professional-level program dedicated to teaching the design and creation of custom furniture. The first part of the program focuses on hand tools. It includes classes on purchasing tools, tool care and sharpening, planing and sawing, and crafting with the exclusive use of hand tools. Students make an octagon (an eight-sided beveled board), several kinds of joints, and two tables. In the second part of the program, students are introduced to the safe use and care of power machinery. They build a wall-hung case with a frame and panel door and an inset side-hung drawer using solid wood construction. They draft and design three projects, learn wood finishing, and complete a large-carcass final piece incorporating advanced techniques (intended as a portfolio piece). No more than three students are in attendance at any given time.

How long it takes: 1 year

What it costs: $700 per month

Center for Furniture Craftsmanship
25 Mill Street
Rockport, ME 04856
(207) 594-5611

The center offers many workshops and classes of various lengths, including an Intensive for those considering furniture making as a profession. The curriculum of the Intensive includes design, drawing, lumber selection, joinery, traditional hand skills, machine techniques, advanced techniques, surface preparation and finishing, shop maintenance, and professional practices. Students learn to develop a design brief, render objects on paper, select wood appropriate to the design, use hand planes, saws, and scrapers, bend laminate, turn spindles, make jigs and fixtures, apply finish, tune and maintain machinery, develop products, price, and market. Each student designs and builds three projects: one requiring hand-cut dovetail and mortise and tenon joinery, one carcass piece with at least one door and one drawer, and one more challenging piece incorporating steam bending, laminate bending, and veneer work.

How long it takes: 12 weeks

What it costs: $3,600

Assistantships, which are unpaid but do include free lodging, are occasionally available. Credit cards are accepted.

Conover Workshops
18125 Madison Road
P.O. Box 679
Parkman, OH 44080-0679
(216) 548-2721
Fax: (216) 548-2721
ConoverWS@aol.com

Conover offers a wide range of workshops, include hand plane, router, planer, and joiner use, wood turning, finishing, hand tool joinery, Shaker box making, kitchen cabinet construction, veneering, and wood coloring. These workshops teach skills such as edge banding, inlaying, decorative finishing, making dovetails, spindle turning, making jigs, and French polishing. For career training, Conover offers an apprenticeship program. This is a goal-oriented program that allows apprentices to learn the trade by working closely with a master crafter on projects such as building a Shaker kitchen, as well as finishing several personal projects. Apprentices are also allowed to audit any of the courses offered during the apprenticeship.

How long it takes: 6 weeks to 6 months

What it costs: Apprentices do not pay any tuition. They pay for
                     their own food and lodging, and are responsible for
                     shop cleanup, machine and tool maintenance, and
                     helping with lunch during workshops.

**The Myerside International School of Antique Furniture
Restoration**
Myerside Grange
Gifford
East Lothian, Scotland EH41 4JA
International telephone: (011-44) 1620-810680

This school is listed here despite the fact that it isn't located in the United States. But it *is*, after all, an international school (and learning a trade in the Scottish hills seems to deserve a listing). The school offers an intensive course that prepares students to set up their own furniture restoration business. Coursework includes timber identification, hand and machine tool handling, woodscrew taps and dyes, veneering, joints, wood turning and carving, wood bending, moldings, inlay and marquetry, finishing and polishing, gilding, metalwork, and workshop organization. The school also runs a commercial antique furniture restoration and furniture-making business, allowing students to experience the working practices, deadlines, and pressures of a "real world" restoration business, and to observe the designing and creation of furniture from start to finish.

How long it takes: 36 weeks

What it costs:　　$13,000 (£8,000)

Cost is approximate and will vary according to the exchange rate. A payment plan is available. The school will help you find housing and will arrange homestays upon request.

Fine Art Woodcarving
P.O. Box 302
Newfane, VT 05345
(802) 365-7255

Fine Art offers intensive wood-carving instruction. Students are introduced to chip carving using the Swiss method, and then they move on to traditional European designs such as Celtic knots, forms from nature, pierced carving, and the human form. Student projects may include lettering, floral forms, rosettes, rope borders, clocks, art nouveau, and classical designs. Although attending this course doesn't provide advanced professional training (unless you return several times), it does provide instruction sufficient to help you get a job in a woodshop as a carver, or to add carving to your furniture-making skills.

How long it takes: 5 days

What it costs:　　$390

Credit cards are accepted.

Miscellaneous Craft and Trade ◆ ◆ ◆

There are six craft subjects in this section: blacksmithing and blade-smithing, jade carving, glassblowing, neon tube bending, sign painting, and saddlemaking. They range from very businesslike and bottom-line-oriented vocations barely on the edge of alternative to careers that verge on the fine arts. If you're interested in making your living with your hands, but you have no specific subject in mind, check them out.

California Contemporary Craft Association
P.O. Box 2060
Sausalito, CA 94966
(415) 927-0321

The association offers an apprenticeship program that places students with master craftspeople in the San Franciso Bay Area. The program provides beginning craft artists with the unique opportunity to be part of a craft business on a daily basis. Students work on projects in the master's studio and learn techniques of small business operation, maintenance of tools and equipment, and marketing and exhibiting. The association provides applicants with lists of craftspeople currently accepting apprentices. The applicants then meet with the masters, visiting their shops and arranging the apprenticeship. Once students are satisfied they've made a good match with a master, the association draws up a contract that describes the needs and expectations of both master and apprentice. Students choose to work in one of five fields: Furniture Design, Glass, Metal, Fiber, and Clay.

How long it takes: 3 to 12 months

What it costs: Per month for full-time study—$750
                    Per month for part-time study—$400

Students can earn a tuition rebate by working at minimum wage on the master's projects. Full-time students can earn up to $250 per month in rebate, part-timers can earn $125.

Worcester Center for Crafts
25 Sagamore Road
Worcester, MA 01605
(508) 753-8183
Fax: (508) 797-5626
craftcenter@worcester.org
www.craftcenter.worcester.org

The center offers certificate trainings in four studio areas: Fibers, Clay, Metals, and Wood. The Fiber program focuses on weaving and surface design. The curriculum includes classes on dye technology, textile inks, pattern drafting, weave structures, direct methods of surface application, appliqué, beading and embroidery, ikat, batik, shibori, tapestry, and clothing design. The Metals program covers design, toolmaking, stone setting, hollowware, jewelry making, blacksmithing, casting, forming, enameling, and fabrication. The Wood program includes the study of fine furniture making, from the creation of unique commission pieces to limited small-production items. Classes cover design, wood carving, joinery techniques, mechanical drawing, construction techniques, wood turning, finishing, and conceptual problems. The Clay program teaches hand building and wheel throwing techniques, and glaze and clay body development. Classes include design, clay formulation, electric kilns, production techniques in clay, and kiln design and construction.

Each of the programs also includes classes in business practices, designed to help students develop a range of business skills, from producing portfolios to pricing and marketing to managing their own craft business.

How long it takes: Each program—2 years

What it costs: Each program—$14,000

Scholarships and work/study grants are available.

Oregon College of Art and Craft
8245 Southwest Barnes Road
Portland, OR 97225
(800) 390-0632
(503) 297-5544
www.ocac.edu

The college offers a comprehensive certification program in crafts. In addition to classes in drawing, design, art history, writing for artists, and business practices, students usually focus on two or three craft areas, including Book Arts, Ceramics, Fibers, Metal, and Wood.

The Book Arts concentration teaches traditional and innovative techniques to create limited editions and one-of-a-kind books. Classes include Printmaking, Bookbinding, Letterforms, Design Issues, and Marbling.

The Ceramics concentration teaches students to work with clay as a sculptural and functional medium. Classes include Firing Techniques, Glaze Calculation, Plaster Processes, Ceramic Sculpture, English Slipware, and Wax Inlay Decoration.

The Fibers concentration incorporates two areas of study: woven/constructed textiles, and surface design. Students learn weaving on tapestry and multiharness looms, felting and basketry, embellishing with dyes, pigments, and resists, silkscreen printing, and pieced imagery.

The Metal concentration teaches students to create fine art jewelry, small-scale sculpture, and hollowware. It includes courses on metalsmithing, fabrication, stone setting, casting, electroforming, enameling, and production design.

In the Wood concentration, students create original furniture. Classes include drawing and visualization, chairs and upholstery, plywood construction, using hand tools, developing specialized hardware, and antique tool restoration.

How long it takes: 3 years

What it costs: $10,320 per year

Financial aid is available.

Conner Prairie
13400 Allisonville Road
Fishers, IN 46038
(317) 776-6000
Fax: (317) 776-6014

Conner Prairie offers four levels of training in blacksmithing. The basic levels are primarily project-oriented: students learn to make small hooks, fireplace pokers, chains, ladles, and forks. In the more advanced levels, the focus is on learning techniques of welding, punching, upsetting, drawing out, and twisting. Possible projects include making belt axes, forging hammers, or other forging tools requiring handles.

How long it takes: Beginning levels—3 weeks
                     Advanced level—10 weeks

What it costs: Beginning levels—$225 per level
                     Advanced level—Price varies

Appalachian Center for Crafts
Tennessee Technological University
1560 Craft Center Drive
Smithville, TN 37166
(800) 255-8881
(615) 597-6801
(615) 372-3888

The center offers certificate programs in Ceramics, Fiber, Glass, Metal, and Wood. The Ceramics program emphasizes a strong foundation in materials, processes, problem solving, and historical and contemporary ceramic traditions within the context of fine art. The Fiber program is designed to introduce and refine technical skills. It covers weaving, surface design, piecework, color and pattern, structure and form, composition, and historic, ethnic, and contemporary fiber art. The Glass program provides a thorough technical foundation in glass skills. It helps students develop a personal aesthetic and exposes them to a variety of career opportunities in glass through hands-on classes, continual experimentation, visiting artist workshops, and slide presentations. The Metal program teaches students the technical foundations and historical background needed to create new work, ranging from jewelry to large-scale sculptural pieces. The Wood program emphasizes furniture design and construction, focusing on mastery of technique, knowledge of material, and the formulation of a personal direction.

How long it takes: Variable—usually 2 years

What it costs: $3,600 to 7,600 per year

Tennessee residents pay less than half the above.

Financial aid is available.

The Forgery School of Blacksmithing
13 Imnaha Road
Tijeras, NM 87059
(505) 281-8080

The Forgery School offers basic and intermediate/advanced courses in Blacksmithing. The basic course is designed for the novice. It covers all basic aspects of blacksmithing, including hammer control, lighting and tending a coal-fired forge, drawing, upsetting, twisting, splitting, punching, drifting, tool steel forging and heat treating, scrolling, riveting, and forge welding.

The intermediate/advanced course helps students perfect their basic skills and learn scroll design and development, collaring, riveting, mortise and tenon joinery, spring fullers, touchmark stamps, and how to design, forge, and heat-treat hammerheads, specialized punches, and chisels.

How long it takes: Beginning course—1 week
                        Intermediate/advanced course—1 week

What it costs: Beginning course—$600
                   Intermediate/advanced course—$600

Turley Forge
Route 10, Box 88C
Santa Fe, NM 87501
(505) 471-8608

Turley Forge trains students in blacksmithing. Instruction includes decorative ironwork, toolsmithing, and making hardware. Students learn essential blacksmithing techniques such as fullering, twisting, bending, hot rasping, forge brazing, forge welding, drawing, upsetting, punching, and sledge striking. Class projects include making fire tools, steel tools, tongs, utensils, hinges, door latches, and scrollwork. In addition to the hands-on work, the training includes lectures that teach students about shop layout and practice, tool acquisition, cost estimating, basic ferrous metallurgy, patinating, and heat treatment practices. Graduates receive a Turley Forge certificate and a letter of reference for prospective employers.

How long it takes: 3 weeks

What it costs: $1,500

Bill Moran School of Bladesmithing
Texarkana College
2500 North Robison Road
Texarkana, TX 75599
(903) 838-4541, ext. 237
Fax: (903) 838-5030

The school offers training in bladesmithing, teaching students to make quality hand-forged blades in an ongoing series of classes. The first class, Introduction to Bladesmithing, teaches students about metal selection, designs, hammer forging, annealing, grinding, and tempering. The second class, Handles and Guards, covers full tang and narrow tang handles, guards, butt caps, decorative file work, spiral dagger handles, silver inlay work, and finished blades. Damascus Steel introduces pattern variations and manipulations—by the end of this class, students are expected to be able to consistently produce Damascus blades of excellent quality in a variety of patterns. Folding Blades I and II teach folding knife construction, including design and locking and non-locking blades. The school's other courses include Silver Smithing, Primitive Knives, and Engraving.

Although the school does offer a certificate to each student who completes a Bladesmithing course, there is not one final bladesmith certification. Students are free to take as many or as few of the courses as they wish—the program length and cost, below, include all the classes.

How long it takes: 9 weeks

What it costs: $4,450

Savage Neon, Inc.
840 Oella Avenue
Ellicott City, MD 21043
(410) 465-8001
Fax: (410) 465-5899
www.savageneon.com

Savage Neon trains Neon Tube Benders. The training program focuses on helping students quickly and easily discover the intricacies of manipulating hot glass and understand the "personality" of the glass. The curriculum includes classes in Glass Tube Bending, Designing and Fabricating neon signs, Installation Procedures, and Estimating and Pricing.

The Tube Bending class covers block and script lettering, pictorial designs, abstract art forms, and channel letters. Design and Fabrication includes pattern design and layout, electrode choice and positioning, sign mounting techniques, and pumping, bombarding, and filling. The Installation Procedures class examines NEC- and UL-approved installations and the process of obtaining sign permits. And the Estimating and Pricing course covers all types of neon projects, repairing neon, and neon equipment. Savage Neon maintains a nationwide network of over forty companies seeking to hire neon course graduates.

How long it takes: 6 weeks

What it costs: $4,000

Credit cards are accepted.

The Studio of the Corning Museum of Glass
One Museum Way
Corning, NY 14830
(607) 974-6467
Fax: (607) 974-6370
Amyglass@aol.com

The studio provides practical instruction in the art and craft of glassworking. The studio is the educational facility of the Corning Museum of Glass, which houses one of the most extensive collections of glass objects in the world. Although the instruction is not a vocational training program, the advanced classes do provide the necessary foundation for a glassmaking career. Beginning courses teach students how to make simple blown vessels, develop fundamental skills such as gathering, marvering, and puntying, use the Venetian style of glassblowing, construct solid sculptures with lamp working, and make beads. In advanced classes, students construct thinly blown vessel bodies and delicate mereses, create miniature objects with virtually unlimited detail, use an updated version of the ancient process of core forming, develop forms and variations, and master goblet and cane making.

How long it takes: Variable—classes are between 1 and 10 weeks long

What it costs: $360 to $440 per class

Credit cards are accepted.

Urban Glass
647 Fulton Street
Brooklyn, NY 11217
(718) 625-3685
Fax: (718) 625-3889
UrbanGlass@aol.com

Urban Glass offers a certificate program in glassmaking. The program begins with two required classes: Glass Survey I and Glass Survey II. Glass Survey I includes studio work in slumping and basic kiln casting, weekly exercises that teach fundamental skills and techniques, and slides and class discussions. Glass Survey II teaches hot casting and mosaics, how to budget and cost out final products, and more slides and class discussions. Students then develop a high level of technical competence in one of the following specialized areas: Glassblowing, Lampworking, Casting, or Neon.

The Glassblowing specialty includes classes in Venetian technique, large vessels, mold blowing, and solid sculpting. The Lampworking specialty includes instruction in making glass jewelry and small-scale sculpture, and mastering tube bending, side seals, and tube flaring using both colored borosilicate and Moretti soft glass. The Casting specialty teaches sand casting, sand preparation, using inclusion, annealing, mold making, glass preparation, and ladling. The Neon specialty focuses on the artistic applications of neon bending, splicing, and designing.

How long it takes: The certificate requires completion of 7 12-week classes, some of which may be taken simultaneously.

What it costs: $355 to $625 per class

Credit cards are accepted.

Sierra Saddlery School
P.O. Box 1791
Bishop, CA 93515
(800) 443-2848
(619) 872-2505
Fax: (760) 873-3479
learn@sierravocational.com
rainbow@telis.org

The school trains students to build custom saddles. Classes cover hide properties, saddle hardware, leather hand tools, saddle tree preparation, layout techniques, placement and installation of rigging, saddle construction (including cutting, fitting, skiving, shaping, smoothing, adjusting, blocking, plugging, and stitching), and leather carving and stamping. In addition to technical skills, the school teaches how to evaluate the rider's needs for a custom seat, recognize and correct fitting problems, understand the horse's back and internal organs, and how to price and market properly to build a successful small business. Upon graduation, students will have made two complete custom saddles to keep or sell, will have a full set of saddle patterns and, as saddlemaking requires advanced leatherwork skills, will also be able to make harnesses, bridles, breast collars, saddlebags, chaps, gun holsters, purses, and other leather items. The school also offers graduates the opportunity to return at any time to refresh their skills—for free.

How long it takes: 10 weeks

What it costs: $7,200

Brown's Saddlery
HC 76, Box 2430
Garden Valley, ID 83622
(208) 462-3787

Brown's Saddlery teaches a limited number of students how to create custom handmade saddles. The school trains students to build comfortable seats and free-swinging stirrups, use stamping, carving, and drawing, and master simple tricks of the art that ensure quality construction throughout the saddle. The Saddlery also teaches the business aspects of saddlemaking, including marketing, advertising, and buying. Each student will complete two saddles of their own during the training. The school accepts only one student per session, and emphasizes that it is only interested in people whose heart's desire is to become a saddlemaker.

How long it takes: 1 month

What it costs: $8,000

Cost includes room and board.

Northwest Technical College
Detroit Lakes
900 Highway 34 East
Detroit Lakes, MN 56501
(800) 492-4836
(218) 847-1341

Northwest offers training programs in Sign Making and Sign Lettering and Design. The sign-making program, Sign Making: Neon and Sign Fabrication, teaches neon production techniques—from basic bending skills to working with lettering and graphics, through hands-on work in the neon lab and production-specific lectures. Students learn how to make patterns, install lights, prepare and construct backgrounds, and use a variety of tube sizes and colors. Classes include Neon Safety, Neon Pattern Making, Block Neon, Script Neon, Production Bending, Bombarding, Transformers and Wiring, Layout and Cost Analysis, Microcomputers, and Contemporary Career Topics.

The Sign Lettering and Design program covers design, layout, lettering, airbrushing, sandblasting, and gold leaf lettering. Classes include Casual Lettering, San Serif Letter Theory, Speed Ball Techniques, Showcard/Banner Techniques, Wall and Window Lettering, Truck Lettering, Commercial Sign Design and Lettering, Storefront Design and Lettering, Highway Sign Design, Technical Mathematics, Human Relations, and Contemporary Career Topics. Students work with a variety of media, including glass, paper, wood, vinyl, and metal.

How long it takes: Neon and Sign Fabrication—2 years
Sign Lettering and Design—2 years

What it costs: Neon and Sign Fabrication—$2,730
Sign Lettering and Design:—$2,530

Financial aid is available.

Butera School of Art
111 Beacon Street
Boston, MA 02116
(617) 536-4623

The school offers a comprehensive program in the art of sign painting. The techniques and skills learned in the sign-painting course at Butera can be applied in television and movie work, promotions, displays, bill-boards, office doors, windows, charts, posters, and trucks. Students are taught to use a diverse group of media, including wood, plastics, metal, gold and silver leaf, and glass. The program involves mastery of the most commonly used alphabets, brush control, color, shading, layout, design, color, arrangement and copy, indoor and outdoor advertising, and estimating jobs. Courses include Shading, Glass, 3-Dimensional Lettering, Airbrushing, Pinstriping, Surface Gilding, Truck/Van Lettering, Screen Process Printing, and Shop Set-Up. Placement assistance is available.

How long it takes: 2 years

What it costs: $21,200

The School of Holography
1134 West Washington Boulevard
Chicago, IL 60607
(312) 226-1007

The school offers a comprehensive course of study in holography—the production of three-dimensional representations down to molecular exactness—both as an art form and a developing technology. Many skilled holographers work in scientific or engineering fields, and many more use holography in their art. In some ways, holography is similar to photography—it provides a representation that can be used for art, study, illustration, research, and so on. Classes at the school include Holography, Display Pulsed Holography, Holographic Interferometry, Optics, Photochemistry, and Pseudocolor Holography.

How long it takes: 8 10-week classes

What it costs: $175 to $375 per class

Jade Carving Workshops
Deborah Wilson
RR#4, S-4, C-70
6002 Bella Vista Road
Vernon, BC V1T 6L7
Canada
(604) 542-0630
(250) 542-0630
Fax: (250) 542-0630

224 ◆ You're Certifiable

Okay, these workshops are in Canada, and we're trying to limit the programs in this book to the United States. But there aren't so many jade carving schools that we can afford to be picky. And Deborah Wilson, who runs the school, was called one of the best of the world's contemporary jade sculptors by *National Geographic*. She offers very small classes (no more than two students), all the necessary tools, and individualized instruction. She teaches all the steps involved in making a jade sculpture: selecting the jade, designing a piece, and all stages of carving. Although this isn't a career school as such, there is a market for high-quality jade carving that students may be able to tap into. Students interested in jade carving as a career will want to repeat the workshop several times.

How long it takes: 6 days

What it costs: U.S. $700

Chapter 9

✳ ✳ ✳ ✳

Food and Drink

e don't want to influence your choice of schools by telling you
which are our personal favorites. But as far as *chapters* go, this
one is hard to beat: it contains both beer brewing and candymaking. It
also includes cake decorating and whole foods and macrobiotic cooking schools—not too shabby for a relatively short chapter. If you're
interested in working with delicious things, or teaching or consulting
about food for health and wellness, this chapter will introduce you to
some tempting career schools.

If you're interested in more traditional chef schools, there are two
excellent books you should read: *The Guide to Cooking Schools* (Shaw
Guides, 1998) and *Peterson's Culinary Schools: Where the Art of Cooking
Becomes a Career* (Peterson's, 1998).

Beer Brewing • • •

Never let it be said that love of beer can't lead to a rewarding vocation—it can. But you need more than passion to become a successful

brewer. You must also be interested in the gory details—wort production, fermentation, yeast use, and so on. The brewing schools in this section teach everything from chemistry to microbiology to taste testing. So, while an experienced beer palate is a plus, your beer can't be the only thing with a head on its shoulders—brewing training can be quite rigorous. But think how rewarding.

Brewing for Professional Brewers
University Extension
University of California, Davis
Davis, CA 95616
(800) 752-0881
(530) 757-8777
Fax: (530) 757-8558

UC Davis offers a Professional Brewer certificate program designed to prepare students to enter the brewing industry. The curriculum covers grain handling, malt analysis, brewhouse processes, the control of wort quality, yeast and fermentation processes, heat transfer and the effects of insulation, theory and practice of carbonation, mixed gas technology, and refrigeration in the brewery. Students learn about such topics as barley varieties, wort boiling, beer maturation, foam stability, beer flavor, and modern malt-based products. Although a degree is not required for acceptence, students must have completed college-level work in math, biology, chemistry, physics, or engineering.

Graduates of the Professional Brewers program can enroll in an advanced program, the Master Brewers Program in Brewing Science and Brewery Engineering.

How long it takes: Professional Brewers—6 weeks
Master Brewers—22 weeks

What it costs: Professional Brewers—$4,500
Master Brewers—$8,800

Credit cards are accepted and a payment plan is available.

Brewing School
American Brewers Guild
1107 Kennedy Place, Suite 3
Davis, CA 95616
(800) 636-1331

(530) 753-0497
Fax: (530) 753-0176
abgbrew@mother.com
www.masterbrewer.com
www.abgbrew.com

The Brewers Guild offers a Craftbrewers Apprenticeship program that prepares students for positions as brewers in brewpubs and microbreweries. The apprenticeship is divided into three sections. The first section consists of intensive formal instruction in brewing science, including classes on chemistry, microbiology, and engineering. The second section provides practical on-site training as a working brewer at a host brewery with a Guild-approved mentor. And the final section is spent reviewing the on-site experience and preparing for the business of craftbrewing. Specific topics covered in the training include wort production and cooling, milling, mashing, and lautering techniques, postfermentation treatments, sterile filtration, yeast handling, brewing equipment, and sampling techniques.

How long it takes: 11 weeks

What it costs: $7,950

Siebel Institute of Technology
4055 West Peterson Avenue
Chicago, IL 60646
(773) 279-0966
Fax: (773) 463-7688
siebelinstitute@worldnet.att.net
www.siebel-institute.com/welcome

The institute offers a professional brewers certification program that prepares students for employment in a variety of brewing positions, particularly in microbreweries or brewpubs. The course is comprised of six modules: Short Course in Brewing Technology, Practical Brewery Engineering, Essential Quality Control, Brewing Microbiology and Microscopy, Sensory Evaluation of Beer, and Microbrewery and Pub Brewery Operation. The Short Course in Brewing Technology includes classes in raw materials, wort handling, fermentation, storage and finishing, sanitation and cleaning, quality control, beer tasting and evaluation, and trends and developments in brewing. Practical Brewery

Engineering covers brewery mathematics, gases, fluids, heat, electricity, and brewery design. The Essential Quality Control course teaches about laboratory safety, titrations, water treatment, malt analysis, cereal adjuncts, hops and hop products, wort, fermentation, pH measurement, and cleaning solutions. In the Brewing Microbiology and Microscopy course, students learn about microorganisms, the importance of bacteria in brewing, the nature of yeast, microscopy, and beer sampling techniques. The Sensory Evaluation class covers the beer flavor wheel, sensory techniques for new product development, recognizing off flavors, and applying descriptive panels, and includes daily tastings. The Microbrewery Operation course covers safety, milling, mashing, lautering, wort cooling, fermenting, filtering, kegging, bottling, and maintaining quality and consistency.

The institute also offers a Brewery Apprenticeship program for graduates of the certification course—or just the Short Course—who want hands-on experience. Various brewpubs and microbreweries throughout the country participate in the program.

How long it takes: Certification course—8 weeks
Apprenticeship—4 to 8 weeks (usually)

What it costs: Certification course—$8,295
Apprenticeship—$250 per week

Scholarships are available.

Candymaking and Cake Decorating • • •

Although the candymaking and cake-decorating programs are brief, they do offer sufficient preparation for entry-level employment or, if you're determined and enterprising, self-employment. In addition to working for a cake shop, bakery, restaurant, or caterer, you could rent a kitchen part-time and start a local confection-making business. If you're interested in finding other candymaking or cake-decorating trainings, many traditional cooking schools offer individual courses in the subject—look through the directories of cooking schools mentioned in the introduction of this chapter to find a list of possibilities.

Richardson Researches, Inc.
23449 Foley Street
Hayward, CA 94545
(510) 785-1350
Fax: (510) 785-6857
info@richres.com
www.richres.com

Richardson offers four training courses in Chocolate Making: Continental Chocolates, Chocolate Technology, Confectionery Technology, and Lite/Reduced Calorie/Sugar-Free/No Sugar Added/and Fat-Free Confections. The Continental Chocolates course offers hands-on participation to students who want to learn the techniques of making gourmet confections. Skills taught include chocolate handling, tempering, and hand-dipping of such treats as the European truffle (a chocolate-brandy crescent covered with chocolate and sprinkled with vermicelli), shelled praline (a toasted hazelnut surrounded by pralines in a chocolate shell), and mocha triangle (a blend of coffee, milk chocolate, and walnuts).

The Chocolate Technology course aims to give students a basic understanding of the principles of chocolate and hard butter coating technology, from cocoa bean to finished chocolate. Classes cover Cocoa Bean Cleaning, Roasting, Winnowing, and Grinding, Conching, Milk Powder and Crumb, and Chocolate Molding, Enrobing, Tempering, and Storage. Students are also required to taste and examine commercially available chocolates.

The Confectionery Technology course teaches students to make pulled and clear hard candy and deposited and extruded fondant creams, to prepare pectin, agar, and gumi-type jellies, to make various caramel and fudge formulas, and to prepare aerated confections such as marshmallows and nougats.

The Lite/Reduced Calorie/Sugar-Free Confections course covers the manufacture of lite, reduced calorie, sugar-free, no sugar added, and fat-free hard candy, jelly bean coating, extruded fondant, nougat, caramel, toffee, truffle, and taffy.

How long it takes: Continental Chocolates—5 days
Chocolate Technology—5 days
Confectionery Technology—5 days
Lite/Reduced Calorie/Sugar-Free—4 days

What it costs:	Continental Chocolates—$1,395
	Chocolate Technology—$1,495
	Confectionery Technology—$1,495
	Lite/Reduced Calorie/Sugar-Free—$1,495

The Wilton School
Chestnut Court Shopping Center
7511 Lemont Road
Darien, IL 60561
(630) 963-7100

The school offers a Masters Course in cake decorating. Students learn basic techniques including side borders, border variations (such as shells, scrolls, string work, and garlands), numerous flower designs, painting in icing with color, figure piping, cake design, sugar molds, and how to use decorating accessories. Students complete the course by creating a multitiered wedding cake. Other seminars, which can be taken in conjunction with the Masters Course, include Introduction to Gum Paste and Pulled Sugar, both of which involve the creation of decorative flowers. Wilton also offers a course in chocolate decoration in which students learn the fine art of melting, molding, crafting, and decorating with chocolate.

How long it takes:	Masters Course—2 weeks
	Chocolate Course—5 days
What it costs:	Masters Course—$675
	Chocolate Course—$465

Credit cards are accepted.

Country Kitchen SweetArt, Inc.
3225 Wells Street
Fort Wayne, IN 46808
(219) 482-4835

Country Kitchen offers a professional cake-decorating course. The course includes instruction on how to make buttercream flowers (including orchids, daffodils, dahlias, and more), three styles of figure piping (simple, 3-D, and sculptured), color mixing, cake writing, airbrush use, and how to make stencils. Students also learn popular cupcake ideas, border work, and a practical and profitable approach to wedding cake design. In addition to the professional course, students can take classes in creating designs with wafer paper, molding, crimping, and embossing with rolled buttercream, and painting with cocoa.

How long it takes: 1 week

What it costs: $295

International School of Confectionery
9209 Gaither Road
Gaithersburg, MD 20877
(301) 963-9077
Fax: (301) 869-7669
ESNotter@aol.com

The International School offers courses in pastry preparation and decoration. Although they do not provide explicitly professional training, they can prepare students for confectionery careers. The core courses taught at the International School focus on sugar and chocolate decoration. Students learn how to create flowers, swans, doves, ribbons, and baskets with fruits out of pulled and blown sugar. Advanced students can expect to design male and female figurines, peacocks, marine life and a rearing horse. Students also learn the art of mold making with wax, silicone rubber, and putty, and contemporary chocolate techniques such as silk screening, transfer sheets, and raking with color. Other courses include petit four "little baked ones" production, cake making, wedding cake decoration, fun with icing, plated desserts, and chocolate showpieces.

How long it takes: 1 to 5 days per class

What it costs: $240 to $720 per class

Macrobiotic and Whole Foods Cooking ◆ ◆ ◆

Whole food and natural cooking emphasizes organic ingredients, healthy preparation, and life-promoting menu planning, as well as delicious taste. In addition to training students to offer their services as personal chefs or through caterers and restaurants, some of the whole foods programs focus on training cooking teachers to offer individual or group instruction. The macrobiotic programs teach cooking, of course, but also cover macrobiotic education, consulting, diagnosis, and guidance, preparing students for careers as professional chefs, managers of macrobiotic centers, and nutritional/dietary consultants.

The Culinary Arts Institute
7981 Redwood Highway
Cotati, CA 94931
(707) 794-8781

The institute offers an intensive training program leading to certification as a Whole Foods Cooking Specialist. The training consists of three courses: Basic, Intermediate, and Advanced. The Basic Course teaches the fundamentals of whole foods cooking and organic gardening, with classes on vegetarian stocks and infusions, the use of herbs and spices, recipe conversion, sanitation, and organic herb, vegetable, and edible flower gardening. The Intermediate Course has classes in mastering therapeutic diets, ethnic cooking (from Mediterranean to Southeast Asian), hands-on cooking for groups, and whole foods teaching skills. And the Advanced Course prepares the student to set up a professional kitchen, cater, become a private chef, and create a business and marketing plan. Successful completion of the program will qualify graduates to work as private chefs, whole food caterers, and cooking instructors.

How long it takes: 9 months

What it costs: $3,800

Credit cards are accepted.

Vega Institute
1511 Robinson Street
Oroville, CA 95965
(800) 818-8342
(530) 533-4777
Fax: (530) 533-4999
vegastudy@cncnet.com
vegastudy@vega.macrobiotic.net
www.vega.macrobiotic.net

Vega offers a Macrobiotic Cooking Teacher training, a Kitchen Apprentice program, and a Caregiver Cook professional training. The Macrobiotic Cooking Teachers' Training prepares students to offer macrobiotic cooking classes. Students design complete macrobiotic cooking courses, including course titles, menus, shopping lists, publicity, lesson plans, and budgets. They also take classes that cover subjects such as developing the spirit of a cooking teacher, in-depth knowledge of macrobiotic nutrition and ingredients, macrobiotic cooking techniques, student-teacher practice demonstrations, and power vegetarian cooking and nutrition. Finally, students attend a master's healing diet cooking intensive, which teaches them to use a macrobiotic healing diet.

The Kitchen Apprentice program trains macrobiotic cooks. Students learn macrobiotic kitchen organization and maintenance skills, Vega-style cooking skills, traditional pickle making, food processing, theory and philosophy, quantity cooking, and menu mastery.

And the Caregiver Cook training program prepares students to give compassionate service to people with life-threatening illnesses. The curriculum covers in-depth study of the Vega approach to healing cooking, creating meals with mindfulness, attention, and love, establishing a kitchen conducive to healing, detoxifying death, daily meditation practice for stability and clarity, and assisting with family issues during healing.

Students also learn how to facilitate good appetite, weight gain, and energy improvement, create a healing atmosphere, apply home remedies, arrange rooms and homes to facilitate the flow of healing, and use natural exercise for the bedridden.

How long it takes: Teachers' Training—4 weeks
Kitchen Apprentice—6 months
Caregiver Cook—2 weeks

What it costs: Teachers' Training—$1,980
Kitchen Apprentice—$1,500
Caregiver Cook—$1,195

Cost includes accommodations. Credit cards are accepted.

The School of Natural Cookery
P.O. Box 19466
Boulder, CO 80308-2466
(303) 444-8068
Fax: (303) 415-0700
snc@sprynet.com

234 ◆ *You're Certifiable*

The school offers two courses for students who want to cook professionally: Personal Chef Training and Main Course Teacher Training. All students begin their studies with the Fundamental course, an in-depth study of the technique and theory of cooking whole grains, beans, vegetables, sea vegetables, sauces, soups, stocks, tofu and tempeh, seitan, and simple desserts. Knife skills, meal composition, improvisational cooking, and some ethnic cooking are also introduced.

The Personal Chef course trains students to cook for small groups or in private homes, emphasizing the ability to respond to different diets. Students learn how to cook in any kitchen, with the foods at hand, for families of all ages, for people who are recovering from illness, at parties, spas, retreat centers, and so on. The Teacher Training program prepares students to teach the Main Course, a whole foods cooking class. Students observe the Main Course being taught, participate in classroom discussion, lecture, manual review, and marketing, and practice teaching the course in their own areas. Completion of this program allows students to offer this cooking class in their own community.

How long it takes: Fundamentals—5 weeks
Personal Chef—1 month
Teacher—variable

What it costs: Fundamentals—$3,500
Personal Chef—$800
Teacher—$1,340

Credit cards are accepted and financial aid may be available.

Kushi Institute
P.O. Box 7
Becket, MA 01223
(800) 975-8744
(413) 645-8744
Fax: (413) 623-8827
kushi@macrobiotics.org
www.macrobiotics.org

The institute offers a macrobiotic career training program, designed to prepare students for a career in the field of macrobiotic cooking, education, and guidance. Students learn to help clients change their diet and lifestyle to one that supports health and vitality, and to enable clients to adapt the macrobiotic diet to their unique situations. Students receive training in the macrobiotic diet and lifestyle, macrobiotic diagnosis and counseling, macrobiotic cooking, and shiatsu. They also learn how to set up a macrobiotic center and run educational programs. Specific classes include daily cooking classes, menu planning, using home remedies, and Oriental/macrobiotic diagnosis. In addition to the macrobiotic career training, the institute offers week-long workshops, women's health retreats, and hosts the annual International Macrobiotic Summer Conference.

How long it takes: 3 months

What it costs: $2,900

Room and board are included.

The Natural Gourmet Institute
48 West 21st Street, 2nd Floor
New York, NY 10010
(212) 645-5170
(212) 627-2665

The school offers a chef's training program that prepares students for a career in health-supportive natural foods cooking in restaurants, catering, food consulting, health spas, and private cooking. The training program focuses on the selection, identification, and preparation of whole foods, French and Oriental knife skills, food balancing and menu planning, healing cuisines, pastry arts, special diet cookery, regional and ethnic cuisines, converting recipes, improvisational cooking, and career development. Classes include Sensational Sea Vegetables, A Healthy Look at Chocolate, Curries and Masalas, Gourmet Cuisine, Self Cleansing, Wholistic Nutrition, Ayurvedic Meals for All Doshas, Homeopathic Medicine Chest, and the Healing Nature of Herbs. The school also offers internships and a lifetime placement program.

How long it takes: 600 hours in 4, 9, or 15 months

What it costs: $10,550

The school offers payment plans, a long-term financing program, and accepts credit cards.

Chapter 10

✳ ✳ ✳ ✳

Herbal and Alternative Medicine

I f you're interested in healing but see yourself as a sort of alternative doctor, prescribing—or, we should say, recommending—herbs, tinctures, liniments, and other healthful preparations, this is the chapter for you. An increasing number of people are interested in alternatives to the discomfort, dehumanization, and expense of conventional medicine. Although most practitioners of alternative medicine can't prescribe medicine, they can offer advice and direction. If you want to guide people back to health, suggesting herbs and supplements, diet and lifestyle changes, and other beneficial actions, you may find what you're looking for in herbal and alternative medicine.

Some of the programs, such as a few in aromatherapy and flower essences, are fairly brief. But others involve years of training and include clinical work, extended internships, and other almost-conventional requirements. There are even some alternative medicine careers that have entirely conventional requirements: they lead to degrees in acupuncture and traditional Chinese medicine. If you're interested in either, call the Council of Colleges of Acupuncture and Oriental Medicine at (301) 608-9175, 1010 Wayne Avenue, Suite 1270, Silver Spring,

MD 20910, or The American Association of Oriental Medicine at (610) 266-1433, 433 Front Street, Catasauqua, PA 18032—both will send you a list of schools. Also see *Planning Your Career in Alternative Medicine* (Dianne J. B. Lyons, Avery Publishing Group, 1997).

Ayurveda ◆ ◆ ◆

Ayurveda is the ancient Indian art and science of healing and rejuvenation. It promotes wellness and natural well-being through self-healing, using cleansing, detoxification, diet, meditation, herbs, and lifestyle changes to help clients balance their constitution. Although more than a hundred colleges in India train Ayurvedic physicians, there is currently no equivalent training in the United States. There are, however, programs that train Ayurvedic practitioners—as opposed to physicians—to offer advice and expertise to clients. If you're interested in an ancient medical tradition that combines elements of spirituality, medicine, and lifestyle advice—the word "Ayurveda" means "the science of daily living"—consider the following training programs.

California College of Ayurveda
135 Argall Way, Suite B
Nevada City, CA 95959
(916) 265-4300
Fax: (916) 265-4003

The California College of Ayurveda certifies Clinical Ayurvedic Specialists, who identify areas of disharmony between a client's actions, constitution, and environment, and prescribe a program of care to reestablish harmony and help the client return to health. The training is divided into two levels: Fundamental Principles and Practices, and Clinical Study, Case Management, and Internship.

Fundamental Principles and Practices consists of three sessions. The first session focuses on the study of history, philosophy, five element theory, Tridosha theory, constitutional analysis, subdoshas, the energetics of food, and physical examinations. The second session includes study of Ayurvedic psychology and the mental humors, the three gunas, herbal preparation and usage, ama, detoxification, and rejuvenation. The third session includes study of the srotas, membranes, prana, pulse diagnosis, mantra therapies, the eight limbs of Yoga, and pranayama.

Students then begin the Clinical Study, Case Management, and Internship level. Students study the treatment and management of digestive, respiratory, and urinary disease from an Ayurvedic and a Western perspective. They learn practice management and development to help them become successful after graduation. And, finally, students participate in a Clinical Internship, in which they evaluate and treat a minimum of ten patients under the direction of one of the staff doctors in the college clinic.

How long it takes: 2 years

What it costs: $4,950

A number of payment options are available.

American Institute of Vedic Studies
P.O. Box 8357
Santa Fe, NM 87504-8357
(505) 983-9385
Fax: (505) 982-5807
vedicinst@aol.com
www.vedanet.com

The institute offers a correspondence course in Ayurvedic Healing. The course covers all the main aspects of Ayurvedic theory, diagnosis, and practice, with a special emphasis on herbal medicine. It trains students to become Ayurvedic Health Educators, able to counsel clients on basic health and constitutional needs. The course includes classes on Ayurvedic Anatomy and Physiology, Diagnostic Methods of Pulse, Tongue, Abdomen, Questioning, and Observation, Examination of the Subtle Body, Ayurvedic Therapeutic Measures, Treatment of Prana, and Patterns of Doshic Accumulation. The course includes study questions, practical exercises, and detailed tests.

The institute also offers courses in Vedic Astrology and Ayurvedic Psychology.

How long it takes: Correspondence course—students work at their own pace.

What it costs: $300

Credit cards are accepted.

Ayurveda Holistic Center
82A Bayville Avenue
Bayville, NY 11709
(516) 628-8200
Fax: (516) 628-8200
mail@ayurvedahc.com
http://ayurvedahc.com

The center offers Ayurvedic Practitioner certification both for people already working as health care professionals (MDs, RNs, Yoga teachers, holistic practitioners) and for those planning to start a professional Ayurvedic practice. In the first section of training, students learn Ayurvedic anatomy and physiology, herbology, abhyanga, nasya, aromatherapy, hatha yoga, sound and gem therapy, Vedic psychology, and spiritual counseling. The training then covers the body systems—circulatory, digestive, respiratory, nervous, immune, metabolic—as well as skin disorders, cancers/growths, and eye and mouth disorders. Finally, students learn beauty care, Vedic architecture, Feng Shui, and how to set up an Ayurvedic business. Certification is granted when students properly practice and understand Ayurvedic routine, display adequate knowledge through homework, exams, and internships, and integrate spirituality, ethics, humility, and respect with classroom knowledge. The training is offered both as a correspondence program and as in-person classes.

How long it takes: 2 years

What it costs: $4,000

Credit cards are accepted and payment plans are available.

Herbology ❖ ❖

Herbology includes traditional Chinese herbology, Western herbology, and the medicinal knowledge and folk herbal traditions of many groups—particularly indigenous groups—worldwide. Most of the herbology programs offer training in a combination of the above: students may learn about the chemical constituents of herbs, pulse and tongue diagnosis, anatomy and physiology, iridology, and how to wildcraft (gather herbs from the wild).

Dry Creek Herb Farm and Learning Center
13935 Dry Creek Road
Auburn, CA 95602
(530) 878-2441

Dry Creek offers an Earth Centered Herbal Apprenticeship program that trains students to cultivate and apply the healing properties of herbs. The program combines hands-on classes with a take-home correspondence course. The coursework covers herbal philosophies, plant identification, harvesting roots, spiritual attunement with plants, tea and tincture formulation, and making liniments, salves, poultices, compresses, and capsules. Other topics include herbal first aid, flower essences, aromatherapy, herb gardening, wildcrafting, legal herbalism, and herbal careers. Optional field trips, individual projects, and guest teachers are also made available to apprentices. Students who complete the apprenticeship program receive two certificates: one from the farm and one from Rosemary Gladstar-Slick, the originator of the correspondence course.

How long it takes: 9 months

What it costs: $1,395

Credit cards are accepted and a payment plan is available.

Natural Healing Institute of Naturopathy
P.O. Box 230294
Encinitas, CA 92023
(800) 559-4325
(760) 943-8485
Fax: (760) 436-9642

The institute offers certification training in clinical herbology. The program teaches the properties of over three hundred Eastern and Western herbs, describing the traditional uses of each herb and the modern research that documents therapeutic effectiveness, safety, and any possible side effects or contraindications. The program trains students to identify, collect, and correctly prepare both medicinal herbs that grow in the wild and those purchased through quality suppliers, using them to make teas, salves, balms, tinctures, and other herbal formulas. Classes include Preparing Herbal Remedies, Creating an Herb Garden, Beginning, Intermediate, and Advanced Herbology, and a Supervised Practicum.

The institute also offers certification training in hypnotherapy.

How long it takes: 300 hours

What it costs: $2,532

The California School of Herbal Studies
Box 39
Forestville, CA 95436
(707) 887-7457

The school offers a certificate class in therapeutic herbalism. The curriculum provides a thorough grounding in all aspects of herbal studies, including botany and field identification, harvesting techniques, medicine making, phytochemistry and phytopharmacology, therapeutic aromatherapy, ethical wildcrafting, and the business of herbalism. The school focuses on worldwide healing traditions, with an emphasis on a bioregional model of herbalism that can be applied in the students' own backyards. The courses go beyond the study of plant remedies for symptom relief to the function of herbs as fundamental elements of holistic transformation and disease prevention. The school also offers a Second-Year Apprenticeship program for students who want to take advanced classes and participate in a supervised student clinic.

How long it takes: 9 months

What it costs: $4,995

Work-study positions are available.

Institute of Chinese Herbology
3871 Piedmont Avenue, #363
Oakland, CA 94611
(510) 428-2061
Fax: (510) 428-2061
kmorris@slip.net

The institute offers an audiotaped home study comprehensive herbalist training course that consists of three sections. Section I is an introduction to Chinese Medicine and Herbs, teaching such subjects as the theory of disease, the function and dysfunction of the organs, tongue diagnosis, herbs and formulas, dosages, and the legal aspects of practicing herbology. Section II includes classes on the art of diagnosis, key concepts in Chinese herbology, and therapeutic principles of Chinese herbology. Section III presents the six major classifications of organ dysfunctions, including lungs, spleen, stomach, heart, kidney, and gynecological. After completing the course, thirty written case studies, and a take-home exam, students are eligible for Herbalist Certification. An advanced Herbal Certification program is also available.

How long it takes: 125 hours

What it costs: $1,215

Credit cards are accepted.

American School of Botanical Medicine
3150 Mission Drive
Santa Cruz, CA 95065
(408) 476-6377

The school offers a certificate course in Botanical Medicine designed to prepare students for clinical practice. The two-year course combines traditional Chinese medicine with Western herbalism and European phytotherapy. It teaches botanical properties, human physiology, and inspires students to think and live like herbalists and healers.

First-year courses include the history of herbology, herbal remedies and formulary, Ayurvedic Tridosha theory, the Chinese theory of five elements, Chinese differential diagnosis, and materia medica. In addition to theoretical, diagnostic, and botanical training, students learn to prepare compresses, liniments, oils, syrups, teas, tinctures, and pills. Second-year courses include advanced Oriental diagnosis, the four radicals, symptom-sign diagnosis, specific diseases and treatments, and the art of simpling. A certificate is awarded upon completion of the coursework plus approved classes in anatomy, botany, chemistry, physiology, meridian therapy, counseling skills, and fifty hours of clinical internship.

How long it takes: 2 years (part-time)

What it costs: $4,900

Credit cards are accepted and installment plans are available.

Christopher Hobbs Foundation
603 34th Avenue
Santa Cruz, CA 95062
(408) 476-6377

The foundation offers an herbalist training course that encompasses both Western phytotherapy and traditional Chinese medicine in seven sections of training. The first section, Introduction to Herbalism and Local Medicinal Plants, is an introduction to phytotherapy, Ayurveda, and traditional Chinese medicine. The second, Harvesting and Medicine Making, covers wildcrafting and processing herbs, and hands-on work in medicine making. The third, Fundamentals of Traditional European Medicine, provides general theory, an organ systems overview, and discussion of constitutional types and herbal energetics. The fourth section, Fundamentals of Traditional Chinese Medicine for Western Herbalists, also discusses general theory, organ systems, constitutional types, and herbal energetics, as well as the East-West connection. The fifth, Materia Medica and Therapeutics, covers body systems such as the nervous, immune, hormonal, digestive, liver, and urinary systems. The sixth, Herbal Gardening and Clinical Diagnosis, teaches students to garden with herbs and use a variety of diagnostic techniques, including tongue, pulse, abdominal, Western, and iridological diagnosis. And the last section, Clinical Practice, covers establishing a practice, working with patients, herbal formulation review, and setting up a pharmacy. Students are also expected to practice with patient volunteers and class members, and participate in herb walks and a hands-on gardening experience.

How long it takes: 7 months

What it costs: $1,545

Credit cards are accepted.

EastWest School of Herbology
P.O. Box 712
Santa Cruz, CA 95061
(800) 717-5010
(408) 336-5010
Fax: (408) 336-4548
www.planetherbs.com

244   *You're Certifiable*

The EastWest School offers a home study herbalist training program that prepares students to become herbal consultants. The training consists of two parts, the Herbal Medicine course and the Professional Herbalist course. The Herbal Medicine course covers the history of herbology, Ayurveda Tridosha theory, Chinese theory, differential diagnosis, herbal formulary, herbal remedies, and herbal therapeutics. The Professional Herbalist course includes advanced lessons, such as the essential principles of disease and diagnosis in the Western, Ayurvedic, and Chinese herbal systems, an extensive and comprehensive materia medica (of over five hundred herbs), advanced diagnostic approaches, and the art of simpling.

How long it takes: Herbal Medicine—12 lessons, 6 months
                       Professional Herbalist—24 lessons, 18 months

Because these are correspondence courses, students may take as long as necessary to complete them: the lengths of time noted above represent averages.

What it costs: Herbal Medicine—$185
                     Professional Herbalist—$520

Credit cards are accepted.

Rocky Mountain Center for Botanical Studies
P.O. Box 19254
Boulder, CO 80308
(303) 442-6861
Fax: (303) 442-6294

The center offers a professional herbalist training course. Students develop therapeutic skills through hands-on experience and classes in natural herbal therapies presented in two residential training programs: Western Herbalism and Clinical Herbalism. The Western Herbalism training includes courses in botany, materia medica, herbal pharmacy, nutrition, anatomy and physiology, pathology, ethnobotany, pharmacognosy, and business management, ethics, and practice.

After completing the Western Herbalism course, students are eligible for enrollment in the more advanced Clinical Herbalism course. The Clinical Herbalism curriculum includes classes in organ systems, Eastern/Western diagnostics, toxicology, herb/drug interactions, and clinical case studies. Students are also required to participate in a practicum in the center's supervised student-run public clinic.

How long it takes: Western Herbalism—1 year
Clinical Herbalism—4 months classwork plus a
9-month practicum

What it costs: Western Herbalism—$4,800
Clinical Herbalism—$2,800

Credit cards are accepted. Payment plans and a discount for enrolling in both years at once are available.

Northern Prairie Center for Education and Healing Arts
130 North Fair Street
Sycamore, IL 60178
(815) 899-3382

The center offers a training program in phytomedicines and related topics leading to a career in therapeutic herbalism. Students learn to evaluate conditions and formulate appropriate herbal-based treatment plans, assess and evaluate common client needs, master basic professional practices such as intake interviews and giving and receiving referrals, and use business practices such as marketing and record keeping. The courses include Flower Essences, Herbalism, Classification of Medicinal Plants, Phytotherapy, Materia Medica, Assessment Modalities (such as Iridology, Constitutional Body Typing, and Applied Kinesiology), and study of the digestive, cardiovascular, respiratory, urinary, immune, and other body systems.

How long it takes: 9 months

What it costs: $3,200

Credit cards are accepted and a payment plan is available.

Northeast School of Botanical Medicine
P.O. Box 6626
Ithaca, NY 14851
(607) 564-1023

The Northeast School of Botanical Medicine trains students to become clinical herbalists. Students learn to distinguish between acute and

246 • *You're Certifiable*

chronic ailments, use a systematic method of diagnosis, develop counseling skills, suggest other forms of treatment and testing when appropriate, and understand herbal formulation. Classes include Anatomy and
Physiology, Clinical Evaluation/Diagnostic Skills, Counseling skills,
First Aid, Herbal Pharmacy/Medicine Making, Herbalist as Educator,
Materia Medica, Networking and Resources, Wild Edibles, Student
Clinic, and a Business Practicum. Students also learn plant identification and wildcrafting through a number of field trips, including weekly
hikes in the local area and weeklong camping trips. The school offers free
advice and herbal consultation through first aid clinics, in which students are encouraged to participate. The school also accepts a limited
number of apprentices.

How long it takes: 3 days per week for 6 months
                       1 weekend per month for 7 months

What it costs: 6 month program—$1,450
                       7 month program—$860

Blazing Star Herbal School
P.O. Box 6
Shelburne Falls, MA 01370
(413) 625-6875

Blazing Star offers a comprehensive apprenticeship program that trains
students to become accomplished herbalists. The coursework includes
wild plant identification, ethical wildcrafting, using herbs as food and
medicine, and the art of herbal preparation and therapeutics. The facil-
ities at Blazing Star include extensive gardens and an herbal library. The
school also offers weekend workshops in subjects such as Herbs for
Allergies and Hayfever, Women's Herbal Health Care, Herbal First Aid,
and Planting by the Moon.

How long it takes: 10 months

What it costs: $1,400

A payment plan is available.

Rocky Mountain Herbal Institute
P.O. Box 579
Hot Springs, MT 59845

(407) 741-3811
rmhi@rmhiherbal.org
www.rmhiherbal.org

The institute offers a professional training program in traditional Chinese herbal sciences. The program is case-oriented and prepares students to consult with and counsel clients, assess health problems, and prepare herbs and formulas. The core curriculum focuses on assessing patterns of disharmony, TCM tongue inspection, abdominal and pulse palpation, body-type analysis, herbal pharmacopoeia, applying TCM principles to foods and Western herbs, and herbal formulation. Other topics covered are plant taxonomy, ordering herbs and inspecting quality, office procedures, legal and ethical issues, epidemiology and current controversies, electromagnetic fields and health, and food allergies and addictions. The institute also offers advanced courses to graduates that teach how to handle a wider range of clinical problems, integrate current health research with TCM, deal with environmental and chemical sensitivities, and refine clinical analysis skills.

How long it takes: 18 months, including 4 weeks of residential intensives

What it costs: $4,875

Green Terrestrial
P.O. Box 266
Milton, NY 12547
(914) 795-5238
Fax: (914) 795-5238

Green Terrestrial offers an herbology apprenticeship program in which students deepen their understanding, knowledge, and connection to Partner Earth through ongoing practical work with the natural world. Apprentices are steeped in the Wise Woman ways of healing, wholing, and nourishing themselves, others, and the earth, as they learn through a combination of technical classroom information and hands-on experience. The curriculum includes plant identification, wildcrafting, organic herb cultivation, herbal preparations and formulas, herbal first aid and medicine, and creating an herb business. Other classes cover herbal networking, flower essences, herbs for women, chronic disease, the immune system, winter discomforts, plants as teachers, nourishing herbs, and plant allies.

How long it takes: 7 months

What it costs: $725 to $950

The American Herbal Institute
3056 Lancaster Drive, Northeast
Salem, OR 97305
(888) 437-2539
(503) 364-7242

The institute offers a home study course in the traditional Western use of herbs. The course is divided into six lessons: Herbology I, Herbology II, Nutrition, Anatomy and Physiology, Herbal Remedies Lab, and How to Practice Medicine without a License. Herbology I teaches a basic understanding of herb use for medicinal purposes. Herbology II covers herbal therapies, properties, formulations, dose determinations, and cleansing. Nutrition includes lessons covering the use of vitamins, minerals, amino acids, enzymes, supplements, and herbs. Anatomy and Physiology introduces the basic workings of the human body. The Herbal Remedies Lab consists of twenty-three herbal medicinal preparation projects, taught with video instructions. And How to Practice Medicine without a License provides instruction on some of the legal issues involved in practicing.

How long it takes: Correspondence course—students work at their
                  own pace.

What it costs: $600

Credit cards are accepted and a payment plan is available.

The School of Natural Healing
P.O. Box 412
Springville, UT 84663
(800) 372-8255
Fax: (801) 489-8341
snh@qi3.com
www.webnetex.com/snh

The school offers a mixed home study and in-person Master Herbalist Program that trains students to become qualified healers and teachers of herbology. The course starts with a ten-session home study Herbalist program that introduces students to the foundations of herbology and the body's inherent power to heal, and trains them to use herbal therapy to remove the causes of disease. The second part of the training is the Master Herbalist program, which is divided into eight home study courses and an in-person certification seminar. The program includes coursework in herb identification, selection, harvesting, horticulture, and usage, and herbal formulation and preparation. Course titles include Internal Cleansing, Herbal Psychiatry, Optic Nerve Regeneration, Allergies, Anatomy, Cold Sheet Treatment, Herbal Preparation, and Chemical Constituents of Herbs.

How long it takes: The 18 levels of home study training: students work at their own pace. The in-person certification seminar is 6 days.

What it costs: $1,980

Credit cards are accepted.

Wisconsin Institute of Chinese Herbology
6921 Mariner Drive
Racine, WI 53406
(414) 886-5858

The institute offers a Chinese herbology training program that emphasizes the benefits of individual herbs, traditional Chinese herbal formulas, and Chinese and American patent formulas. The course consists of three levels of study. Level I covers disorders of the lungs, liver, spleen, and stomach. Students learn the physiological functions of the organs, and their disharmonies and possible treatments according to Chinese medicine. This level introduces sixty-seven herbs, twenty-one formulas, and fifteen case studies. Level II covers obstetrics, gynecology, disorders of the lower burner, rheumatology, bi-syndromes, heart and spirit disorders, dermatology, injury and trauma, cancer, and HIV. Students learn how to use herbal formulas that are applied topically for internal disorders, as well as plasters, liniments, and TDP lamps. Level III requires the completion of a senior thesis, clinical internship, fieldwork, thirty-five case studies, and coursework in Western anatomy and physiology.

How long it takes: 2 years

What it costs: $3,210

Homeopathy ✦ ✦ ✦

Homeopathy is based on the concept that "like cures like," that illness can be treated with a substance that produces an effect similar to the symptom or problem being treated. These substances, contained in minute doses in homeopathic remedies, stimulate the body's defense mechanisms and immune system, helping the client fight off disease. Although homeopathy is considered alternative in the United States, this wasn't always the case: in the early part of the century, there were dozens of homeopathic colleges around the country. And in some European countries, homeopathy is still considered fairly mainstream (for example, in England, Queen Elizabeth II is a strong supporter of homeopathy).

Evolution of Self School of Homeopathy
2700 Woodlands Village Boulevard, #300-250
Flagstaff, AZ 86001
(520) 525-2228
Fax: (520) 525-2228

The school offers two levels of certification: Certified Trained Homeopath and Certified Master Homeopath. Students develop skills in observation, case taking, and remedies. Students are taught through independent studies and through live, in-class case analysis and patient follow-up. Some Kabbalah studies are also included, as an aid for spiritual development.

How long it takes: Certified Trained Homeopath—4 years
Certified Master Homeopath—6 years

What it costs: Certified Trained Homeopath—$19,600
Certified Master Homeopath—$29,400

Institute of Classical Homoeopathy
1336-D Oak Avenue
St. Helena, CA 94574

(707) 963-7796
Fax: (707) 963-1383
ich@community.net
www.community.net/~ich/

The institute offers professional training in classical homoeopathy. The curriculum includes Philosophy and Principles of Classical Homoeopathy, Materia Medica, Medical Sciences and Psychology, Clinical Practice and Case Analysis, and Practice Management and Ethics. Philosophy and Principles is the foundation of the program. It emphasizes the philosophies of Samuel Hahnemann, the originator of homoeopathy, and also covers the works of classical homoeopathic physicians such as Kent, Dunham, Boger, and Close. Materia Medica covers over two thousand homoeopathic remedies, how they apply in the contexts of first aid and acute and chronic disease prescribing, and how they relate to one another. Medical Sciences and Psychology offers instruction in anatomy and physiology, pathology, clinical science, medical terminology, and psychology. Clinical Practice and Case Analysis encompasses the study of the repertory (the homoeopathic index of symptoms) and case analysis through class discussion and observation of approved homoeopaths in the institute's clinic. And Practice Management and Ethics includes methods of establishing clinics and integrating homoeopathic practice in other health care settings.

Students are also required to complete 150 hours of clinical experience and submit one or two advised and eight unadvised cases for evaluation.

How long it takes: 4 years

What it costs: $13,600

Payment options are available.

The Colorado Institute for Classical Homeopathy
2299 Pearl Street, #401
Boulder, CO 80302
(303) 440-3717
Fax: (303) 440-6525
bseideneck@aol.com
www.coloradohomeopathy.org

The institute offers a classical homeopathy certification program consisting of three phases. Phase I covers history and philosophy, repertory, case taking, case analysis, and materia medica. Students learn to refine observation skills, evaluate clients as integrated individuals, incorporate underlying psychological patterns into analysis, and understand the origin, function, and characteristics symptoms that define the application of homeopathic remedies in treatment. Phase II covers philosophy, homeopathic practice methodology, further study of the materia medica, and clinical experience and training. Students learn to integrate the principles of homeopathy into a clinical context, choose the most precise remedy for the patient, understand the intricate relationship between remedies, and work with experienced homeopathic practitioners in a clinical setting. Phase III covers more advanced materia medica and clinical experience and training, therapeutic management of chronic conditions, practice management, and case supervision. Students learn how to use complementary patterns of remedies, how to deal with situations in which conventional and alternative therapies are being used simultaneously, and practice management skills. They also develop the skill and confidence needed to practice.

Students are required to have taken basic college-level anatomy and pathophysiology, and be certified in CPR and first aid before completion of the course.

How long it takes: 2½ years

What it costs: $7,900

New England School of Homeopathy
356 Middle Street
Amherst, MA 01002
(413) 256-5949
Fax: (413) 256-6223
nesh@nesh.com
www.nesh.com

The school offers a professional homeopathy course designed to train students to prescribe constitutionally in a homeopathic practice setting. The course emphasizes the Herscu method of understanding homeopathy through the study of the cycles or pattern each remedy presents, and the segments or subpatterns that run through the cycle. The program includes courses in case taking, case analysis, materia medica, and the repertory. The school is affiliated with *The New England Journal of Homeopathy*.

How long it takes: 3 years

What it costs: $7,800

Credit cards are accepted.

Northwestern School of Homeopathy
10700 Old County Road 15, Suite 300
Plymouth, MN 55441
(612) 794-6445
Fax: (612) 525-9518

The school offers a practitioner training program in classical homeopathy that emphasizes seven subjects: philosophy, materia medica, repertory, case taking, case analysis, clinical training, and personal development and practice management. Students are introduced to both common and obscure remedies, learn how to use advanced computer repertories, and analyze hundreds of cases, including both live clinical cases and paper cases, to master the art of deciding upon appropriate remedies. They also observe instructors with clients, handle cases with instructor supervision, and eventually gain enough skill to handle most cases unsupervised. Students must complete some coursework in the biomedical sciences (such as biology, physiology, chemistry, and anatomy) at an accredited college prior to completing the training.

How long it takes: 3 years

What it costs: $14,700

Teleosis School of Homeopathy
Clocktower Building
3 Main Street
Chatham, NY 12037
(518) 392-7975
Fax: (518) 392-6456
teleosis@igc.org

The school trains students to become practicing clinical homeopaths. The training consists of three parts: a Certificate Program that teaches students all the necessary skills needed to become a practicing homeopath, a Clinical Program that provides advanced clinical training, and a Postgraduate Clinic that supports students' transition into practice. The Certificate Program includes instruction in homeopathic philosophy, case taking, analysis, and management, materia medica, repertory studies, personal development, and a heavy emphasis on developing a sound understanding of the most commonly used remedies. Graduates of the Certificate Program can practice homeopathy without completing the advanced trainings. The Clinical Program covers materia medica of the smaller remedies, advanced case management and analysis, philosophy, practice management, and ethics. And the Postgraduate Clinic requires that students handle sixteen clinical cases under the supervision of a supervisor. Completion of a BA program or at least one semester of biology and chemistry are prerequisites for acceptance into the program.

How long it takes: Certificate Program—300 hours in 2 years
Clinical Program—270 hours in 2 years
Postgraduate Clinic—hours vary, runs concurrently
with the 2-year Clinical Program

What it costs: Certificate Program—$5,000
Clinical Program—$5,000
Postgraduate Clinic—$2,900

Payment plans are available.

Miscellaneous Herbal and Alternative Medicine ❖ ❖ ❖

Most of the programs in this section train aromatherapists and flower essence practitioners, who use essential oils extracted from flowers, herbs, and roots to promote healing, relaxation, and physical and emotional fitness. If this is your primary interest, also check out the Herbology section, above—many of the herbalism schools offer individual courses in aromatherapy and flower essences. Other trainings in this section combine some features of alternative medicine, such as the use of homeopathic remedies or acupuncture meridians, with other systems, such as biofeedback or color healing—or offer a variety of alternative medical training programs.

Medical Astrology

Dr. Eileen Nauman
P.O. Box 2513
Cottonwood, AZ 86326
(520) 634-9298
Fax: (520) 634-9298
docbones@sedona.net

Eileen Nauman offers certification in medical astrology through two intensive seminars. The first, Beginning Medical Astrology, covers zodiac signs, cardinal, fixed, and mutable signs, tools to cure various conditions, beginning homeopathy, use of the Med-Scan Method, making prayer bundles, and diagnosing from a natal chart. The second seminar, Advanced Medical Astrology, teaches students how to use Uranian planets and the Cosmobiology wheel to discover potential medical/health problems in a client's life, to master the fine points of the Med-Scan Method, to incorporate flower and gem essences, homeopathic remedies, herbs, vitamins/minerals, and to use Native American healing techniques.

Students must be familiar with astrological aspects in a natal astrology chart before they are eligible to attend the first seminar: if you aren't, give Nauman a call and she'll refer you to a professional astrologer in your area who can teach you the basics.

How long it takes: Beginning Medical Astrology—5 days
Advanced Medical Astrology—5 days

What it costs: Beginning Medical Astrology—$650
Advanced Medical Astrology—$650

Credit cards are accepted.

Connecticut Institute for Herbal Studies

87 Market Square
Newington, CT 06111
(860) 666-5064
Fax: (860) 666-5064

The institute offers certification courses in Herbal Studies, Western Clinical Herbalism, Aromatherapy, and Bach Flower Essences. The Herbal Studies course takes place in Beijing, China—round-trip airfare, accommodations, interpreters, and meals are included in the tuition—and includes study of herbs, formulas, and treatment strategies for epigastric pain, constipation, diabetes, and infertility. The Western Clinical Herbalism course includes a business practicum, tincture and medicine making, men's health issues, first aid, clinical evaluation, the digestive system and diet, and the respiratory system (allergies, asthma, colds, coughs, and flus). The Aromatherapy training focuses on the history, uses, and basic care and safety of oils. And the Bach Flower Essence course includes training exercises, direct experience with the thirty-eight Bach essences, etheric and psychospiritual healing, therapeutic applications, and initiating and documenting a case study. The institute also offers a variety of other workshops and seminars, such as Pulse and Tongue Diagnosis, Apitherapy, Healing Herbs of the Caribbean, and Craniosacral Therapy.

How long it takes: Herbal Studies—2 weeks
Western Clinical Herbalism—4 weekends
Aromatherapy—1 weekend
Bach Flower Essences—4 weekends

What it costs: Herbal Studies—$2,495
Western Clinical Herbalism—$750
Aromatherapy—$175
Bach Flower Essences—$595

Credit cards are accepted.

International Academy of Bioenergetic Practitioners

2160 West Drake Road, #A-1
Fort Collins, CO 80526
(970) 224-2850
Fax: (719) 520-3227
www.phazx.com

Bioenergetics is a technology that detects the stressors that create distress and ill health in a person's life, and identifies the most effective healing remedy. Although it was originally based on electroacupuncture, which involves the use of an ohmmeter to measure the body's response to the stimulation of the meridians, Bioenergetics now includes the use of a modified biofeedback machine to balance the body both energetically and through the use of appropriate supplements and homeopathic remedies.

The academy offers two levels of training for aspiring Bioenergetic Practitioners. The Class I training is a home study course. It teaches the basics of Bioenergetics, homeopathy, herbs, Chinese meridians, nutrition and wellness, and vitamins and minerals. It covers the use of a BioTron meridian tester, and teaches students to identify and measure the meridian points, and verify biocompatibility and the utilization of supplements. The BioTron tester is included in the tuition, so students get hands-on experience while doing the coursework.

Class II training combines home study and on-site instruction in four semesters of coursework. In the first semester, students learn the history of electroacupuncture, physiology and the Chinese model, and homeopathics. The second semester includes the study of more advanced homeopathics and homotoxicology. The third semester covers allergies and stressors and Bioenergetics and health. And the fourth semester includes energetics practice and two theory classes.

Two hands-on labs are required for Class II training: early in the training, students learn proper testing technique, later they learn to verify testing technique. Optional practice labs, monthly discussion forums, and other in-person trainings are also available.

How long it takes: Class I—Home study, no time limit
Class II—Maximum of 2 years

What it costs: Class I—$2,195
Class II—$3,995

To be a Class II practitioner, a graduate must purchase a biofeedback unit. The recommended unit costs $25,000. Credit cards are accepted and lease options are available.

The Institute for Esogetic Colorpuncture and Energy Emission Analysis
1705 14th Street, Suite 198
Boulder, CO 80302
(303) 443-1666
(415) 461-6641

Esogetic Colorpuncture is a system of colored acu-light therapy, which combines the energetic practices of Chinese medicine, the modern biophysics of light, and certain spiritual or esoteric principles. Colored light is applied to specific points on the skin—acupressure points and other body points—using an acu-light wand that emits various light frequencies throughout the body's energy pathways. This helps balance the nervous system, detoxify the body, relieve pain, and stengthen specific organs. Colorpuncture uses Kirilian Energy Emission Analysis, a method of aura photography, to determine which light treatments would best serve to balance the client's energy system. After treatment, a second photo is taken to assess the impact of the treatment.

The training consists of four levels: Introduction to Colorpuncture, Basic Colorpuncture Training, Advanced Colorpuncture Training, and Kirilian Energy Emission Analysis. Introduction to Colorpuncture introduces basic theories and simple treatments for energetic detoxification, balancing, dream activation, and consciousness expansion. Basic Colorpuncture Training is a practitioner certification course that includes training in a large body of treatments, extensive theoretical information, and methods for determining treatment protocols without kirilian photography. Advanced Colorpuncture Training is in-depth study for certified practitioners focusing on such areas as Transmitter Relays, Ellipse Therapies, Conflict Solution Therapy, Foot Reflex Colorpuncture, and Infrared Therapies. The final level, Kirilian Energy Emission Analysis, is a series of three seminars that teach about emission states, topography, basic and advanced steps of kirilian interpretation, and give students an opportunity to gain hands-on experience taking and interpreting kirilian photos.

How long it takes: Introduction to Colorpuncture—2 days
Basic Colorpuncture Training—14 days
Advanced Colorpuncture Training—a series of
3- and 4-day seminars
Kirilian Energy Emission Analysis—8 days

What it costs: Introduction to Colorpuncture—$200
Basic Colorpuncture Training—$1,550
Advanced Colorpuncture Training—Varies
Kirilian Energy Emission Analysis—$1,000

School of Natural Medicine
P.O. Box 7369
Boulder, CO 80301
(303) 443-4882

(303) 443-4848
Fax: (303) 443-8276
SNM@boulder.net
farida@boulder.net
www.purehealth.com

The school trains Natural Physicians, who use iridology, medicinal and nutritive herbs, flower essences, and naturopathic therapies to teach clients about their state of health and to guide them through therapeutic programs that restore natural body functions. The program consists of three home study courses—in Iridology, Naturopathy, and Herbal Medicine—and an intensive in-person Summer School program.

The Iridology and Foundations of Natural Medicine course trains students to understand how the colors, fiber structures, markings, and pigments of the iris of the eye display the holistic inner ecology of the body systems, organs, glands, and tissues. The Naturopathy course teaches the foundations of naturopathic healing, including the philosophy of purification, acute and chronic disease, nutrition, fasting, water cure, naturopathic sanitariums, how the five elements create and cure disease, and life habits. The Herbal Medicine Course offers an in-depth study of over one hundred herbs, covering nutrition, formulas, chemistry, botany, subtle healing, body systems, and specific herbal treatments. The materia medica has over thirty-seven categories of information for each herb, such as Ayurveda, Chinese medicine, flower essences, aromatherapy, homeopathy, chakras, spiritual properties, habitat, wildcrafting, and astrology. These home study courses are supplemented by workshops, clinical trainings, experiential programs in Puerto Rico and India, and wildcrafting programs.

The Summer School classes and workshops include a Transcen-Dance seminar, Iridology and the Foundations of Natural Medicine, Advanced Iridology and Natural Medicine, Wildcrafting, Advanced Herbology, and Naturopathy, and one week of Clinical Training during which students observe and practice work with clients.

How long it takes: The 3 home study courses can be completed at your own pace, although the school recommends that students set a study goal of 18 months to 3 years, depending on previous experience. The Summer School is held during the last 3 weeks in August every year.

What it costs: Iridology—$630
Naturopathy—$525
Herbal Medicine—$525
Summer School—$1,890
Complete program—$3,150

Credit cards are accepted and a payment plan is available.

The Australasian College of Herbal Studies
P.O. Box 57
Oswego, OR 97034
(800) 487-8839
(503) 635-6652
Fax: (503) 697-0615
australasiancollege@herbed.com
achs@herbed.com
www.herbed.com

The Australasian College offers correspondence certification courses in Natural Therapies, Flower Essences, Iridology, and Homeopathy, and diploma courses in Herbal Studies, Aromatherapy, and Homeobotanical Therapy. Although all of the courses can be used as career preparation, the three diploma courses are the most vocationally oriented.

The Herbal Studies diploma program is designed for students who want a professional working knowledge of Herbal Medicine. Students learn the therapeutic effects of seventy medicinal plants and the body systems they directly influence. Classes include Anatomy and Physiology, Materia Medica, Veterinary Herbal Treatments, Skin Care, Wild Herbs, Therapeutic Groups, Differential Diagnosis, and Clinical Practice.

The Aromatherapy diploma course teaches students the art of using plant oils externally and internally for preventive health care, first aid, healing, and relaxation. Classes include Essential Oils (ranging from anise to ylang-ylang), Disease Conditions and Treatments, Anatomy and Physiology, Chemistry, Massage, and Blending.

The Homeobotanical Therapy course is professional training for students who wish to make a career in Natural Healing. A diploma is awarded to students who complete the Homeobotanical Therapy course plus either the Natural Therapies certification or the Herbal Studies course.

How long it takes: Herbal Studies—1 year
Aromatherapy—1 year
Homeobotanical Therapy—2 years

What it costs: Herbal Studies—$882
Aromatherapy—$750
Homeobotanical Therapy—$1,900

Credit cards are accepted and payment plans are available.

Flower Essence Society
P.O. Box 459
Nevada City, CA 95959
(800) 736-9222
Fax: (916) 265-0584
classes@flowersociety.org
www.flowersociety.org

The Flower Essence Society offers a practitioner intensive training course. This comprehensive course covers the theory and practice of flower essence therapy, a field trip to a pristine wildflower meadow, and interpersonal work. The certification also requires completion of two case studies—students treat two clients with flower essence therapy and present the results to the society. Before taking the Practitioner Intensive, students must complete the FES Introductory course or have equivalent knowledge and experience in flower essence therapy.

How long it takes: Introductory Course—1 weekend
Practitioner Intensive—7 days

What it costs: Introductory Course—$200
Practitioner Intensive—$980

Credit cards are accepted.

Jeanne Rose Aromatherapy
219 Carl Street
San Francisco, CA 94117-3804
(415) 564-6785
Fax: (415) 564-6799

Jeanne Rose Aromatherapy provides three levels of training, culminating in certification as an Aromatherapist and Master Herbalist. The first level, Aromatherapy, requires completion of a course introducing the art and science of aromatherapy. The second level, Advanced Aromatherapy, requires the additional completion of a correspondence course in Aromatherapy Studies, in which students study over two hundred essential oils, learn distillation and the therapeutic use of oils by application, inhalation, and ingestion, prepare to treat a variety of physical and mental conditions, and make body-care treatments. The third level of classes requires all the above plus completion of a thirty-six lesson home study Herbal Studies course and intensives by two teachers other than Jeanne Rose.

How long it takes: Aromatherapy—16 hours
                           Advanced Aromatherapy—50 hours
                           Herbal Studies—up to 2 years

What it costs: Aromatherapy—$450
                           Advanced Aromatherapy—$350
                           Herbal Studies—$450

Credit cards are accepted and payment plans and discounts for ordering more than one class at a time are available.

Artemis Institute of Natural Therapies
875 Alpine Avenue, Suite 5
Boulder, CO 80304
(303) 443-9289
Fax: (303) 443-6361

Artemis offers a clinical aromatherapy certification program that teaches students about the fragrances, color energetics, psychological actions, chemical constituents, bioenergetic properties, and biomedical actions of essential oils. Students learn specific formulating, blending, and administrative techniques of aromatherapy, how to discern the purity and quality of genuine essential oils, and clinical skills for preventive treatment of systemic conditions and curative treatments of specific disorders. Classes include Cultural and Medical History of Aromatherapy, Philosophy and Principles of Aromatherapy, The Essential Oil Pharmacy, Energetic Pharmacology of Essential Oils, Biochemical Pharmacology of Essential Oils, Essential Oil Materia Medica, Fragrance Psychology, Essential Oil Administration, Diagnostic Principles and Methods, Therapeutics, and Esthetic Aromatherapy Applications.

How long it takes: 6 weekends in 6 months

What it costs: $1,150

A payment plan is available.

The Atlantic Institute of Aromatherapy
16018 Saddlestring Drive
Tampa, FL 33618
(813) 265-2222
Fax: (813) 265-2222
Sylla@AtlanticInstitute.com
http://AtlanticInstitute.com

The Atlantic Institute offers an aromatherapy practitioner correspondence course and several in-person introductory courses. The correspondence course consists of ten sections, covering such topics as the history of aromatics, essential oil production and purity, essential oil chemistry, the effects of essential oils on human physiology, psychoaromatherapy, pharmacology, treatment methods and applications, contraindications, and a detailed study of fifty-five essential oils and their biospecific therapeutic uses. The in-person courses are Basic Aromatherapy, Advanced Aromatherapy, The Chemistry of Essential Oils, and Principles of Natural Perfumery. The institute also offers correspondence courses in natural perfumery and natural beauty treatments for face and body.

How long it takes: Practitioner Certification course—1 to 6 months
In-person courses—2 days

What it costs: Practitioner Certification course—$475
In-person courses—$200 to $275

Bach Flower Essences Education Programs
Nelson Bach USA Ltd
100 Research Drive
Wilmington, MA 01887
(800) 334-0843
(516) 536-4165
Fax: (978) 988-0233
www.nelsonbach.com

The Bach Flower Essences programs train students to use the power of flowers to naturally relieve the emotional factors that impede physical healing. They learn to address the central emotional causes of disease and alleviate psychological stress with essences composed of thirty-eight flowering plants, trees, and special waters. In a series of three seminars, students learn about type and mood essences and the subtle differences between them, how to choose the right Bach Flower Essences for use with clients, and how to begin a practice as a Bach Practitioner. These seminars are offered at various locations around the United States, and in fifteen countries worldwide. The first two seminars offer training in the fundamentals of flower essences, and the third seminar is the practitioner training.

How long it takes: Seminar I—2 days
Seminar II—2 days
Seminar III—4 days, plus 6 months of home study

What it costs: Per seminar—$185

Credit cards are accepted.

Institute of Aromatherapy
3108 Route 10 West
Denville, NJ 07834
(973) 989-1999
Fax: (973) 989-0770
essence@aromatherapy4u.com
www.aromatherapy4u.com

The institute offers an aromatherapy consultant diploma program comprised of classwork, written and oral examinations, case studies, and a research paper. Over half of the class time consists of three courses: Essential Oils in Relation to the Body Systems, Aromatic Materia Medica, and Lab Work, which cover general and perfume blending, consultation practice, and case discussions. Other classes include Essential Oils, Essential Oil Extraction and Yields, Essential Oil Adulteration, Quality and Testing, Toxicity and Contraindications, Methods of Application, Dilutions and Dosages, Aromachemistry, and Carriers for Essential Oils. Finally, students learn consultation guidelines and procedures and business practices and ethics to help them succeed in their own businesses.

How long it takes: 200 hours

What it costs: $3,995

Institute of Dynamic Aromatherapy
1202 5th Avenue North
Seattle, WA 98109
(800) 260-7401
(360) 894-0609
(206) 286-5225

The institute offers both a correspondence course and an intensive in-person certificate/diploma course in dynamic aromatherapy, a holistic discipline that integrates principles of aromacology, human anatomy and physiology, and the art and science of the use of essential oils. Practitioners of dynamic aromatherapy learn to enhance clients' wellness and empower them to take charge of their own health and well-being. The correspondence course consists of twelve sections, including classes on the characteristics and classifications of essential oils, chemotypes, methods of applications, dosages, common disorders, consultation techniques, blending techniques, the physiology of olfaction, and how to establish an aromatherapy practice. The intensive covers much of the same material, including courses in aromatic materia medica, natural cosmetics, doctrine of signatures, basic pathology, natural remedies for women and children, and developing a practice.

How long it takes: Intensive program—12 weeks
                        Correspondence course—6 to 12 months

What it costs: Intensive program—$550
                   Correspondence course—$375

Credit cards are accepted.

Chapter II

✱ ✱ ✱ ✱

Media

Most media careers are not alternative. They may be interesting, but they're fairly conventional. Still, we figured that a book on alternative careers should include *some* discussion of media-related careers. After all, plenty of alternative people—artists, intellectuals, egotists, visionaries—gravitate toward some facet of the media. So we culled the best or most interesting of the media careers and focused on alternative and/or vocationally oriented programs. We included no MFAs, no degrees in journalism or communications, no four-year film schools, and no drama or theater programs (which would be alternative enough, but not so vocationally oriented). Instead, we included programs that focus on preparing you to make a living in the belly of the media beast: animation, broadcasting, filmmaking, and publishing.

Animation ・・・

Graphic design, we decided, was just too mundane to include. And fine art was too profound. But animation was juuuuust right. Not only does it involve cool art and cooler software, but it's a growing field: for the moment at least, getting a toehold in the business isn't too difficult. If you're interested in animation, you've probably already spent many hours doodling pictures in classrooms. Maybe it's time to pay someone to show you how to make a living at it.

If you're interested in a more formal, college-based animation training program than the following, check out *The Complete Guide to Animation and Computer Graphic Schools* (Ernest Pintoff, Watson-Guptill Publications, 1995). You can also write the National Cartoonists Society at Columbus Circle Station (P.O. Box 20267, New York, NY 10023) for a list of schools.

3D Exchange Animation Training
999 East Stanley Boulevard, Suite B
Livermore, CA 94550
(510) 371-4500
Fax: (510) 371-4501
www.exchange3d.com

3D Exchange offers certificate training in the use of LightWave 3D, a professional animation program. The training includes intensive instruction in both modular and layout techniques, as well as classes in the history of animation, character plug-ins, internal plug-ins, and studio tours. Students learn the processes, teams, tools, techniques, and emerging trends of animation.

How long it takes: 30 weeks

What it costs: $8,000

Credit cards are accepted.

The American Animation Institute
4729 Lankershim Boulevard
North Hollywood, CA 91602
(818) 766-0521

The institute offers professional instruction in screen cartooning, but does not have a certificate program; students take individual classes until they believe they are prepared for the job market. There are two introductory classes: Introduction to the Art and Industry, and Basic Animation Mechanics. The Introduction course includes an overview

268 ◆ You're Certifiable

of screen cartooning in Los Angeles, and discusses current employment opportunities. The Basic Animation course introduces the functions and capabilities of the animation camera, the use of animation bars and peg systems with tilts and pans, the composition and reading of the exposure sheet, and flipping, rolling, and stacking drawings. Advanced classes include Inbetweening and Assistant Animation, Layout, Storyboarding, Background Painting and Design, Character Design, Life Drawing, and Anatomy and Figure Construction.

The institute is administered by Local 839, a labor union representing writers, artists, craftspersons, and technicians involved in making animated cartoons.

How long it takes: 3 to 12 weeks per class

What it costs: $60 to $210 per class

Computer Arts Institute
310 Townsend Street, #230
San Francisco, CA 94107
(415) 546-5242
Fax: (415) 546-5237

The institute offers a vocational program in 3D Modeling and Animation. Students learn animation design, storyboarding techniques, creating photorealistic explosions and flames, creating animated characters, preparing interactive presentations for CD-ROM and the Internet, creating two-dimensional animations, line art, logos, and gradients, and modeling and animation for multimedia, computer gaming, broadcast, film, and video. Specific animation software taught includes Infini-D, 3D Studio Max, Fractal Design Painter, Lightwave 3S, and PhotoShop for Animators.

How long it takes: 26 weeks

What it costs: $6,320

Center for Electronic Art
250 4th Street
San Francisco, CA 94103
(415) 512-9300
info@cea.edu
www.cea.edu

The center offers a certificate program in computer animation that covers computer fundamentals, design, the theory and business of animation, digital media, two- and three-dimensional animation tools, and animation production. Classes include Animation Production Workshop, Electric Image, Form Z, 3D Studio Max, Detailer, and Careers in Computer Animation. Students learn storyboarding, editing, layout, key framing, shooting, postproduction, and how to use techniques such as decal mapping, fog lights, particle systems, velocity graphs, and polygon explosions. In advanced classes, students work together in production teams to follow the process from conceptualizing through modeling, rendering, and outputting a finished, portfolio-quality piece. The center also offers programs in multimedia, the Internet, desktop publishing, and Web publishing.

How long it takes: 1 year

What it costs: $3,110

Cost is approximate (fees are paid class by class).

Credit cards are accepted.

Video Symphony
1701 Verdugo Boulevard
Burbank, CA 91506
(818) 559-4273
(818) 558-1900
d3d@videosymphony.com
www.videosymphony.com

Video Symphony offers a wide range of animation training programs, including a SoftImage 3D Immersion Camp. This intensive course is designed to provide beginning animators with extensive knowledge of 3D production and SoftImage, one of the most common and powerful 3D animation software packages. Video Symphony very strongly recommends that students take the Immersion Camp in concert with a SoftImage Demo Reel Production Class, in which students develop a professional-quality demo reel that showcases their animation, modeling, texturing, and lighting talents. Other courses include Alias|Maya Essentials, 3D Studio Max, LightWave 3D, Power Animator, and Motion Capture.

How long it takes: SoftImage 3D Immersion Camp—10 weeks (though students may take 6 months at no extra charge)
Demo Reel Production—up to 4 months

What it costs: SoftImage 3D Immersion Camp—$3,995
Demo Reel Production—$3,500
Combined Immersion Camp and Demo Reel Production—$5,995

Credit cards are accepted and payment plans are available.

School of Communication Arts
3220 Spring Forest Road
Raleigh, NC 27616
(800) 288-7442
(919) 981-0972
Fax: (919) 981-0946
sca3d@aol.com
www.ncsca.com

The school offers two levels of computer animation training: Computer Art and Animation for beginning students, and 3D Computer Animation for advanced students. The Computer Art and Animation program includes instruction in digital paint imaging and image manipulation software for 2D computer art, print production, and texture mapping for 3D models. It also includes in-depth training in 3D Studio MAX, a computer animation software package with which students learn 3D computer modeling and animation techniques and production and postproduction basics. The 3D Computer Animation program is an advanced-level course that covers "high end" computer animation, video and motion picture animation production, the use of SoftImage and Alias on Silicon Graphics workstations, and advanced skills in all facets of 3D computer animation including modeling, character animation, and special effects.

In the course of completing either program, students will develop a portfolio containing color prints of still images rendered from animation sequences and a broadcast quality demo reel of finished animation. The School also has a job placement and career development center.

How long it takes: Computer Art and Animation—6 to 7 months
3D Computer Animation—6 to 7 months

What it costs: Computer Art and Animation—$7,740
                   3D Computer Animation—$10,490

Financial aid is available.

The Joe Kubert School of Cartoon and Graphic Art
37 Myrtle Avenue
Dover, NJ 07801
(973) 361-1327
Fax: (973) 361-1844

The school offers courses in Cartoon-Graphics and Cinematic Animation. Both courses begin with a foundation program that includes classes such as Narrative Art, The Human Figure, Layout, Lettering, Methods and Materials, and Introduction to Animation. The Cartoon-Graphics course continues the training in many of those areas, adding classes in Story Adaptation, Color Illustration, Advertising Illustration, Sketching and Layout, Sequential Storytelling, and the Business of Art. The Cinematic Animation course builds on the foundation program with classes in Character Development, Storyboards, the Oxberry Camera, In-Betweening, The Animated Film, and The Business of Film Art.

How long it takes: Cartoon-Graphics—3 years
                     Cinematic Animation—3 years

What it costs: Cartoon-Graphics—$34,500 to $36,000
                   Cinematic Animation—$34,500 to $36,000

Financial aid and scholarships (including one offered by Marvel Comics) are available.

Watkins Film School
Watkins Institute College of Art and Design
601 Church Street
Nashville, TN 37219
(800) 288-1420
(615) 251-7910
Fax: (615) 242-4278
www.watkinsinstitute.org

The school offers a professional certificate program in filmmaking with a concentration in Animation. The program requires courses in film history, film art, production, beginning screenwriting, figure drawing, animation, and an internship. The program emphasizes planning and creating animation shorts in various forms such as cel, cutout, claymation, 3-D modeling, and pan and scan, and gives students the opportunity to produce animated films.

Watkins also offers training in film producing, directing, screenwriting, cinematography, theatrical design, and editing. See Filmmaking for more information.

How long it takes: 2 years

What it costs: $15,360 (non-Tennessee resident)
                     $7,680 (Tennessee resident)

Financial aid is available.

Broadcasting ◆ ◆ ◆

We first intended to include only broadcasting programs that train students to become on-air personalities: DJs, newscasters, sports announcers, meteorologists, and so on. We figured maybe a reader would become the next Dr. Laura or Howard Stern (in fact, Robin Quivers, Stern's sidekick, is a graduate of one of the following programs). But then we noticed that some of the production training programs—teaching students to do sound engineering, video producing, editing, script- and copywriting, camera operating, and so on—are also interesting, if a bit less public. So we threw those in, too.

Conservatory of Recording Arts and Sciences
2300 East Broadway Road
Tempe, AZ 85282
(800) 562-6383
(602) 858-9400
Fax: (602) 829-1332

The Conservatory offers a Master Recording Program that consists of six primary courses: Audio Recording and Production, Music Business, MIDI/Computer/Electronic Music Recording, Sound Reinforcement, Troubleshooting/Maintenance, and Internship. The Audio Recording and Production course teaches basic recording techniques, equipment use and maintenance, record and tape processing, and music production, and gives students the opportunity to work on projects for film and video. Music Business covers contracts, publicity and public relations, copyrights and publishing, and other business-related matters. The Electronic Music Recording course covers computer basics, synthesizers and drum machines, computer recording sequencers, sampling theory, and sound storage. Sound Reinforcement covers hardware, testing, and systems design, and includes a recording project. Troubleshooting/Maintenance covers digital multimeters, oscilloscopes, tone generators, and signal problems. The final course is an internship. Students submit a list of five studios to the conservatory, which then works to arrange an internship at one of the locations on the list, giving priority to the highest preference.

How long it takes: 22 weeks

What it costs: $6,565

Payment plans and financial aid are available.

The Academy of Radio and TV Broadcasting
16052 Beach Boulevard, Suite 263
Huntington Beach, CA 92647
(714) 842-0100

4914 East McDowell Road, Suite 107
Phoenix, AZ 85008
(602) 267-8001

The academy offers two training programs: a Radio Broadcasting program and a Television/Video Production program. The Radio Broadcasting training provides hands-on experience working in fully equipped studios, preparing students for careers as air personalities, newscasters, sportscasters, and producers. Courses cover voice coaching, copywriting, music directing, sportscasting, voice-overs, and talent and style development. The Television/Video Production program offers training in camera operation, audio operation, lighting operation, graphics, news journalism, production and direction, editing, set design, shot composition, and institutional scriptwriting. Students then prepare a final project, have their work critiqued by industry professionals, and complete outside assignments and research.

How long it takes: Radio Broadcasting—30 weeks
　　　　　　　　　　Television/Video Production—30 weeks

What it costs: Radio Broadcasting—$7,950
　　　　　　　　Television/Video Production—$7,950

Financial aid is available.

Los Angeles Recording Workshop

5278 Lankershim Boulevard
North Hollywood, CA 91601
(818) 763-7400
Fax: (818) 763-7447
http://village.ios.com/~larw

The Recording Workshop offers programs that train recording engineers, video operators, and audio-video production technicians. The recording engineer program trains students in all aspects of recording session procedures, from the initial preparatory stages of equipment setup to the multitrack-to-stereo mixdown. Classes include recording theory, sound system theory, automation, tape alignment, postproduction, and computer workshops. The video operator program trains students in all aspects of video planning, shooting, editing, and postproduction, from the planning and preparation stages through the videotaping process to final on-line editing. Coursework covers lighting, CMX, digital video, Avid, and advanced editing. The Audio-Video Production technician course combines the first half of the Recording Engineer training with the full Video Operator training to give students hands-on experience, and open career possibilities, in both fields. The workshop also offers a Super Program, which combines the full recording and the full video training.

How long it takes: Recording Engineer—600 hours
　　　　　　　　　　Video Operator—300 hours
　　　　　　　　　　Audio-Video Production—600 hours
　　　　　　　　　　Super Program—900 hours

Full- and part-time schedules are available, from 10 to 45 weeks.

What it costs: Recording Engineer—$6,700
　　　　　　　　Video Operator—$3,695

Audio-Video Production—$6,700
Super Program—$9,395

Financial aid is available.

Sound Master Audio/Video Institute
10747 Magnolia Boulevard
North Hollywood, CA 91601
(213) 650-8000

Sound Master offers a complete program in Record Engineering, which covers audio/video postproduction, synchronization, recording studio maintenance, film scoring, MIDI, and CD/DAT mastering. Students learn recording fundamentals such as multitrack recording procedures, microphone types and applications, equalization techniques and procedures, and NAB tape alignment. Advanced classes cover 48-track recording and mixing, setup and lash-up procedures, time code regenerating, video formats and signal path, controlling MIDI special effects devices, checkerboard mixing and editing, disc-based command sequences, on-line and off-line video editing, and film and video scoring.

How long it takes: 10 months

What it costs: $8,950

Financial aid is available.

Connecticut School of Broadcasting
525 Northlake Boulevard
North Palm Beach, FL 33408
(800) 887-2346
(561) 842-2000
Fax: (561) 842-9842
www.media-arts.com

Radio Park
Farmington, CT 06032
(203) 232-9988

80 Ferry Boulevard
Stratford, CT 06497
(203) 378-5155

49 Walnut Park
Wellesley Hills, MA 02181
(617) 235-2050

377 Route 17 South, Penthouse
Hasbrouck Heights, NJ 07604
(201) 288-5800

The school's Radio and Television Broadcasting programs include training in radio and television announcing, commercial interpretation, studio operations, copywriting, broadcast journalism, audio production, broadcast sports, speech/radio-TV acting, television performing, interviewing, and programming/promotions. Students learn to use studio consoles, deliver play-by-play and color commentary, produce studio programming, gather and deliver news stories, and receive instruction in voice, speech, and improvisational speaking.

How long it takes: 32 weeks

What it costs: $5,990

Scholarships are available.

Massachusetts Communications College
142 Berkeley Street
Boston, MA 02116
(617) 267-7910
Fax: (617) 236-7883
www.communications.org

The college offers certificate programs in Recording Arts and Broadcasting. The Recording Arts program includes classes in audio recording, music production, listening and analysis, acoustics and electronics, and principles of computer music. Students in the Broadcasting program can concentrate in radio or television. The basic courses for both concentrations include media writing, radio, introduction to television production, and introduction to computers. The radio concentration then teaches voice and articulation and radio production, and includes a radio internship. The television concentration includes studio production, field production, voice and articulation, and a television internship.

How long it takes: 30 weeks

What it costs: $10,400

Financial aid is available.

Broadcasting Institute of Maryland
7200 Harford Road
Baltimore, MD 21234
(800) 942-9246
(410) 254-2770
Fax: (410) 254-5357
www.gidd.com/bim

The Broadcasting Institute offers a Broadcasting training program in which students major in Radio/TV News (Sports), Radio DJ, or Television Production. In the Radio/TV News (Sports) major, students learn to visit and interview newsmakers, report and practice broadcasting local events, attend press conferences, write and prepare radio and television copy, and learn the basics of preparing and performing a television reporter package. The Radio DJ major teaches all aspects of station operation, including preparing "hot clocks" and devising programming features. The Television Production major trains students to conceive, write, produce, and tape productions common to most stations, and teaches use of portable Minicam equipment. Specific skills taught include interviewing techniques, ad-libbing patter, producing jingles, reading copy, and obtaining a job in the broadcast industry.

How long it takes: 20 weeks

What it costs: $7,145

Payment plans are available.

New England School of Communications
One College Circle
Bangor, ME 04401
(888) 877-1876
(207) 947-6083
Fax: (207) 947-3987

The school offers a certificate training in broadcasting in which students concentrate in either radio and television. All students must complete coursework in FCC rules and regulations, writing commercials and public service announcements for radio and television, public speaking, media studies, and career preparation. Students who are concentrating in radio take additional classes in broadcast announcing, production, voice, and diction. They also receive hands-on training in station operation and programming decisions from sign-on to sign-off. Students who are concentrating in television take additional classes in television production, audio engineering, and television performance.

How long it takes: 1 year

What it costs: $5,570

Financial aid is available.

Specs Howard School of Broadcast Arts
19900 West Nine Mile Road
Southfield, MI 48075
(248) 358-9000
Fax: (248) 746-9777

Specs Howard offers a training program in radio and television broadcasting, with concentrations in radio and video. All students begin by taking courses in video performance, studio operation, career perspectives, news writing, technical television, and television news production. They learn shot composition, diction and articulation, operation of radio transmission devices, sports and weather reporting, and video production techniques. Students concentrating in radio then study vocal performance, commercial production, station training, station operations, commercial copywriting techniques, and radio programming. They also learn to use reel-to-reel equipment and the Roland DM-80 digital editor. Students concentrating in video study scene production, preproduction planning, news production, and video editing techniques. They produce various types of commercials, work as part of a production team to create a weekly news program, transform scripts into productions, and learn to produce dramatic and comedic scenes.

How long it takes: 32 weeks

What it costs: $10,490

Brown Institute
2225 East Lake Street
Minneapolis, MN 55407
(800) 627-6966
(612) 721-2481
Fax: (612) 721-2179
www.brown-institute.com

The institute offers a certificate training program in Radio and Television Broadcasting. Required coursework includes study of radio technology, broadcast advertising, television studio production and editing, and broadcast journalism. Electives include Management Concepts, Principles of Marketing, Broadcast Law, Introduction to Computers, and Broadcast Technology. The program emphasizes on-air practice and hands-on training.

How long it takes: 9 months

What it costs: $7,973

Financial aid is available.

Southwest School of Broadcasting
1031 East Battlefield, Suite 212B
Springfield, MO 65807
(417) 883-4060

The school trains students for careers in radio as disc jockeys, announcers, and producers. The training course is divided into ten sections: Fundamentals of Radio-Television Broadcasting, Broadcast Commercial Writing Techniques, Technical Aspects of Broadcasting, Broadcast Journalism, Fundamentals of Voice, Broadcast Sales and Advertising, Full Studio Operation, Radio and Television Field Trips, Interviewing, and Preparation for Employment. Students learn speech drills, production hand signals, sales promotion, writing copy, editing audiotapes, studio equipment operation, interpretive announcing, foreign language pronunciation, breathing exercises, handling wire copy, and commercial production.

How long it takes: 36 weeks

What it costs: $5,000

Financial aid is available.

The New School of Radio and Television
50 Colvin Avenue
Albany, NY 12206
(800) 649-7682
(518) 438-7682
Fax: (518) 438-3603

The school offers training programs in Radio/Television Broadcasting and Television Production with concentrations in Air Personality/Commercial Production and News/Sports/Talk. Students who choose the Air Personality/Commercial Production concentration study voice training, ad-lib development, and commercial production techniques. They learn advanced techniques on both linear and digital editing systems, and produce a professional audition tape that they can use to demonstrate their skills to prospective employers. The News/Sports/Talk concentration teaches operations of studio equipment, news gathering, writing, and basic shooting and editing techniques. Other courses in the Radio/Television Broadcasting program include Linear Multi-Track Audio Recording, Ad Libbing with Topical Items, Using Computerized News Sources, Writing the Sports Story, Using the Teleprompter, Remote Broadcasts, and Basic ENG Lighting.

How long it takes: 6 months

What it costs: $5,465

Financial aid is available.

Institute of Audio Research
64 University Place
Greenwich Village
New York, NY 10003
(212) 677-7580
Fax: (212) 677-6549

The institute offers a Recording Engineering and Production program designed to prepare students for a career in the recording industry as an assistant recording engineer or an entry level audio technician. Courses include the physics of acoustics and sound, circuit construction and wiring, microphones and sound reinforcement, audio processing devices, digital processing, editing and mixing techniques, and MIDI and synthesis. Specific skills taught include ear training, tape machine alignment, analog-to-digital and digital-to-analog conversions, using software such as Digidesign Soundtools, remixing, and doing audio for film and video. Students get the opportunity to work on recording projects with professional and aspiring bands—from the initial tracking to the final mix. The program also covers business and producing issues, such as recording and producing contracts, publishing and protecting music, and setting up a small business.

How long it takes: 9 months (full time)

15 months (part time)

What it costs: $9,050

Financial aid and payment plans are available.

Sam Ash Music Institute
162 West 48th Street
New York, NY 10036
(212) 719-4572
Fax: (212) 719-1941
http://hudson.idt.net/~saminyc

The institute offers a Total Music Recording program that trains students in all aspects of contemporary recording techniques and procedures. Students learn to use analog, digital, MIDI, and other recording equipment. The program includes instruction in current MIDI recording practices, the basics of music theory and keyboard playing, and computer-based digital audio recording, editing, and CD mastering. Students gain hands-on experience setting up keyboard controllers, using industry standard software sequencers and MIDI patchbays, calibrating tape machines, and performing manual and automated twenty-four-track mixdown onto DAT. The institute also offers an internship that provides students with on-the-job training.

How long it takes: 6 months

What it costs: $4,395

Ohio Center for Broadcasting
4790 Red Bank Expressway, Suite 102
Cincinnati, OH 45227
(513) 271-6060
Fax: (513) 271-6135
ocb@broadcastcntr.org
www.broadcastcntr.org

9000 Sweet Valley Drive
Valley View, OH 44125
(216) 474-9117

The Ohio Center offers a training program in radio and television broadcasting. The course emphasizes the on-air performance skills that are required to find work as a broadcast announcer, and covers other areas such as control room procedures, news and sports writing and reporting, copy writing, and broadcast management. Classes include Speaking Techniques, News Announcing, Broadcast Interviewing Techniques, Video Production, Directing Techniques, Ad-Libbing, ENG News Gathering, and Creating and Producing a TV Audition Tape. The center also offers an internship program at local radio and TV stations for interested students.

How long it takes: 38 weeks

What it costs: $6,097

Financial aid is available.

American Broadcasting School
4511 Southeast 29th Street
Oklahoma City, OK 73115
(405) 672-6511
Fax: (405) 672-6488

6218 South Lewis
Tulsa, OK 76136
(918) 742-1227
Fax :(918) 742-3537
www.radioschool.com

The school offers a professional training for students who want to pursue a career in radio broadcasting. Students learn newscasting, sportscasting, programming, production, copywriting, vocal diction, music mixing, control room operation, and creation and production of radio commercials. Students spend over five hundred hours preparing for and delivering on-the-air shows, newscasts and sportcasts.

How long it takes: 30 weeks

What it costs: $7,995

Financial aid is available.

Madison Media Institute
One Point Place, Suite 1
Madison, WI 53719
(800) 236-4997
(608) 829-2728

The institute offers two career training programs: Radio and Television Broadcasting, and Recording and Music Technology. The Broadcasting program includes courses on electronic media, writing for broadcasting, media history, studio skills, TV/video production, current media trends, and the business of broadcasting. Students learn production techniques, camera work, graphics, and videotape editing.

The Recording and Music Technology program includes courses in music and MIDI concepts, recording/audio technology, music business, music/audio production, and MIDI and synthesizer technology. Students become proficient in the use of mixers, digital recorders, computer sequencers, samplers, microphones, and sound processing equipment.

How long it takes: Radio and Television Broadcasting—30 weeks
Recording and Music Technology—30 weeks

What it costs: Radio and Television Broadcasting—$6,630
Recording and Music Technology—$7,905

Financial aid is available.

Filmmaking ◆ ◆ ◆

If you're a wannabe film producer or director—but not a wannabe film student—this section is for you. The following programs train students to make their own films and work on others' as everything from a producer to a key grip to a production assistant to a director. Some focus on artistic or experimental films, some focus on documentaries, and some focus on commercial films: be sure you know which you're interested in before you enroll in a program. This section does not include any of the many film studies programs that offer bachelor's and master's degrees. If you want a more thorough and academic training, check out *The Complete Guide to American Film Schools and Cinema and Television Courses* (Ernest Pintoff, Penguin Books, 1994) and *Film School Confidential: The Insider's Guide to Film Schools* (Karin Kelly and Tom Edgar, Pedigree, 1997).

Los Angeles City College
Cinema/Television Department
855 North Vermont Avenue
Los Angeles, CA 90029
(213) 953-4545
Fax: (213) 953-4505
cintv@citymail.lacc.cc.ca.us
http://citywww.lacc.cc.ca.us

The college offers three certificate programs in cinema and television: Film Production, Television Production, and Cinema/Video Production. The Film Production program requires coursework in motion picture production, film theory and history, documentary filmmaking, screenwriting, motion picture photography, film and TV sound, directing, editing, budgeting, and scheduling. Other classes cover optics, photo emulsions, microphone placement, Foley and ADR use, flatbed operation, financing, and distribution.

The Television Production program covers the history of radio and TV broadcasting, television lighting and sound, equipment procedures, studio production, television announcing, videotape editing and production, and nonlinear editing. Students learn about cost, ratings, and profits, as well as the use of microphones, mixers, and cameras and how to direct, edit, and work with actors. As part of their coursework, students are required to write, produce, and direct several live-switched productions.

The Cinema/Video Production program focuses primarily on film production and requires many of the same courses as the Film Production course—production, history, screenwriting, photography, sound, and editing. The video portion emphasizes studio and remote production, producing, writing, and directing, and use of cameras and lighting, and videotape editing.

How long it takes: Film Production—1 year
Television Production—1 year
Cinema/Video Production—1 to 1½ years

What it costs: Film Production—$4,250
Television Production—$3,375
Cinema/Video Production—$4,375

California residents pay under $500 for each of the programs. Financial aid is available.

UCLA Extension
Department of Entertainment Studies and Performing Arts
10995 Le Conte Avenue, Room 437
Los Angeles, CA 90024
(310) 825-9064
Fax: (310) 206-7435
espa@unex.ucla.edu

UCLA Extension offers a certificate program in film, television, video, and new media. The program is comprised of two required and four elective courses. The two required courses are Pre-Production and Production for Film and Television, and Post-Production. The electives can be chosen from hundreds of courses in subjects such as Acting, Producing/Business, Production, Film Theory and History, and Appreciation. Specific courses include Acting for the Non-Professional, Scene Study According to Stanislavski, Understanding Feature Film Development, Film Structure for Producers, Directors, and Editors, Production Accounting for Film and Television, Corporate Video Production, Documentary Production, The Fundamentals of Television Production, The Post-Modern Crisis in the Arts, and The Director's Intention: Five Maverick Filmmakers.

How long it takes: 3 years (part-time)

What it costs: $8,000

Financial aid is available.

The Community Film Workshop
1130 South Wabash Avenue, Suite 302
Chicago, IL 60605
(312) 427-1245
Fax: (312) 427-8818
CFWChicago@aol.com

The workshop offers an intensive film production training course. Students must complete a prerequisite that covers the aesthetic elements of motion pictures, film production terminology, and film criticism and analysis before enrolling in the intensive workshop. The workshop then trains students to operate cameras, lights, and sound and editing equipment, preparing them to direct, shoot, edit, and conform the two short color films (one voice-over and one sync-sound) that are required for completion of the course. During the training, each student performs many different crew functions, including working as a sound mixer, boom, gaffer, grip, and script supervisor.

How long it takes: 16 weeks

What it costs: $3,570

Anthropology Film Center
1626 Canyon Road
Santa Fe, NM 87501
(505) 983-4127
anthrofilm@nets.com
www.nets.com/anthrofilm

The center offers an ethnographic and documentary film training program for students who want to write, direct, and produce ethnographic or social-documentary films. The training begins with an introduction to photography, filmmaking, and ethnology, which teaches film technology, vocabulary, theory, procedures, and the role of anthropology and media in cross-cultural communication and multicultural democracies. The course also includes hands-on training in storyboarding, camera and sound use, editing, lighting, budgeting, scheduling, and proposal development.

How long it takes: 9 months

What it costs: $9,600

The Film Program
New York University School of Continuing Education
Pless Building/Lower Concourse
82 Washington Square East
New York, NY 10003
(212) 998-7140
sceinfo@nyu.edu
www.sce.nyu.edu

NYU offers a certificate program in film. Students work as teams under the supervision of professional filmmakers to create original films. Courses include Film Techniques and Technology, Film Production, Cinematography, Production Sound Workshop, Film Editing, Preproduction Workshop, and Directing for Film and Television. Students learn how to use the camera, light a set, tell a story, edit, lay in narration and music tracks, film special effects, and use the techniques of sync-sound production. Electives include Getting into Film and Video, The Business of Writing for the Screen, The Documentary: Directing and Producing, Acting for Film and Television, Outlaw Cinema, and Cinema Classics: Flaherty to Fellini. The program is offered in three formats: summer intensive, daytime intensive, and evening/weekend intensive.

How long it takes: Summer Intensive—6 weeks
Daytime Intensive—11 weeks
Evening/Weekend Intensive—6 months

What it costs: Summer Intensive—$5,500
Daytime Intensive—$5,500
Evening/Weekend Intensive—$2,750

New York Film Academy
100 East 17th Street
New York, NY 10003
(212) 674-4300
Fax: (212) 477-1414
film@nyfa.com
www.nyfa.com

The academy offers a workshop in filmmaking for individuals with little or no experience. Classes include Director's Craft, Crews, Writing,

Sound, Editing, Budgeting and Scheduling, Hands-on Camera, Production Workshop, and a Final Film Project. Skills taught include visual storytelling, editing, screenwriting, arranging shots to create cogent sequences, casting, getting permits, working with props, lighting, using lenses, and screen testing for focus, exposure, and contrast. Students form four-person crews for film exercises and the final film project, in which each student writes, produces, directs, shoots, and edits a ten-minute narrative, documentary, or experimental film. The academy also offers intensive summer courses at Yale, Princeton, UCLA, UC Berkeley, Cambridge, Oxford, and in Paris and Berlin.

How long it takes: 8 weeks

What it costs: $5,775

Northwest Film Center
Portland Art Museum
1219 Southwest Park Avenue
Portland, OR 97205
(503) 221-1156
Fax: (503) 294-0874
registrar@nwfilm.org
www.nwfilm.org

The center offers a certificate program in film that prepares students for a career in the media arts and the world of independent filmmaking. The program consists of a core curriculum, electives, workshops, and an independent final project. The core curriculum includes classes in film production, screenwriting, cinematography, sound editing, postproduction, video production and editing, documentaries, and personal/experimental cinema. Electives cover subjects such as animation, corporate scriptwriting, creative makeup for film, optical printing, production management, and visual design for film. Workshops include Breaking in as a Production Assistant, Directing Actors, Distribution and Marketing, Fundraising for Film/Video, and Non-Linear Editing. The independent final project is a three- to six-minute film that students write, direct, edit, and finance on their own.

How long it takes: 2 to 4 years

What it costs: $11,000

Scholarships and a payment plan are available.

Watkins Film School
Watkins Institute College of Art and Design
601 Church Street
Nashville, TN 37219
(800) 288-1420
(615) 251-7910
Fax: (615) 242-4278
www.watkinsinstitute.org

The school offers a professional certificate program in filmmaking with six possible concentrations: Producing, Directing, Screenwriting, Cinematography, Theatrical Design, and Editing. All the concentrations require core courses in film history, film art, production, beginning screenwriting, and an internship. The Producing program requires additional classes in production management, film finance, distribution, and exhibition, and entertainment business and law. The Directing program requires additional classes in drawing, color fundamentals, storyboard design, directing, and acting for directors. The Screenwriting program requires additional classes in screenwriting, writing for television, adaptations, and script marketing. The Cinematography program requires additional classes in color fundamentals, photography, and cinematography. The Theatrical Design program requires additional classes in color fundamentals, drawing, theatrical design, art direction, costume design, and architectural drawing. And the Editing program requires additional classes in editing and digital editing.

Students in all the programs work as part of a production team to write, produce, direct, design, shoot, and edit their own film, taking a story concept from script to finished product.

Watkins also offers an animation training program. See Animation for more information.

How long it takes: 2 years

What it costs: Tennessee resident—$7,680
Out-of-state resident—$15,360

Financial aid is available.

Publishing • • •

The following programs are included not only because they are in the potentially exciting fields of magazine and book publishing (which are often not so alternative or, for that matter, exciting) but because they are intensive courses that prepare students for employment. They teach students the basics of acquiring, developing, editing, promoting, and designing books and articles—and introduce additional goodies like contract negotiation, choosing paper stock, and working with children's books and multimedia products. And—extremely important—some of them provide a wealth of networking opportunities. Teachers and guest speakers at most of these programs are very plugged in and ripe for stalking . . . er, networking. If you take one of these courses, don't wait until you graduate to make job contacts.

University of Denver Publishing Institute
2075 South University Boulevard, D-114
Denver, CO 80210
(303) 871-2570
Fax: (303) 871-2501
www.du.edu/pi

The institute offers a career training program in book publishing. The course consists of workshops in editing and marketing and lecture/teaching sessions conducted by publishing professionals. In the workshops, students work on a manuscript from a leading publisher, learning editorial skills such as preparation of a reader's report, substantive manuscript editing, copy editing, and proofreading, and marketing skills such as writing publicity releases and advertisements and developing a marketing plan. The workshops also teach the basic principles of book design and manufacture.

The lecture/teaching sessions include courses such as The Role of the Editor, Acquisition of the Manuscript, Editor-Author Relations, The Role of the Literary Agent, Book Design, University Presses, Advertising and Promotion, The Role of the Sales Representative, Subsidiary Rights, Publishing in a Multimedia World, International Publishing, Children's Book Publishing, Legal Aspects of Publishing, and Reference/Information Publishing in an Electronic World. During the last week of the program, an informal job fair is held in which students meet with human resource managers from various publishers and attend a seminar on how to get a job.

How long it takes: 4 weeks

What it costs: $2,750

Publishing Program
University of Chicago
Graham School of General Studies
5835 Kimbark Avenue
Chicago, IL 60637
(773) 702-1724
Fax: (773) 702-6814
s-medlock@midway.uchicago.edu
www2.uchicago.edu/grahamschool/

The University of Chicago offers three levels of training in publishing. The first level consists of three courses: Basic Manuscript Editing, Introduction to Book or Publication Design, and Introduction to Book or Magazine Production. Classes cover proofreading, headings and subheads, capitalization, documentation, and typographic evaluation. Students also learn how to choose paper stocks, build a production schedule, and design publications.

The second level includes classes on the business of publishing, such as How to Start a Trade Magazine, The Business of Book Publishing, and Marketing in the Nineties. Students learn about magazine business planning, advertising sales, editorial costs, manuscript acquisition, contracts, pricing, prepress, subsidiary rights, electronic publishing, and creation and implemention of comprehensive marketing plans.

The third level offers students the opportunity to specialize in editing, writing, or design. The editing specialization includes courses in medical editing, indexing, manuscript editing, the author-editor relationship, and editing on-line. The writing specialization covers plotting the story, building durable fiction, writing picture books, and writing light verse. The design specialization covers multimedia, typography, and design.

How long it takes: Each level is 1 year

What it costs: $1,250 to $1,500 (approximate cost per year)

Radcliffe Publishing Course
Radcliffe College
6 Ash Street
Cambridge, MA 02138
(617) 495-8678
Fax: (617) 496-2333
rpc@radcliffe.edu
www.radcliffe.edu

Radcliffe offers an intensive course in book and magazine publishing. The course provides an introduction to book and magazine publishing, from the evaluation of original manuscripts through the sales and marketing of finished products. Students spend the first part of the program concentrating on book publishing: they learn about manuscript evaluation, bookstore sales, movie deals, editing, design, production, promotion, advertising, and marketing. The second part of the course focuses on magazine publishing. It teaches students about planning, writing, designing, and producing a magazine, and includes classes in circulation projections, direct-mail pieces, advertising campaigns, and budget analysis. Other classes cover book clubs, ethical issues, subsidiary rights, literary agents, children's books, book packaging, magazine ideas, and electronic publishing. Finally, the course offers instruction in career planning and résumé writing.

How long it takes: 6 weeks

What it costs: $3,645

Some financial aid is available.

Center for Publishing
New York University School of Continuing Education
11 West 42nd Street, Room 400
New York, NY 10036
(212) 790-3232
pub.center@nyu.edu
www.sce.nyu.edu/pubcenter

The center offers certificate programs in book publishing and magazine publishing. In the book publishing program, students first complete an overview course that covers the creation of ideas, literary agent submissions, contract negotiations, the editorial process and design, marketing and publicity, and subsidiary rights. Students then choose five electives from subjects such as Copyediting and Proofreading, Book Production and Design, Book Marketing, Financial and Legal Issues, and Electronic Publishing. The structure of the magazine publishing program is similar. Students first attend an overview course that focuses on concept development, editorial content, production, working with writers and freelancers, financial management, circulation, and advertising. They then choose five electives from a variety of classes including Editorial Planning and Management, Technical and Medical Copyediting, Production, Public Relations, Circulation, and Newsletter Publishing.

How long it takes: Each program—variable (commonly 1 year)

What it costs: Each program—$1,700 to $2,700

The Rice University Publishing Program
School of Continuing Studies
P.O. Box 1892
Houston, TX 77251
(713) 527-4803
Fax: (713) 285-5213
rupp@rice.edu
www.rice.edu/rupp

Rice University offers a training program in magazine and book publishing in which students participate in simulations of launching new magazines and working at book publishing houses. In the magazine program, students work as a team to create their own version of an existing magazine, defining its mission, audience, frequency, and editorial and artistic slants. Issues covered include maintaining the magazine's integrity while catering to advertisers, developing features, departments, and columns, creating a media kit to target appropriate advertisers, building subscriptions and newsstand sales, designing the cover and table of contents, and analyzing the competition. At the end of the magazine course, students present their improvements to the actual publisher of the magazine. In the book program, students review and evaluate manuscripts, learn about editor-agent negotiations, compete for the hottest literary properties, design and produce book covers and sales catalogs, write cover and promotional copy for books, and negotiate the sale and purchase of subsidiary and foreign rights. Part of each

294   ◆   *You're Certifiable*

program involves meeting with professionals who come to lecture and recruit.

How long it takes: 2 weeks

What it costs: $2,095

Scholarships are available.

Chapter 12

✖ ✖ ✖

Metaphysical Healing

The healing careers in this chapter are based on energetic, spiritual, intuitive, and psychic systems and techniques. They include clairvoyant reading, aura clearing, spiritual counseling, energy channeling, color and gemstone healing, and much more. You may find it hard to believe that you can transform your interest in the transcendental into a down-to-earth business. But many people have done just that. However, virtually all of them are self-employed—if metaphysical healing is your path, be sure that you're prepared to run a small business. Most beginners in this field seem to leave the success of their practice to the Fates, but those with a bit more initiative and business savvy, and a marketing plan, tend to do more good, serve more clients, and make more money.

Metaphysical Healing ✦ ✦ ✦

Okay. We admit it—this chapter contains only one section. But metaphysical healing is so holistic that we were unable to separate the training programs in any intelligible way. So this section contains color and gemstone healing trainings, which teach you how to apply color and gemstone energy for healing and to help clients with life direction, spiritual attunement, and emotional clarity. It contains Qi-based healing, which is energy healing with an Asian emphasis—these programs tend to discuss the meridians, the five elements, and other elements of traditional Chinese medicine. And it contains every other vocational training based primarily on vibrational, energetic, spiritual, intuitive, and psychic healing techniques. But although we're lumping all these trainings together, they are not all alike. One school may teach clairvoyant reading, auric sensing, and energy work. Another might focus on chakra balancing and cellular healing. And a third may devote itself to intuitive counseling and spiritual unfolding. If you're already familiar with these terms—or you intuitively sense they represent your future career—and want to help others discover the benefits of esoteric healing, the following schools will prepare you for a transcendent career.

The School of Heart Awakening
P.O. Box 4195
Cave Creek, AZ 85327
(800) 370-5479
(602) 488-1731
Fax: (602) 488-5806
heartawk@primenet.com
http://iypn.com/heartawakening/

Heart Awakening is a process of undoing the tangles that block the heart's perception of the truth, with the intention of supporting people in achieving their heart's desires. Certified Heart Awakeners act as mirrors, catalysts, and guides, combining deep unconditional love and intuitive guidance to heal clients' relationships with the Divine.

The process of Heart Awakening includes four steps: intuitive counseling, prayer, energy work, and breakthrough. In intuitive counseling, the practitioner establishes rapport and trust with the client. Prayer uses the presence of the Divine to cleanse and purify all levels of the client's being. Heart Awakeners use energy work to sense and clear those blocks in the aura that represent traumas and deep-rooted mental/emotional patterns. And breakthrough allows the client, feeling safe and surrounded by unconditional love, to let go of suffering and pain.

The school trains students to use physical, emotional, and absentee healing, to heal the aura with energy, prayer, crystals, color, sound, and frequency, to discover and develop their unique spiritual gifts, to work with guides and teachers on the inner planes, to study and apply spiritual principles for daily living, and to develop a healing practice.

Prerequisites for enrollment in the school are one complete Heart Awakening session or attendance at an introductory workshop and a personal interview by the Heart Awakening staff.

How long it takes: 3 years (part-time)

What it costs: $12,600

Credit cards are accepted and payment plans are available.

The Amanae Foundation
700 Hensley Creek Road
Ukiah, CA 95482
(707) 463-2653
Fax: (707) 463-2906
office@amanae.org
www.amanae.org

Amanae is an emotional release technique that opens the doorways closed by deeply held fear, anger, and trauma. The foundation trains Amanae Practitioners, who help clients bypass their mind and ego to shift out deep emotions and traumas held in the body, take a quantum leap into a more conscious and vital union of spirit, mind, and body, and move into their full integrity and magnificence. But students don't just learn a healing technique: they also embark on a journey toward their own highest transformation. The first step toward certification as an Amanae Practitioner is attendance at an intensive workshop that helps students access, feel, and release as much emotional baggage as possible. Students then enroll in the certification program, which includes weekly classes, monthly energy imprinting, five intensive workshops (from three to six days long), regular assessments, sweat lodges, and eighteen practicum sessions with paying clients.

How long it takes: Intensive Amanae Workshop—5 days
                    Certification Course—9 months

What it costs: Amanae Workshop—$830
                    Nine-Month Certification Course—$6,230

Applied Metaphysics Institute
P.O. Box 307
Guerneville, CA 95446
(707) 869-0985
Hannum.AMI@wclynx.com

The institute teaches medical intuition, biofeedback techniques, and Hannum Process Energy Work, a systematized psychic technique that employs nonvisual color projection to effect spontaneous healing. Students also learn innovative methods to clear up allergies (such as the Tapas method, an allergy elimination technique based on acupressure), one-to-one, self, and team healing, and how to resolve present emotional and past life influences on illness. Coursework includes an introduction to the latest research on microbe and toxin interaction, personal energy management, divination methodology, internal viewing, and constructing a systematic healing plan.

The training program is divided into beginning and advanced classes, and there is an apprenticeship program that includes participation in a student clinic.

How long it takes: Beginning Classes—3 months
Advanced Classes—3 months
Apprenticeship Program—1 year

What it costs: $1,575 for the entire program

The Chi Nei Tsang Institute
2315 Prince Street
Berkeley, CA 94705
(510) 848-9558
Fax: (510) 848-0686
cnt@slip.net
www.chineitsang.com

Chi Nei Tsang is a holistic approach to body therapy that includes vital energy cultivation (Chi-Kung), active meditations, and massage therapy techniques. Students of CNT learn the principles of physical, mental, emotional, and spiritual development using techniques of grounding the spirit in pragmatic reality.

The institute's certification program teaches students to practice Chi-Kung and meditation, to recognize and manipulate the internal organs, to observe internal patterns of tension and misalignments of the external structure of the body, to feel the energy-body and address internal and structural problems, to lead clients through meditation and visualization, and to promote emotional release and integration.

In addition to the coursework, students are required to receive thirty-two professional treatments, complete one hundred documented treatments (twenty clients receiving five treatments each), take anatomy and physiology workshops or home study, and attend two weekend workshops. The curriculum meets the standards of the International Healing Tao system to provide graduates with Chi Nei Tsang practitioner certification.

How long it takes: 2 years. Class time is 170 hours, not including weekly group practice sessions, the clinical assistantship program, or occasional weekend workshops.

What it costs: $2,300

Clearsight

1640 5th Street
Suite 200
Santa Monica, CA 90401
(310) 395-1170
Fax: (310) 395-4409
clearsight@earthlink.net

Clearsight offers two certificate training programs: the Clearsight Healing program and the Clearsight Clairvoyant program. The Healing program trains students in the use of laying-on-of-hands to effect change in the human energy field. Students learn to perceive, diagnose, and clear energy blockages that can lead to disease. The Healing program includes both a Master Healer and an Advanced Master Healer certificate training course.

Classes in the Master Healer program include Manifesting Your Archetype, The Cleansing Process, Energetic Healing, and Inspiring the Healer Within. Students are required to complete six documented healings between taking the seminars. Coursework for the Advanced Master Healer program includes Vibrational Healing, Clearing the Birth Process, Healing with the Elements, and Cellular Restructuring and Homeopathic Energy Healing. Students must complete thirty-six documented healings to be eligible for Advanced Master Healer certification.

The Clairvoyant program teaches students to access their innate clairvoyant ability to read auras and chakras. This reading procedure allows the student to become an intuitive counselor, an energy healer, and to perceive the energy changes in the essence of all living things. With practice, students can see auras within three months and can read and understand them within five months. Classes include Energy Awareness Skills, Cleansing, Clearing, and Restructuring Your Life, Seeing the Aura, and Professional Intuitive Skills.

Clearsight also offers a number of advanced programs to graduates of the Clairvoyant and Healing programs: a Teacher Training program for those who wish to teach, a Spiritual Counseling program for those who wish to set up a professional Spiritual Counseling practice, and a Ministership program for those interested in performing rituals such as weddings, baptisms, etc.

How long it takes: Master Healer Program—6 weekends in 1 year
Advanced Master Healer Program—10 weekends in 20 months
Clairvoyant Program—1 year

What it costs: Master Healer Program—$1,200
Advanced Master Healer Program—$2,000
Clairvoyant Program—$3,468

Credit cards are accepted and a payment plan is available.

Colorburst
501 West Glenoaks Boulevard, #215
Glendale, CA 91202
(888) 243-1207
chromalite@aol.com

Colorburst offers training in color healing, or Chromatherapy, focusing on the use of the Chroma-Lite II color wand. Two classes are offered, Chromatherapy I and II. In the first class, students learn to use color to heal various physical imbalances and emotional upsets. In the second, they learn to work on auric bodies to heal emotional imbalances, and to use chromatherapy on reflexology zones. Some of the conditions color therapy addresses are arthritis, carpal tunnel syndrome, headaches, muscle tension, and sore throats. Although color therapy may be best used as an adjunct therapy by someone already practicing a healing profession, Colorburst also offers training for those who want to become chromatherapy trainers and demonstrators, and Chroma-Lite color wand distributors.

How long it takes: Chromatherapy I—1 day
                        Chromatherapy II—1 day

What it costs: Chromatherapy I—$95
                        Chromatherapy II—$95

Credit cards are accepted.

The Learning Light Education and Research Foundation
1212 East Lincoln
Anaheim, CA 92805
(714) 533-2311

Learning Light offers a certification training in Healing, Metaphysics, and Psychic Arts. The program is designed to provide students with the knowledge and skills required to develop a successful metaphysical career. The program offers both a basic and an advanced certificate. The coursework for the basic certificate includes instruction in ethics, the history of metaphysics, meditation, whole body balancing, spiritual growth and connection, universal laws and principles, and an intro-duction to healing and psychic development. The advanced certificate courses train students in comparative religions, advanced universal laws, advanced mental self-improvement, advanced spiritual growth and connection, public speaking, and marketing.

How long it takes: Basic Certificate—1 year
                        Advanced Certificate—1 year

What it costs: Basic Certificate—$1,800
                        Advanced Certificate—$1,800

Financing is available.

School for Advanced Healing
7960 Faraway Lane
Elfin Forest, CA 92029
(888) 755-5599
(760) 761-0006
Fax: (760) 755-5599

The school offers certification in Advanced Healing, a synthesis of techniques used to accelerate healing and enlightenment. The training program begins with an introductory course, The New Basics, which teaches the art of invocation, clairvoyance and high sense perception, unity through relationship, advanced states of consciousness, and powerful healing techniques. The core coursework then trains students to combine hands-on healing with an understanding of human energy fields, chakras, energetic anatomy, and higher states of consciousness. Students are taught to develop subtle sense perception and inner guidance in order to understand the energetic nature of disease and work toward the unlimited possibilities of healing. Certification requires the additional completion of an anatomy and physiology class and fulfillment of a healing/therapy requirement of one healing session per month for two years. The school offers Master Healer and Teacher Training certification courses for graduates.

How long it takes:　New Basics—4 days
　　　　　　　　　　　Core Coursework—2 years (part-time)

What it costs:　　　Basic Training Course—$2,950
　　　　　　　　　　　Core Coursework—$11,800

Credit cards are accepted and payment plans are available.

School of Energy Mastery
1241 Adams Street, Suite 1132
St. Helena, CA 94567
(800) 238-3060
(305) 895-1866
energymastery@interx.net

The school trains healers in the art of Advanced Energy Healing, a practice that rapidly transforms disease while simultaneously uplifting the consciousness of the healer and the client. The first step toward certification as a Master Healer is attendance at an Advanced Energy Healing Basic Intensive, which introduces students to the subtle causes of disease and their relationship to etheric anatomy, the development and use of auric vision for diagnosis, and clairsentient body scanning, and helps students develop expertise in the Awareness Release Technique.

　　Upon completion of the Basic Intensive, students may enroll in the core training program, which focuses on bringing students into contact with their own higher dimensional energies and opening them to the unity of love and oneness of spirit. The training emphasizes five areas: enlightenment, anchoring and holding higher states, sharing and understanding the chakras, healership skills, and visions skills. The curriculum includes intuitive skills such as clairvoyance, clairaudience, and clairsentience, and healing methods such as magnetic and radiatory healing, the Awareness Release Technique, Energetic Unwinding, and the Energetic Dialogue Process.

Finally, students who want to be certified as Master Healers must demonstrate the ability to read all layers of the energy field, transform the energy field at interdimensional levels, hold the client in an expanded state of love and consciousness, and manage a client with a severe or life-threatening disease. They also have to complete a course in anatomy and physiology and a practicum.

How long it takes: Basic Intensive—3 days
Master Healer Program—18 months to 3 years

What it costs: Basic Intensive—$495
Master Healer Program—$9,600

Credit cards are accepted and payment plans are available.

The Body-Energy Center
2730 29th Street
P.O. Box 19708
Boulder, CO 80308
(303) 447-0484
(303) 442-3131
Fax: (303) 442-3141

The center offers two professional training programs: Body-Energy Practitioner Certification training and Chi Kung Healing Touch training. The Body-Energy program trains students to practice Body-Energy Healing, which draws on many modalities, such as Healing Touch, Therapeutic Touch, Chi Kung, Centered Guidance, Shamanistic practices, and Transpersonal and Anthroposophical principles. Students learn aura clearing, chakra opening and balancing, polarity therapy and mind clearance, centered guidance, backwork, Chi Kung meditation, ritual, trauma release, and sacred spiral/medicine wheel philosophy. Business and management skills are also covered.

The Chi Kung Healing Touch training consists of four levels. Level

I covers the anatomy and physiology of Oriental medicine and how it relates to Chi Kung and Healing Touch, the three Tain Tien practices, the Tai Chi Chi Kung form of "Dancing Cloud Hands," and Chi Kung healing forms. In Level II, students learn the theory and practices of the Microcosmic Orbit and the Pa Kua navel form, the Energy Shower, the Chi Kung Finger Drumming techniques, and Eight Extra Meridian Chi Kung Healing. The third level covers the Inner Healing Smile, the Five Elements as they relate to the twelve major meridians, the six healing sounds, and the eight trigram practices of the Pa Kua and their specific medical applications. And Level IV covers the Macrocosmic Orbit, general medical applications of Chi Kung Healing, and the Inner Alchemy process of "The Fusion of Five Elements."

How long it takes: Body-Energy Practitioner Training—108 hours in 1 year
Chi Kung Healing Touch Training—80 hours in 1 year

What it costs: Body-Energy Practitioner Training—$900
Chi Kung Healing Touch Training—$800

Delphi University
P.O. Box 70
McCaysville, GA 30555
(706) 492-2772
Fax: (706) 792-5404
registrar@delphi-center.com
www.delphi-center.com

Delphi offers certificates in Mediumship, Spiritual Healing, Metaphysician Practitioner, and RoHun Therapy. The university contains three schools: the Arthur Ford Academy of Mediumship, the Patricia Hayes School of Inner Sense Development, and the RoHun Institute. The prerequisite for enrollment in the latter two schools is the In-depth Mediumship Training offered at the Arthur Ford Academy.

The academy grants a Certificate of Mediumship to students who learn to use their intuitive and spiritual abilities for healing, mediumship, channeling, aura analysis, automatic writing, psychometry, and intuitive counseling. After completing the course, students will be able to provide guidance, insight, and healing energy to those with questions, emotional issues, or physical problems.

The Patricia Hayes School offers a Metaphysician Practitioner Program that teaches metaphysical skills and methods of treatment for the purpose of healing and spiritual unfoldment. This program helps Metaphysician Practitioners begin or expand their private practices through the application of light, love, and healing. Coursework includes trance healing, past life therapy, lotus sessions, psi-scans, soul travel, and life reading. The training program contains two sections: Advanced Mediumship, which focuses on the study of the astral world and its inhabitants; and Advanced Mediumship II, which focuses on the study of the causal plane (Angelic and Light Beings) and its effect on the physical world. Students who complete the first section are eligible for certification as Spiritual Healers, and those who complete the second receive certification as Metaphysican Practitioners.

The RoHun Institute offers a RoHun Therapy certification program. RoHun is a transformational therapy that blends spiritual and psychological processes to promote individual evolution on both levels. It clears clients' blocks and self-limitations, balances the male-female energies, sets in motion a positive energy field that attracts loving experiences, encourages self-realization and transformation, and helps activate spiritual and psychic abilities. RoHun therapists are etheric surgeons, psychically and spiritually trained to alter faulty thought patterns, adept at opening the spiritual perception of clients, and dedicated to being channels of healing. There are four levels of RoHun classes below the master's level. RoHun I teaches the use of RoHun cards as a psychotherapeutic tool designed to facilitate healing and self-growth. RoHun II teaches the purification process. RoHun III teaches therapy for release, healing, self-insight, and perception of the Higher Self. And RoHun IV teaches techniques to move into greater depth of the unconscious where elements of the shadows are surfaced and excised.

The Church of Wisdom is affiliated with Delphi University, and ordains graduates of RoHun training as ministers upon payment of a $100 ordination fee. Ordination is optional, but it does provide church authority to conduct spiritual counseling therapy and alternative medical therapy, as well as all other functions of a traditional ministry.

In addition to offering certificates, Delphi offers bachelor's, master's, and doctoral degrees.

How long it takes: Mediumship—8 days
Spiritual Healer—7 days
Metaphysican—5 days
RoHun Therapy—5 months to 2 years

What it costs: Mediumship Training—$1,600
Spiritual Healer—$1,500
Metaphysician—$1,200
RoHun I—$750
RoHun II—$1,600
RoHun III—$1,200
RoHun IV—$1,200

DoveStar Institute
50 Whitehall Road
Hooksett, NH 03106-2104
(603) 669-5104
(603) 669-9497
Fax: (603) 625-1919

120 Court Street
Plymouth, MA 02360
(508) 830-0068
Fax: (508) 830-0288

39 Main Street
Attleboro, MA 02703
(508) 222-1683
Fax: (508) 222-3691

4C Northridge Drive
Hilton Head Island, SC 29928
(803) 342-3361
Fax: (803) 342-3639

The institute offers practitioner training in Alchemia, a system of core energy work. Practitioners activate the Universal Fifth Dimensional Energy to help individuals achieve complete, vibrant wellness by tapping their inner capacity for self-healing. Classes include Vibrational Healing, Alchemia Bodywork, Etheric Release, Hypnotherapy, Four Forces, RENEW, and Alchemy and Physiology.

The institute also offers training programs in hypnotherapy and colon hydrotherapy. See the appropriate sections for more information.

How long it takes: 3 months

What it costs: $3,025

The institute accepts credit cards. Some work-study positions are available.

The Academy of Natural Healing
40 West 72nd Street, Suite 117
New York, NY 10023
(212) 724-8782

The academy offers certification training in Natural Healing. The program emphasizes a multidisciplinary approach to healing, integrating a broad range of healing modalities with theological, psychotherapeutic, anthropological, and other studies. Classes include acupressure and reflexology points, the five elements, craniosacral points, shamanism, nutrition and herbs, anatomy and physiology, meal planning, color therapy, creative visualization, chakras/kundalini, and homeopathy. Students also learn to discover what they really want, resolve personal struggles, improve relationships, become spiritually focused, and create financial independence. Entrepreneurial skills are also taught, preparing students to set up their own practice.

The academy offers a Healing Team Apprenticeship program that gives students hands-on, supervised experience working with clients.

How long it takes: 155 hours

What it costs: $2,700

Work-study is available to many students.

Barbara Brennan School of Healing
P.O. Box 2005
East Hampton, NY 11937
(516) 329-0951
Fax: (516) 324-9745
registrar@barbarabrennan.com
www.barbarabrennan.com

The school offers a certificate program that trains professional Healing Science practitioners. Students learn to perceive the aura, balance and strengthen the Human Energy Field, discern illnesses, channel, and use spiritual guidance for healing. The training also familiarizes students with the psychodynamics of the Human Energy Field and helps them discover and awaken the healer within through self-responsibility, personal development, and living within the Universal Principle of Healing. Various deep healing techniques are taught, such as healing with color and sound, Life Task healing, and Core Star healing, as well as more mundane topics such as anatomy and physiology. Graduates are qualified to establish their own private practices in Healing Science.

How long it takes: 4 years (part-time)

What it costs: $20,800

Credit cards are accepted and a payment plan is available.

Eastern Healing Arts Center
Tian Enterprises
3601 Ingleside Road
Shaker Heights, OH 44122-5003
(800) 859-4343
(216) 475-4712
Fax: (216) 752-3348
www.qi-healing.com

The center offers certification programs in Chinese Qigong Instruction and Eastern Healing Arts. Chinese Qigong is a mind/body technique used to improve health, prevent disease, and generate vitality by circulating Qi, or life energy, through the body's energy channels. Both programs are offered as a correspondence courses, which include brief instructor contact for assessment and certification.

The Chinese Qigong Instruction course includes classes such as Qigong Relaxation, Waving Body, Small Heaven, Basic Healing Techniques, Ying-Yang Balance, Common Troubles in Qigong Classes, and How to Help a Student Feel Qi Flow.

The Eastern Healing Arts course covers Qi Induction into the Body, 365 Acupoints, Shao-Lin Stick 36 Forms, Mind Power Special Training, Mystery Healing Techniques, and Successful Ways for Healing Workers.

How long it takes: Qigong Instructor Course—4 months
Eastern Healing Arts—4 months

What it costs: Qigong Instructor Course—$1,250
Eastern Healing Arts—$1,250

Credit cards are accepted and a number of payment plans are available.

The Practical Psychic Institute of Greater Cincinnati
P.O. Box 9874
Cincinnati, OH 45209
(513) 521-4581

The Practical Psychic Institute offers four levels of training that prepare students for private practice as psychic readers and energy healers. Level I, Personal Healing and Meditation, teaches students to communicate psychically from their heart centers, establish their spiritual identities, distinguish and separate their energy from other people's, open, close and clean their chakras, and dissolve energy blocks. Level II, Expanding Psychic and Healing Skills, offers advanced techniques to increase clairvoyance and clairaudience. Instruction includes a comprehensive view of the chakra system, how to work with the layers of the aura, and how to increase healing energy channels through connection with the Healing Master Guide. In Level III, Psychic Reading and Healing Practicum, students learn reader preparation techniques, professional ethics, and powerful healing methods, and complete several professional-level psychic readings. It is after completion of Level III that students are able to provide professional services as psychic readers. Level IV, How to Channel Your Guides, teaches advanced techniques for becoming a conscious channel. Students learn how to interview guides, choose which guides to bring in and which to release, identify and clear karma, and maintain seniority over channeling sessions. The institute offers ongoing professional training to graduates of Level IV.

How long it takes: Personal Healing and Meditation—3 days
Expanding Psychic and Healing Skills—2 days
Psychic Reading and Healing Practicum—3 days
How to Channel Your Guides—3 days

What it costs: Personal Healing and Meditation—$150
Expanding Psychic and Healing Skills—$175
Psychic Reading and Healing Practicum—$195
How to Channel Your Guides—$195

Institute of Multidimensional Cellular Healing
Star Route, Box 5AB
Bastrop, TX 78602-9686
(800) 809-1290
(512) 332-2223
Fax: (512) 332-2223
mch@bastrop.net

The institute offers both home study and in-person practitioner training courses in Multidimensional Cellular Healing. MCH is a technique
for releasing energetic patterns, including thoughts and feelings, from
past lives, past dimensions, and past experiences. Some of the benefits
of MCH include personal empowerment, freedom from recurring destructive emotions, clarification of one's core patterns and soul purpose,
and a clear connection with the Higher Self. MCH practitioners learn
techniques such as nervous system and spinal cord balancing, living light breath, clairvoyant listening, etheric psychic surgery, energetic scanning, and chakra clearing and balancing. Other topics include
group regressions, working with children and animals, dehaunting physical locations, holographic picturing, and recovery of oversoul frag-
ments.

The home study course consists of books, video and audiotapes, a
phone session with an MCH staff member, and finally an in-person,
hands-on training.

How long it takes: Correspondence course—students work at their
own pace. Once they've completed the home study,
they attend a 3-day certification seminar.

What it costs: $777

Credit cards are accepted.

Adona School of Healing
2756 Northeast 95th Street
Seattle, WA 98115
(206) 527-9489

The school offers an Energy Work training program designed to help
students develop proficiency in various methods of healing. Trainees
learn to open energy channels, sense, direct, and transmute energies,

work with chakras and entities, deal with past life and karmic issues, and use psychic surgery, affirmations, and nutritional advice. Classes include The Chakras, Working within the Auric Field, Discovering the Healer Within, Keeping Your Own Space, The Body/Mind Relationship, Affirmations and Visualizations for Healing, and Healing and Wholism of Body/Mind/Spirit.

How long it takes: 3 years (part-time)

What it costs: $5,400

Awakenings and Clairvoyant Training
Glen Head, NY

Administrative Office and Additional Courses:
5816 143rd Street Southwest
Edmonds, WA 98026
(425) 787-6155

Awakenings offers a clairvoyant training certification class that prepares students to become professional readers and healers. Students first attend an introductory workshop, Awakenings One, which teaches the basics of using psychic abilities and healing gifts. They then take the clairvoyant training, an in-depth study of psychic reading and healing that trains student to listen to their own information, read energy levels, and offer professional clairvoyant readings. The program also teaches students to balance their own and others' energy, stay in their power, own their divine identity, and travel into many dimensions. Students develop a variety of techniques, such as DNA reprogramming and connecting people to the Divine, that allows them to provide flexible and professional services.

How long it takes: Awakenings One—2 days
                      Clairvoyant Training—6 months (part-time)

What it costs: Awakenings One—$200
                      Clairvoyant Training—$2,000

Credit cards are accepted.

Lightstreams Diamond and Gemstone Therapy

3272 California Avenue Southwest
Seattle, WA 98116
(206) 932-1671
Fax: (206) 933-0291
lightstreams@earthlink.net
www.earthlink.net/~lightstreams

Diamond and Gemstone Therapy is a set of techniques that uses therapeutic-quality diamonds and gemstones to enhance well-being, clarify goals and life directions, identify and work with core issues, change habitual or dysfunctional patterns, and heighten spiritual awareness.

Lightstreams offers a training program in which students learn to use diamonds and gemstones to help clients clear energetic blockages and accumulations, recognize their bodies' blueprint for perfect health, open communication between various aspects of the self, and nourish and strengthen weak areas. The program consists of three levels of training. In Level I, Basic Therapeutics, students acquaint themselves with the six most commonly used gemstones, sensitize themselves to gemstone energy, learn some simple therapy techniques, and practice sensitivity exercises and visualizations. In Level II, Earthstones, students learn about elementary diagnostics, twelve commonly used therapeutic earthstones, which gemstones to use for which issues, body energetics, and how to use gemstones with intention. In Level III, Color Ray Stones, students gain knowledge of eight color ray gemstones, thirty-eight new gemstones, the different vibrations of color stones and colors in general, and continue to sensitize themselves to gemstone energy and understand body energetics. Finally, Lightstreams offers an internship that trains students to do gemstone therapy with pets, create a gemstone pharmacy, use gemstones with energy fields, for spiritual growth, business, and detoxification, prescribe gemstone necklaces, and set up their own therapy business.

How long it takes: 6 months

What it costs: $360

Chapter 13

✳ ✳ ✳ ✳

Outdoors and Active

Almost every outdoor and active career is alternative, especially when compared to a desk-bound corporate job. But many outdoor careers—commercial fisherman, organic farmer, park ranger—aren't in fields that have vocational certification programs. And many other active careers, particularly those in sports and recreation—such as being a tennis, hang-gliding, or golf instructor—require that you already be highly proficient in the field. The outdoor and active career training programs in this chapter, on the other hand, help students with little or no expertise in a field attain a professional level of ability. Of course, it would be silly to enroll in a commercial diving school without some little diving experience—at least enough to know you don't hate the water. But for the most part, the following programs presume little or no previous training. If you want a physically oriented career but your leisure activities aren't marketable, consider the following schools.

This chapter also includes one program that didn't fit well in any category: Clown School. So we'll just mention up front that it's buried in the Miscellaneous section if you're interested.

Diving ◦ ◦ ◦

There are many specialties within the commercial diving field: underwater construction, salvage, testing, photography and video, and emergency medicine. Although some of the work is sort of antialternative, such as building offshore oil platforms, all of it takes place underwater—it doesn't get much less conventional than that. If you're interested in a physical field with many opportunities and you've enjoyed some diving in the past, you may enjoy one of the many commercial diving jobs.

College of Oceaneering
272 South Fries Avenue
Wilmington, CA 90744
(800) 432-3483
(310) 834-2501
Fax: (310) 834-7132
www.diveco.com

The college offers three professional commercial diving programs: MedTech Diving, SpecTech Diving, and WeldTech Diving. The MedTech program prepares students for a career in emergency medical care. The program includes EMT training and advanced diving medicine courses.

The SpecTech program prepares students to work in underwater inspection, nondestructive testing, underwater still photography, videography, ultrasonic testing, and magnetic particle inspection. Students pursuing this concentration are most commonly employed as inspectors of underwater structures.

The WeldTech program teaches underwater and topside burning, and wet shielded metal-arc welding. The work of underwater welders includes cleaning and preparation of weld surfaces, burning, and fabrication of jigs and supports.

How long it takes: MedTech—1 year
SpecTech—1 year
WeldTech—1 year

What it costs: MedTech—$16,500
SpecTech—$16,500
WeldTech—$16,500

Santa Barbara City College Marine Diving Technology
721 Cliff Drive
Santa Barbara, CA 93109
(805) 965-0581, ext. 2426
Fax: (805) 963-7222
odale@gate1.sbcc.cc.ca.us
www.sbcc.cc.ca.us

The college offers a Marine Diving Technology program that allows students to concentrate in Professional Commercial Diving or Recreational Diving. The Commercial Diving program covers all aspects of commercial diving, hyperbarics, bell/saturation diving emergency medicine, and remote operated vehicles.

The Recreational Diving program offers much of the same training, but graduates are more likely to become diving instructors or dive masters, or work in the SCUBA industry in retail, marketing, management, equipment repair, and emergency medicine.

How long it takes: Professional Commercial Diving—1 year
Recreational Diving—1 year

What it costs: Professional Commercial Diving—$6,419
Recreational Diving—$6,239

Federal financial aid is available.

Louisiana Technical College
P.O. Drawer 2148
Morgan City, LA 70381
(504) 380-2436
Fax: (504) 380-2440

Louisiana Tech offers a training program in commercial diving. Students learn about the physics and physiology of hyperbaric environments, and gain hands-on experience in equipment maintenance and operation. The curriculum includes air decompression, diving medicine, recompression chamber operation, rigging, logs, records, and standards, environmental hazards, underwater work, mixed-gas diving, operations planning, and job-seeking skills.

How long it takes: 3 months

What it costs: $1,440

The Divers Academy of the Eastern Seaboard
2500 South Broadway
Camden, NJ 08104
(800) 238-3483
(609) 966-1871
Fax: (609) 541-4355
http://diveweb.com/diversacademy

The Divers Academy offers a commercial diving training program. Courses include Diving Physiology, Decompression, Hyperbaric Chamber Operation, Deep Sea Diving Techniques, Cutting and Welding, Demolition, Rigging, Salvage, Inland Diving, Mixed Gas Diving, Saturation, First Aid and CPR, Underwater Photography, Remotely Operated Vehicles, Non-Destructive Testing, and Employment Opportunities. Specific topics include environmental hazards and marine life, hand jetting, low and high explosives, wreck removal, waterway evaluation, sheet pile inspection, deep dive systems, suit repair, emergency rescue, and ultrasonic testing.

How long it takes: 20 weeks

What it costs: $7,100

Financial aid and payment plans are available.

The Ocean Corporation
10840 Rockley Road
Houston, TX 77099
(800) 321-0298
(281) 530-0202
Fax: (281) 530-9143
admissions@ocorp.com
www.ocorp.com

The Ocean Corporation offers four training courses in Professional Diving: Commercial Diver, Ultimate Diver, Non-Destructive Testing/ Inspection, and Medical Technician. The Commercial Diver training includes instruction in safety and first aid, rigging, decompression, emergency procedures, mixed-gas physics and medicine, bell/saturation systems, welding, and hazardous waste operations.

The Ultimate Diver training includes commercial air diving,

mixed-gas/bell diving, underwater welding and cutting, hazardous waste operations, emergency response, and remote operated vehicles. Students also learn chamber operations, mixed-gas physics, underwater welding, and magnetic particle, liquid penetrant, and ultrasonic inspection.

The Non-Destructive Testing/Inspection course includes courses in magnetic particle, liquid penetrant, ultrasonic, and remote inspection techniques.

The Medical Technician training includes coursework in assisted ventilation, intubation, treating shock, intravenous fluid therapy, bandaging and splinting, helicopter evacuation, pulmonary overinflation syndromes, and oxygen toxicity.

How long it takes: Commercial Diver—22 weeks
                      Ultimate Diver—30 weeks
                      Testing/Inspection—8 weeks
                      Medical Technician—5 weeks

What it costs: Commercial Diver—$7,900
                      Ultimate Diver—$9,900
                      Testing/Inspection—$3,000
                      Medical Technician—$3,000

Financial aid is available.

Divers Institute of Technology
4315 11th Avenue Northwest
Seattle, WA 98107-0667
(800) 634-8377
(206) 783-5542
Fax: (206) 783-2658

The institute offers a training program in commercial diving. Courses include Communications, Decompression, Diving Physics and Physiology, Medical Aspects of Diving, First Aid and Safety, Rigging, Deep Sea Diving, Hot Water System, Offshore Oil Industry, Salvage, Cutting and Welding, Underwater Photography, Underwater Television and Video, Mixed Gas, Haz-Mat, Saturation, Non-Destructive Testing, Inspection Reports, and Employment Opportunities. Students learn about emergency rescue, crane signals, marine life, search procedures, pipe laying, mud pumping and sealing, boat salvage, metallic arc cutting techniques, surface decompression, magnetic particle testing, and report drawing, sketching, and writing.

The institute allows graduates to return for refresher training at no cost except for consumables used.

How long it takes: 7 months

What it costs: $10,500

Payment plans and financial aid are available.

Guiding and Leadership ◆ ◆ ◆

Most of the programs in this section train river raft guides, who lead groups of thrill-seeking tourists safely through white water and beyond. In addition to rafting and safety skills, many river guide schools also teach students to cook in the outdoors, lead group activities, and provide river-specific educational information. Other programs train ski and mountain guides and outdoor leaders, who lead groups in a variety of outdoor environments and activities.

Many guides only work seasonally, but it's almost always possible, if it's your only livelihood, to do it full-time—if this is your goal, be sure to bring it up when you contact the schools. And some guides combine two or more of the outdoor activities, working as river guides in the summer and ski guides in the winter, for example.

Outdoor Leadership Training Seminars
P.O. Box 20281
Denver, CO 80220
(800) 331-7238
(303) 333-7831
rmedrick@OLTS-BT.com

Outdoor Leadership offers an outdoor leader training program that introduces a complete range of outdoor skills and environments. Instruction includes training in inner game awareness, tai chi, nature ritual and celebration, deep ecology, ecopsychology, vision quest, communications, peer counseling, and program design and facilitation. Field training includes rock climbing, backpacking, mountaineering, ice and snow climbing, ski mountaineering, back country skiing, rafting, canyoneering, desert travel, wilderness medicine, and avalanche awareness and prediction skills. Other skills taught include map navigation, defining goals, breathing and balance awareness, meditation, chanting, and leadership skills. Outdoor Leadership also offers various short-term seminars such as River Gods and Goddesses, Rio Chama Herbal Discovery Trip, Canyon Quest and Spiritual Warrior Training, Women's Canyon Quest, and The Wilderness Warrior for Men.

How long it takes: Beginners—8 months
Advanced Students—5 months

What it costs: 5-month course—$3,800
8-month course—$5,100

Payment plans are available.

American Mountain Guides Association
710 Tenth Street, Suite 101
Golden, CO 80401
(303) 271-0984
Fax: (303) 271-1377
info@amga.com
www.climbnet.com/amga

The AMGA trains rock, alpine, and ski guides. Students must have experience in the discipline for which they're training to be eligible for the following programs.

Students in the alpine guide program learn how to guide frozen waterfalls, prepare and orient clients, select appropriate equipment, manage time and pace, and evaluate anchor construction. The also learn about risk management and client care, technical guiding skills, navigation and route finding, roping strategies, and rescue techniques. Students practice all of these skills in a variety of terrains, including alpine, winter waterfall, steep snow, crevassed and highly broken glaciated environments.

The rock guide program provides instruction in client orientation and preparation, equipment selection, time and pace management, anchor construction, rope management, rappelling and lowering with clients, ascending methods, risk management, developing strategies for multiple clients on longer routes, and application of techniques based on terrain transition. Students get a chance to learn and climb in diverse terrains and environments.

Topics covered in the ski guide program include snowpack evaluation, hazard awareness and risk management, avalanche forecasting and rescue, route finding, group management, client assessment and care, record keeping, navigation, winter survival, and decision making. Students also learn about snow and ice climbing techniques, rope management skills, lowering and rappelling, performing improvised rescues, and overnight ski tour and snow camping techniques.

How long it takes: Alpine Guide Program—45 days
Rock Guide Program—28 days
Ski Guide Program—27 days

What it costs: Alpine Guide Program—$8,290
Rock Guide Program—$5,530
Ski Guide Program—$5,000

Some scholarships are available.

Outdoor Adventure River Specialists (OARS)

P.O. Box 67
Angels Camp, CA 95222
(209) 736-4677
Fax: (209) 736-2902
reservations@oars.com
www.oars.com

OARS offers a training program in river guiding. The course covers equipment maintenance and repair, menu planning, food preparation, emergency medicine, search and rescue techniques, and river ethics. The core of the program is comprised of swift-water navigation, swift-water rescue, boat rigging, camping and campsite selection, and equipment care and repair. Classes cover such subjects as oar and paddle boat techniques, route selection and safety, ropes, knots, anchors, dealing with accidents and evacuations, load placement, rigging frames, anchoring boats overnight, kitchen and tent placement, minimum impact strategies, flash floods, camp talk, boat patching, and emergency oar, paddle, and tent repair.

How long it takes: 8 days

What it costs: $795

Adventure Connection
P.O. Box 475
Coloma, CA 95613
(800) 556-6060
(916) 626-7385
Fax: (916) 626-9268

Adventure Connection offers a training program in river guiding that consists of on-the-water experiences, lectures, group meetings, and guest lectures. The course of study includes river menu planning, equipment maintenance and repair, food preparation, and search and rescue techniques. Students leave the program with a general knowledge of white water rafting that prepares them for entry-level positions as guides.

How long it takes: 1 week

What it costs: $800

Ahwahnee Whitewater
P.O. Box 1161
Columbia, CA 95310
(800) 359-9790
(209) 533-1401
Fax: (209) 533-1409

Ahwahnee offers a training program in river guiding. The program teaches river dynamics and navigation, safety and rescue, effective decision making, planning and organizing safe and successful outings, oar and paddle boat guiding, river etiquette, rigging and derigging equipment, and river camp setup.

How long it takes: 8 days

What it costs: $760

The American River Touring Association (ARTA) River Trips
24000 Casa Loma Road
Groveland, CA 95321
(800) 323-2782
(209) 962-7873
arta-info@arta.org

ARTA offers a training program in river guiding that focuses on paddling and rowing in swift, steep, and small-volume rivers. Students learn advanced paddle techniques, oar-paddle combination rafts, technical white water, swift water rescue, and advanced rescue and rope work. Upon completion, qualified graduates are offered positions as assistant guides for ARTA's commercial trips. ARTA also offers shorter-term educational workshops, and recreational rafting trips in the Sierras, Cascades, Rockies, and Grand Canyon.

How long it takes: 12 days

What it costs: $1,080

Durango Rivertrippers
720 Main Avenue
Durango, CO 81301
(303) 259-0289
Fax: (303) 385-0645

Durango Rivertrippers offers a training program in river guiding. Students spend the first half of the program on the water with a certified instructor, learning how to read the water. During the second half, they guide the raft themselves, with the instructor observing. The curriculum includes rigging boats, put-ins and take-outs, handling accidents, first aid, working with oar and paddle boats, and learning how to read currents, eddies, and rapids.

How long it takes: 10 days

What it costs: $400

Mild to Wild Rafting
11 Rio Vista Circle
Durango, CO 81301
(970) 382-0545
(800) 567-6745
mildwild@rmii.com
www.mild2wildrafting.com

Mild to Wild offers a training program in river guiding. Classes cover swift water rescue, risk management, planning and scouting, river etiquette, crew orientation, and raft rigging. Students learn about boat handling, safety measures, the advantages and disadvantages of different types of rafts, reading rivers and currents, paddling and rowing, and handling emergencies. They also learn to handle river obstacles such as eddies, ferries, holes, waves, laterals, low head dams, tongues, and sleepers.

How long it takes: 10 days

What it costs: $500

Rocky Mountain Outdoor Center
10281 Highway 50
Howard, CO 81233
(800) 255-5784
(719) 942-3214
Fax: (719) 942-3215
73354.2030@compuserve.com
www.rmoc.com

Rocky Mountain offers a training program in river guiding. Topics covered include proper use of equipment, rigging paddle rafts, river features, river reading strategies, maneuvering the raft, safety techniques, paddle talk to guests, trip organization, trip leader responsibility, river rescue and emergency procedures, and how to minimize outdoor resource impact. Students learn types of hazards and rapids, eddy turns and peel outs, passenger positioning, river commands, paddle signals, evacuation routes, rope throwing and belays, and how to deal with hypothermia. Students spend roughly thirty hours aboard a raft guided by an instructor and twenty hours guiding the raft themselves with an instructor aboard.

How long it takes: 10 days

What it costs: $550

Whitewater Voyageurs
P.O. Box 346
10240 Highway 50
Poncha Springs, CO 81242
(800) 255-2585
(719) 539-7618
Fax: (719) 539-7610

Whitewater offers a training program in river guiding. In addition to teaching rafting skills, the training emphasizes the ability to think well under pressure, develop motivational skills, and use inherent leadership abilities. The program includes classroom study, on the water training, and medical certification, which is required to be a guide on the Arkansas river where the training takes place.

How long it takes: 17 days

What it costs: $325

Canyonlands Field Institute
P.O. Box 68
Moab, UT 84532
(800) 860-5262
(435) 259-7750
CFlinfo@canyonlandsfieldinst.org
www.canyonlandsfieldinst.org

The institute offers a training program in river guiding. The program covers river ecology, boat rigging, rowing skills, safety practices, low-impact camp routines, righting flipped rafts, rescue scene management, multipoint anchors, and basic medical skills. Students also learn about protecting public lands, risk management, and how to enhance visitor satisfaction. Specific classes include Wilderness Safety and CPR, Guiding Desert Waters, Canyon River Rescue, and River Skills. Canyonlands also hosts an Outdoor Science School for youth, a Graduate Residency Program in Environmental Education on the Colorado Plateau, and numerous weekend workshops and trips.

How long it takes: 4 months

What it costs: $1,565

Miscellaneous Outdoors and Active ◆ ◆ ◆

This section includes just two careers: hot air balloon piloting and professional clowning. Hot air balloon pilots usually offer family adventures, sunset tours, romantic rides, and other recreational ballooning activities. And the clown school, affiliated with Ringling Brothers, is a professional clown training.

Adventure Flights
19301 Jasmine Court
Lake Elsinore, CA 92530
(909) 678-4334
Fax: (909) 678-2011

Adventure Flights offers a training course in Commercial Piloting of Hot Air Balloons in which students learn to fly both passengers and cargo. The curriculum includes safety, venting, and landing procedures. Students also learn balloon piloting instruction techniques.

How long it takes: 7 to 10 days

What it costs: $2,995

Cost includes balloon, all equipment, insurance, and chase crew.

World Balloon
4800 Eubank Northeast
Albuquerque, NM 87111
(505) 293-6800
Fax: (505) 294-5619

World Balloon offers a professional training course in Hot Air Balloon Piloting. Students are instructed in technical and safety skills, and given reviews and a series of quizzes to prepare them for the FAA written examination. Students receive a combination of on-ground classroom learning and over thirty-five hours of instruction in the air. Upon completion of the program, students are prepared to take the FAA examination for certification as a commercial hot air balloon pilot.

How long it takes: 3 to 5 weeks (depending on the weather)

What it costs: $7,560

Ringling Bros. and Barnum and Bailey Clown College
P.O. Box 39040
Sarasota, FL 34238
(800) 755-9637

326 ♦ *You're Certifiable*

The Clown College trains clowns. The school is dedicated to the preservation and perpetuation of the "grand, glorious, and gaffawrious" art of clowning. The training program begins with structured classes that cover the history of clowning, classic clown routines, slaps and falls, and the physicality of clowning. The more advanced training offers individual instruction, helping students develop their own routines and material. Courses include Character Development, Improvisation, Makeup, Pantomime, Mask, Gag Development, Skills, Acrobatics, Dance, Costume Construction, and Prop Construction. Students develop a multidimensional clown character, learn new ways to imaginatively interpret a given situation, learn about the three basic categories of clown makeup (Whiteface, Auguste, and Character), write and structure clown gags, and learn the essentials of comedic gymnastics, stilt walking, unicycling, and juggling. Students are required to audition for the school; however, no experience is required, "just a sound body and a silly mind."

How long it takes: 8 weeks

What it costs: Tuition is free—the circus treats the program as a feeder school. You will, however, spend $140 per week for housing, and $600 for materials.

Chapter 14

✳ ✳ ✳ ✳

Therapy

There's more to therapy than traditional couch-based psychoanalysis. There are alternative therapeutic modalities that rely less on the expertise of the counselor than the resources of the client. There are therapies that focus on dealing with specific issues and problems instead of psychological understanding or resolution. There are therapies that speak directly to the senses: sound, touch, movement, or a sense of inner knowing. And there are therapies that are just plain . . . alternative. These training programs will train you to help people move through their blocks and issues, and facilitate inner work, self-actualization, and awareness.

The categories in this chapter are Breathwork and Rebirthing, Hypnotherapy, and Miscellaneous. The Miscellaneous section is particularly large and diverse, containing therapeutic methods such as shamanic counseling, movement therapy, a home-based program for special-needs children, sex therapy, Focusing, and rapid eye therapy.

Not included in this chapter are training programs in music, art, and dance that require master's degrees. If you're interested in music therapy training, contact the National Association for Music Therapy

(8455 Colesville Road, Suite 930, Silver Spring, MD 20910, [301] 589-3300) or the American Association for Music Therapy, Inc. (P.O. Box 80012, Valley Forge, PA 19484, [610] 265-4006). For degrees in art therapy, contact the American Art Therapy Association, Inc. (1202 Allanson Road, Mundelein, IL 60060, [874] 949-6064). And for information about dance therapy, write the American Dance Therapy Association (2000 Century Plaza, Suite 108, 10632 Little Patuxent Parkway, Columbia, MD 21044).

Breathwork and Rebirthing

The training programs in this section teach students to help clients tap into the power of breath for health, happiness, and self-discovery. Although the various methods all focus on the breath, some combine breathing with music and art, some with bodywork, and some with verbal counseling. If you're curious about offering transformative, enlightening, and healing breathwork to individuals or groups, be sure to get information from a number of the schools to find the one that most closely matches your interests.

Grof Transpersonal Training
20 Sunnyside Avenue, A-314
Mill Valley, CA 94941
(415) 383-8779
Fax: (415) 383-0965

Grof Transpersonal Training offers a certification program in Holotropic Breathwork, a technique of self-exploration and healing based on ancient spiritual practices, modern consciousness research, various depth psychologies, and transpersonal psychology. The method uses accelerated breathing, evocative music, focused energy release, and mandala drawing to unleash the spontaneous healing potential of the psyche in nonordinary states of consciousness. Courses include the Healing Potential of Non-Ordinary States of Consciousness, Abnormal Psychology and Architecture of Psychopathology, the Practice of Holotropic Breathwork, Understanding and Treating the Crises of Transformation, Addiction and Spirituality, Cross-Cultural Work with Symbols and Shamanic Practice, and Perinatal and Transpersonal Themes in Art and Culture.

Students must experience at least five Holotropic Breathwork sessions before applying to the practitioner training. The basic training program includes attending workshops and seminars, seven training modules, and a certification seminar. Finally, an apprenticeship program is available to students who wish to lead their own workshops.

How long it takes: Basic Training Program—150 hours
Seven Modules—6 days each
Certification Seminar—2 weeks

As the training involves deep personal work, the minimum time for completion is 2 years from the time at which the trainee begins attending modules.

What it costs: Basic Training Program—$1,500 to $2,500
Seven Modules—$895 to $995 each
Certification Seminar—$2,300

Mendocino School of Holistic Massage and Advanced Healing Arts
2680 Road B
Redwood Valley, CA 95470
(707) 485-8197

The school offers two rebirthing certification programs: Rebirther and Master Rebirther. The Rebirther course trains students to facilitate the uncovering and resolution of pre- and perinatal trauma in adults, children, and infants. The course covers current perspectives on pre- and perinatal psychology and introduces innovative methods to access the psyche and heal the inner child. Classes include Imprinting and Core Assumptions, Pre- and Perinatal Psychology, Cellular Memory and Early Imprinting, Personal Negatives, and Conception and Beyond. Completion of a practicum and ten rebirthing sessions with the instructor are required for certification.

The Master Rebirther training course provides advanced training in Water Rebirthing, a method of pre- and perinatal regression therapy. Master classes include Integrative Holistic Massage, Advanced Study of Pre- and Perinatal Trauma, a Practicum, and Self-Employment Training.

How long it takes: Rebirther—100 hours
Master Rebirther—180 hours

What it costs: Rebirther—$660
Master Rebirther—$1,300

Middendorf Breath Institute
4335 Vermont Street
San Francisco, CA 94107
(415) 255-2174
(415) 255-2467

The institute offers a certification program in Middendorf Breathwork, an artistic form of somatic education based on connecting with the natural breath to allow the essence of the Self to unfold to its true definition. The program combines personal work on one's self with training to apply the work in group classes and individual hands-on sessions. Students learn to sense the five breathing spaces and the direction of the central breath forces, experience and understand breath rhythms, vocalize breath movement, explore the connection between breath and the creative foundation of Self, and integrate the training experience into daily life and a professional practice. Thirty-four sessions with a certified Middendorf practitioner are included as part of the training program. Prerequisite for the program is a basic knowledge of anatomy and psychology, particularly Jungian work.

How long it takes: 3 years (part-time)

What it costs: $12,600

SUNDOOR Foundation for Transpersonal Education
Box 669
Twain Harte, CA 95383
(800) 755-1701
(209) 928-1700
Fax: (209) 928-4800

The foundation offers a Breathwork Practitioner training. The program requires that students first attend SUNDOOR's Fire Initiation Training—a course in leadership, personal development, and spiritual expansion that helps students eliminate past negative patterns, regain a sense of purpose, and connect with a universal energy source for guidance and direction.

Then students begin the certification program itself, which trains practitioners of SUNDOOR Breathwork, an empowerment practice that taps into the breath to unlock the life energy, vital enthusiasm, and clarity necessary to achieve dreams. Breathwork Practitioners help their clients release old patterns of failure, clarify their life purpose, enhance and expand the connection to their spiritual core, and experience renewed vigor and excitement in all facets of life.

SUNDOOR also offers a Firewalk Instructor certification training. See Miscellaneous Consulting and Counseling for information.

How long it takes: Fire Initiation training—7 days
Breathwork Practitioner training—8 days

What it costs: Fire Initiation training—$995
Breathwork Practitioner training—$995

Credit cards are accepted and payment plans are available.

The International Breath Institute
2525 Arapahoe Avenue, E4-287
Boulder, CO 80302
(303) 444-8615
Fax: (303) 442-0559
comments@transformbreathing.com
www.transformbreathing.com

The institute offers training in TransformBreathing Energy Management System, or TEMS. This system combines TransformBreathing—a physical and psychospiritual approach to radiant health, emotional balance, mental clarity, peak performance, and joy—with movement, music, interactive exercises, subconscious exploration, emotional repatterning, autogenic training, neural reassociation, and mental restructuring. The TEMS training consists of four modules: TransformBreathing for Health, Joy, and Aliveness; Emotional Maturity and Energy Management; Inspiration, Intuition, and Insight; and Facilitator Certification Seminar. In the first three modules, participants experience the benefits of TEMS in their own life, and in the fourth module, they learn to instruct others in TEMS as certified TransformBreathing Facilitators. Classes in the first three modules include Subliminal Affirmation, Imagery and TransformBreathing, Rites of Balance, Kinesthetic Associative Reprogramming, Breathing Analysis, Identifying and Opening Inner Pathways for Inspiration, Developing a Model for Miracle Consciousness, and Experiencing Altered States. The goals of the Certification Seminar include transcending self-limiting concepts, experiencing transpersonal states, and learning to conduct and market individual and group TransformBreathing sessions.

How long it takes: 2 days per module

The Facilitator Certification Seminar includes an optional third day to help students with presentation and teaching skills.

What it costs: Module I—$395
                       Each, for Modules II and III—$600
                       Facilitator Certification Module—$700
                       All 4 Modules—$2,000

Credit cards are accepted and a payment plan is available.

Rebirth International
P.O. Box 118
Walton, NY 13856
(607) 865-8254
Fax: (607) 865-8247

Rebirth International offers a professional rebirther training course based on the experience of spiritual purification techniques using earth, air, fire, water, mind, and spiritual community. Courses include Prosperity Consciousness, The Ultimate Truth Process, The Science of Personal Aliveness, The Business of Self Improvement, Philosophy of Immortality, and Vision Quest. Rebirth International also offers advanced trainings—a three-week training, a year-long training, and a three-year training—and seminars covering relationships, prosperity, weight control, and fire walks.

How long it takes: 1 week

What it costs: $800

The cost includes food and lodging.

Installment plans are available.

Relationships Unlimited
P.O. Box 3399
Redmond, WA 98073
(800) 373-1718

(425) 868-3335
peter@rebirthing.com
www.rebirthing.com/peter

Relationships Unlimited offers a rebirthing school that trains rebirthing practitioners to facilitate clients' rebirthing through sessions that include both verbal counseling and the rebirthing breathing process. Students learn to use rebirthing to increase people's ability to feel and resolve the effects of their past, increase their levels of physical and spiritual energy, and cleanse the tensions held in their bodies. The curriculum includes guiding the breath, energy release and body sensations, dry and wet rebirthing, birth and relationships, the unconscious death urge, and rebirthing as a business.

How long it takes: 1 month

What it costs: $1,800

The BodyMind Academy
1247-120th Avenue, Northeast
Bellevue, WA 98005
(425) 635-0145
(425) 367-9060

The academy offers a BodyMind Breathwork Practitioner training course that incorporates rebirthing and other breathwork modalities, touch sensitivity, deep reassurance, Trustwork, Emotion Repatterning, and Visionwork. Students learn to guide clients through three areas: Breath, Emotion, and Emotion Release; Releasing Birth Trauma, Injury, and Abuse; and Purpose, Vision, and Commitment. Breath, Emotion, and Emotion Release covers breath and trust, emotion release stages, warm water breathwork, family roles and rules, and breaking family taboos about feeling. Releasing Birth Trauma, Injury, and Abuse includes courses on contacting and rescuing the inner child, healing imagery, releasing grief and pain, reexperiencing and releasing birth trauma, and addictions and breathwork. And Purpose, Vision, and Commitment covers personal healing process, personal mythology, releasing Mom, releasing Dad, emotional maturity, bliss and balance, life purpose, and claiming your vision.

The academy also offers a Counseling Hypnotherapy Practitioner training program. See Hypnotherapy for more information.

How long it takes: BodyMind Breathwork Practitioner—304 hours

What it costs: BodyMind Breathwork Practitioner—$3,000

Credit cards are accepted and payment plans are available.

Hypnotherapy • • •

Hypnotherapy is the inducement of a state of altered consciousness in which the subconscious mind becomes more accessible and open to therapeutic and other helpful suggestions. The goals of hypnotherapy range from losing weight to natural anesthesia (yes, some people do undergo surgery or dentistry using only hypnoanesthesia) to overcoming psychological blocks to achieving the potential for removing unwanted habits. Hypnotherapy is not stage hypnosis, and it's not Machiavellian mind control—in fact, it's not even all that alternative. Hypnotherapy has been around since the eighteenth century, and the American Medical Association officially recognized it back in the 1950s.

There are a number of organizations that certify hypnotherapy schools. The preeminent one seems to be the American Council of Hypnotic Examiners. That doesn't mean every worthwhile school is certified by ACHE, but their requirement of a minimum of 150 hours of training for practicing hypnotherapists seems like good sense to us. This is a career in which certification and licensing are increasingly important: ask schools where they stand.

The Alchemy Institute of Healing Arts
2310 Warwick Drive
Santa Rosa, CA 95405
(800) 950-4984
(707) 579-7984
www.hollys.com/alchemy (includes over 200 pages of articles)

The institute offers a certificate course in Alchemical Hypnotherapy, a method of hypnotherapy that relies on the Higher Self as the primary source of healing. Practitioners learn strategies for contacting, testing, and working with Inner Guides through trance, movement, and shamanic practices. They learn to help clients contact past-life memories within the collective unconscious to access creative abilities, resolve trauma, and change karma. And they learn to integrate subpersonalities, which resolves conflicting desires and goals, resulting in the unification of the will and the achievement of dreams.

The institute offers three levels of certification training: students can become Master Hypnotists, Hypnotherapists, and Alchemical Hypnotherapists. Topics covered in the Master Hypnotist certification include trance induction, posthypnotic suggestion, etheric plane communication, regression, ancient shamanic techniques, communicating with different aspects of the personality, referrals, marketing, and office management. Topics covered in the Hypnotherapist training include pain and disease control, trance induction, discovery of hidden subpersonalities, alchemical bodywork, cellular clearing techniques, weight management, clearing the trauma of sexual abuse, and working with the Inner Adolescent. The Alchemical Hypnotherapist training and certification require the mastery of additional Alchemical techniques, assisting at a basic Alchemical training, and receiving five documented Alchemical sessions.

How long it takes: Master Hypnotist—150 hours
Hypnotherapist—200 hours
Alchemical Hypnotherapist—350 hours

What it costs: Master Hypnotist—$2,805
Hypnotherapist—$3,525
Alchemical Hypnotherapist—$4,670

The institute offers an early payment discount.

Alchemical Hypnotherapy Institute of Sacramento
1215 High Street, #101
Auburn, CA 95603
(916) 446-9629
(916) 889-8505

The institute offers a training program similar to that taught by the Alchemy Institute of Healing Arts (above). The program focuses on providing powerful tools to help clients contact inner resources and resolve spiritual, emotional, and behavioral issues. Each student works with a minimum of three professional trainers, to ensure exposure to a variety of therapeutic styles. Certification training includes a Hypnotherapist certification, a Clinical Hypnotherapist certification, and

336 • *You're Certifiable*

an Alchemical Hypnotherapist certification. The Alchemical training consists of assistant teaching the Clinical Hypnotherapy program, and having ten Alchemical sessions.

How long it takes: Hypnotherapist—200 hours
Clinical Hypnotherapist—250 hours
Alchemical Hypnotherapist—350 hours

What it costs: Hypnotherapist training—$2,200
Clinical Hypnotherapist training—$675
Alchemical Hypnotherapist training—$725
(approximately)

An installment plan is available.

Center for Hypnotherapy Certification
455 Newton Avenue, #1
Oakland, CA 94606
(800) 398-0034
(510) 839-4800
Fax: (510) 836-0477
mgordon@hypnotherapycenter.com
www.hypnotherapycenter.com

The center offers three levels of hypnotherapy courses that train students to become Certified Hypnotherapists and Advanced Certified Hypnotherapists. The first level includes classes such as Habit Control, Making Hypnosis Tapes, Hypnoanesthesia, Inner Guidance Techniques, Improving Speaking and Presentation Skills, Mind-Mapping for Creative Vision, and Marketing and Business. The second level covers transformational healing, trauma release, spirit release, cognitive therapy, focusing, and accelerating performance levels. And the third level includes instruction in subpersonality healing, reframing, healing imagery and metaphor, hypnosis for childbirth, surgery, chronic illness, shamanistic and metaphysical healing, and prosperity programming.

How long it takes: Certified Hypnotherapist—100 hours
Advanced Certified Hypnotherapist—150 hours

What it costs: Certified Hypnotherapist—$1,300
Advanced Certified Hypnotherapist—$600

Credit cards are accepted and a payment plan is available.

Hypnosis Clearing House
3702 Mt. Diablo Boulevard
Lafayette, CA 94549
(510) 283-3941
Fax: (510) 283-3940
HCH@support.net
www.support.net/hch

The Clearing House offers four levels of hypnotherapy training resulting in certification as a Master Hypnotist, Hypnotherapist, and Clinical
Hypnotherapist. The first level of coursework includes basic induction
and deepening techniques, interviewing skills, hypnotic phenomena,
and a survey of theoretical approaches. Level II covers cross-cultural
issues, habit control and reframing, Jungian perspectives, skill rehearsal,
and past-life therapy. Level III discusses intuition and trance states,
dreamwork, shamanism, legal and ethical issues, and how to establish a
successful business, and includes clinical case presentations and supervision. The final level includes coursework on codependence and addiction, inner family work, death and dying, working with relationship
issues, and marketing yourself as a hypnotherapist.

How long it takes: Master Hypnotist—150 hours
Hypnotherapist—200 hours
Clinical Hypnotherapist—250 hours

What it costs: Master Hypnotist—$2,025
Hypnotherapist—$2,700
Clinical Hypnotherapist—$3,375

Credit cards are accepted and a payment plan and student loans are
available.

Hypnosis Motivation Institute
18607 Ventura Boulevard, Suite 310
Tarzana, CA 91356
(800) 682-4464
(818) 344-4464
(213) 873-6979

HMI offers a training program that leads to a career as a Certified
Hypnotherapist. Courses include Hypnotic Inductions, Maternal and

Paternal Approaches, Anchoring, Use of Paradox, Psychodynamics of Dreams, Medical Model of Hypnosis, Child Hypnosis, Hypno-diagnostic Tools, Physical and Emotional Sexuality, Substance Abuse, Crisis Intervention, Counseling and Interviewing, and Building a Successful Practice. In addition to coursework, the institute offers supervised client contact, and clinical case conferences, and provides residents with a therapy office, secretarial services, and weekly supervision so they can start their private practice while still in school. Although students receive certification before the final step—the Clinical Residency—the institute considers the residency program the most important part of the training. HMI also offers a videotaped home study course.

How long it takes: 1 year

What it costs: $9,860

Payment plans and student loans and grants are available, and credit cards are accepted.

Hypnosis Training Institute of Santa Barbara
P.O. Box 31208
Santa Barbara, CA 93130-1208
(800) 874-9766
(805) 684-8448
Fax: (805) 566-9684

The institute offers five courses that lead to professional certification as a Master Hypnotist, Hypnotherapist, and Clinical Hypnotherapist. The first three courses—Professional Hypnotism Training, Principles and Practice of Hypnotherapy, and Hypnotherapist Training—teach beginning to advanced principles and methods of hypnotherapy. They also cover step-by-step techniques for dealing with particular issues and problems, and instruct students on how to start, promote, and build their own business as a Master Hypnotist. The fourth course, Hypnotherapy in Healing and Pain Control, teaches how to use hypnotherapy as an adjunct to medical treatment, how to enable clients to live fuller and more satisfying lives, and how to help clients discover and use their own healing power. This course leads to a diploma as a Hypnotherapist. The fifth course, Studies in Clinical Hypnotherapy, teaches a variety of advanced therapeutic techniques and shows students how to work with corporations and other businesses. Upon completion of this course, students are awarded diplomas as Clinical Hypnotherapists.

How long it takes: Each of the 5 courses—50 hours in 3 weeks

What it costs: Professional Hypnotist Training—$750
Each Additional Course—$850

Credit cards are accepted.

Hypnotherapy Training Institute
4730 Alta Vista Avenue
Santa Rosa, CA 95404
(800) 256-6448
(707) 579-9023
(415) 456-5641
Fax: (707) 578-1033
hypno@sonic.net
www.sonic.net/hypno

The institute offers an eclectic training in many systems and techniques of hypnotherapy, including transpersonal hypnosis, hypnotic dreamwork, NLP, advanced ideomotor methods, MasterMind hypnosis, and Eriksonian techniques. The institute offers three levels of certification, training students to become Master Hypnotists, Hypnotherapists, and Clinical Hypnotherapists. The Master Hypnotist training begins with a course on establishing realistic goals, developing hypnotic rapport, using hypnotic metaphors, controlling addictions and habits, and using grounding and centering techniques. Students then learn about quantum cellular hypnotherapy, establishing and collapsing anchors, producing anesthesia, systematic desensitization, emotional clearing strategies, and spiritual hypnosis.

The Hypnotherapist certification requires advanced training in regression strategies, protective ideomotor methods, Gestalt, hypnotic dreamwork, psychosynthesis, parts therapy, and analytical hypnotherapy. It also introduces the business and marketing strategies necessary to build a successful practice. And the Clinical Hypnotherapist training covers the Churchill Imprint Method for transforming subconscious beliefs, core energetics, hypnoanalysis, Mulder's sandbox process, the cartography of human consciousness, experiential sessions of holotropic breathwork, and practice sessions.

How long it takes: Master Hypnotist—150 hours
Hypnotherapist—200 hours
Clinical Hypnotherapist—250 hours

The Institute offers both regular and accelerated-format classes.

What it costs: Master Hypnotist—$2,085
Hypnotherapist—$2,780
Clinical Hypnotherapist—$3,475

Credit cards are accepted.

Hypnotism Training Institute of Los Angeles
700 South Central Avenue
Glendale, CA 91204
(818) 242-1159
Fax: (818) 247-9379

HTI trains Master Hypnotists, Certified Hypnotherapists, and Certified Clinical Hypnotherapists. The Master Hypnotist training includes courses in induction techniques, trance management, posthypnotic reinduction, overcoming resistance, waking hypnosis, rewriting old scripts, instantaneous hypnosis, and developing a successful practice. It also covers age regression, abreactions, emotional ventilation, subconscious reeducation, and the reprogramming of fixed ideas from childhood. The Hypnotherapist course focuses on all aspects of healing as well as the control and elimination of pain. The Clinical Hypnotherapist course is a residency in which students gain clinical experience working with clients in a supervised setting.

How long it takes: Master Hypnotist—150 hours
Hypnotherapist—200 hours
Clinical Hypnotherapist residency—4 months

What it costs: Master Hypnotist—$2,250
Hypnotherapist—$750
Clinical Hypnotherapist residency—$750

International Association of Past Life Therapists
19744 Beach Boulevard, Suite 356
Huntington Beach, CA 92648
(714) 536-1953

Fax: (714) 960-1343
http://home.earthlink.net/~ccarbone

The association offers a Certified Past Life Therapist home study course that includes three videos, an audiotape, a script book, a Therapist's Survival Book, and a personal course study book. Students learn to use Past Life Therapy as a tool for helping people achieve their goals and overcome barriers such as phobias, bad habits, and nonproductive relationships. Students also get tips on marketing, advertising, building clientele, and networking.

How long it takes: Correspondence course—students work at their own pace; most finish in several weeks.

What it costs: $195

Credit cards are accepted.

Institute for Educational Therapy
P.O. Box 8533
Berkeley, CA 94707
(800) 694-4438
(510) 528-3738

The institute combines Eriksonian hypnotherapy and Neuro Linguistic Programming with traditional therapeutic techniques such as client education and skill building in a certification program that trains Strategic Hypnotherapists. By combining hypnotic interventions with client education, trainees learn to help clients consciously evaluate their problems, become aware of behavior patterns, and make changes on both the unconscious and the conscious levels. Students study a number of techniques, learn to group the techniques together to form mutually reinforcing "technique clusters," and finally are taught to bring the clusters together into a treatment plan. Some techniques and subjects taught are age regression, bypass resistance, unconscious decision points, unconscious mind as cotherapist, mind mapping, and interruption of negative patterns.

The training is comprised of three levels: Hypno-Tech, Hypnotists, and Master Hypnotist.

How long it takes: 50 hours per level

What it costs: $550 per level

Intuitive Hypnotherapy Institute and Sacred Counseling Center
P.O. Box 11697
Berkeley, CA 94712
(510) 843-6591

The institute offers two certification programs: Intuitive Hypnotherapy, and Sacred Counseling. Intuitive Hypnotherapy focuses on the applications of hypnosis for psychologically healthy individuals, helping them deal creatively with recurring life challenges, generate resources for change, and manifest full, rich lives. Basic hypnotherapy courses include verbal and kinesthetic trance induction techniques, image formation and transformation, interactive trance, inner guides, trance rehearsal, shamanic induction, animal allies, and trance writing and drawing. Advanced hypnotherapy training includes therapeutic reframing, parts therapy, pain management, hypno-healing, core transformation, soul retrieval, healthwise hypnosis, and spiritual hypnosis. The institute offers a comprehensive training manual and a business and promotional start-up kit at no extra cost.

The Sacred Counseling Ordination is for people who have completed the hypnotherapist course, or are already working as professional counselors, and want to center their work in the revitalization of spiritual energies for personal and planetary healing. The training is offered as an individual tutorial: suggested work includes spiritual journaling, sacred sensing in everyday life, creative self-expression, community service, a pilot project with clients, and designing and promoting your sacred service.

How long it takes: Hypnotherapy Training—100 hours
Advanced Hypnotherapy Training—100 hours
Sacred Counseling Ordination—500 hours

What it costs: Hypnotherapy Training—$695
Advanced Hypnotherapy Training—$695
Sacred Counseling Ordination—$200 (approximately)

L & P School of Professional Hypnotherapy
12941 Gilbert Street, Suite D
Garden Grove, CA 92641
(800) 974-9766
(714) 539-6005

The school offers six certificate training courses: Professional Hypnotist and Clinical Hypnotherapist, Advanced Hypnotic Techniques, Analytical/Counseling, Behavioral Hypnotherapy, Age Regression and Past Life Therapy, and Hypnotherapeutic Approach to Human Sexuality and Dysfunction. The Professional Hypnotist course covers the nine-step induction process, deepening techniques, semantics, removal of habit patterns, dental hypnosis, NLP techniques, and legal and ethical aspects of hypnotherapy. Advanced Hypnotic Techniques teaches advanced deepening techniques, bracketing and anchoring, color therapy, script writing, and advanced techniques in metaphors. Analytical/Counseling includes courses in psychoanalytical psychology, personality disorders, family history, treatment modalities, transference and countertransference, and counseling techniques. Behavioral Hypnotherapy focuses on the principles of transactional analysis, the ego states, life scripts, gestalt psychology, and behavior modification. Age Regression and Past Life Therapy includes classes on theories of past lives (such as karma, reincarnation, and life between life), therapeutic applications, contrasting past life regression with past life therapy, the Bardo technique, and the Cathedral technique. And the Hypnotherapeutic Approach to Human Sexuality and Dysfunction course offers classes in desensitizing the therapist, dysfunctions, communication, male performance patterns, couples counseling, and script writing for dysfunctional clients.

How long it takes: Professional Hypnotist—48 hours
Clinical Hypnotherapist—162 hours
Other Certificates—30 to 60 hours

What it costs: Professional Hypnotist—$800
Clinical Hypnotherapist—$2,245
Other Certificates—$465 to $750

Credit cards are accepted and payment plans are available.

Leela Foundation
P.O. Box 936
Stinson Beach, CA 94970
(415) 868-9800
Fax: (415) 868-0900
elileela@aol.com

The foundation teaches the Leela Method, or No-Mind Psycho-therapy—a process of awakening from the trances of suffering and misidentification in order to produce an ever quieter mind, a deep sense of peace and bliss, the ability to face and heal emotional wounds, and an improved relationship with all life. Students can become certified Leela Trainers through a series of four levels of training that also result in five additional certifications: Clinical Hypnosis, Advanced Clinical Hypnosis, Leela Therapy, Enneagram Training, and Clinical and Eriksonian Hypnosis Training.

The foundation's foundational course, The Enneagram and Self-Realization, introduces the nine trances of the Enneagram—a map of character fixation that offers a divine reflection of people's true nature. This introductory course is a prerequisite for all the other Leela courses, but does not result in certification.

The Level II course, Leela Foundation Retreat and Professional Training, guides participants in the use of No-Mind as a therapeutic context, and uses the Enneagram and Eriksonian Hypnosis to recognize and uncover the structure of the ego. Certification in Clinical Hypnosis is available to students who complete this course.

The Level III course, Advanced Leela Retreat and Professional Training, expands upon the therapeutic techniques and deepens the insights of previous trainings. At the completion of Level III, certification in Advanced Clinical Hypnosis and as a Leela Therapist is available.

Level IV, Training for Trainers, requires that students retake Levels I through III, participating as an assistant to help others learn and deepen their own understanding. This level prepares students for eligibility for teaching certificates as an Enneagram Trainer and a Trainer in Clinical Hypnosis and Eriksonian Hypnosis.

Finally, a limited number of graduates of Level IV are accepted in the Leela Trainer program, which involves a minimum of one more year of training and completion of a special project.

How long it takes: Level I—5 days
Level II—3 weeks
Level III—2 weeks
Level IV—1 year

What it costs: Level I—$495
Level II—$925

Level III—$1,375
Level IV—$2,400

Credit cards are accepted.

Living Essence Foundation
454 Las Gallinas Avenue, #308
San Rafael, CA 94903
(415) 492-1186
lef@infoasis.com
www.infoasis.com/people/lef

The foundation offers a professional hypnotherapy training program that is divided into three levels of study. In the first level, students learn to induce deep states of relaxation, deepen the experience of clients in trance states, be with clients in natural empathy, facilitate "Self Inquiry," liberate obscuring emotions, thoughts, and physical sensations, and dissolve core feelings of separation in relationships. The second level teaches students to dissolve the projections that create entanglements and addictions in romantic relationships, bring clients to a deep and clear sense of true life purpose, dissolve fears and limiting beliefs about money and material possessions, eliminate addictive desires, and move beyond limiting fears. And in the third level, students learn to help clients recognize the essential benevolence of life, dissolve the judgments that cause separation, and develop a deeper relationship with, and understanding of, the physical body, pain, and disease.

How long it takes: Level I—6 days
Level II—6 days
Level III—6 days

What it costs: Level I—$750
Level II—$600
Level III—$600

Natural Healing Institute of Naturopathy
P.O. Box 230294
Encinitas, CA 92023
(800) 559-4325
(760) 943-8485
Fax: (760) 436-9642

The institute's Hypnotherapy program includes coursework in induction, visualization, posthypnotic suggestion, age regression, and ideomotor communication. Students learn to use hypnosis to help clients with weight control, smoking cessation, pain management, addiction and phobia treatment, and pediatric and obstetric issues.

The institute also offers certification training in Clinical Herbology. See the Herbology section for more information.

How long it takes: 200 hours

What it costs: $1,495

Palo Alto School of Hypnotherapy
2443 Ash Street, Suite D
Palo Alto, CA 94306
(800) 774-9766
(650) 321-6419
www.pasoh.com

The school offers two certification programs: Clinical Hypnotherapy and Medical Hypnotherapy. The Clinical Hypnotherapy course includes inductions, pain control, natural childbirth, metaphor intervention, Reiki and body energy, addictive behaviors and phobias, laughter therapy, and manifesting abundance and prosperity. The Medical Hypnotherapy course covers immediate and emergency care, surgical anesthesia, imagery for cancer, managing the side effects of chemotherapy, hypnodontics, and sports injuries. The school offers additional training in hypnoanesthesiology, emergency medical therapy, inner child therapy, and past life regression.

How long it takes: Clinical Hypnotherapy—150 hours
                      Medical Hypnotherapy—40 hours

What it costs: Clinical Hypnotherapy—$1,125
                      Medical Hypnotherapy—$750

Payment plans are available, and credit cards are accepted.

NLP Comprehensive
5695 Yukon Street
Arvada, CO 80002
(800) 233-1657

(303) 442-1102
Fax: (303) 442-0609
learn@nlpcomprehensive.com
www.nlpcomprehensive.com

NLP Comprehensive offers certification as an NLP Practitioner and an NLP Master Practitioner. In the Practitioner training, students learn to recognize and utilize people's deeply held beliefs, values, and criteria to align actions and behaviors for the greater good of the system—be it an organization, individual, educational institution, or other system. The Master Practitioner certification program offers advanced training, teaching students to detect and use strategies and submodalities, beliefs and criteria, metaprograms, motivation, and sequences of states.

How long it takes: NLP Practitioner—20 days
NLP Master Practitioner—20 days

What it costs: NLP Practitioner—$2,700
NLP Master Practitioner—$2,700

A payment plan is available.

Transpersonal Hypnotherapy Institute
1705 14th Street, Suite 139
Boulder, CO 80302
(800) 366-9417
(303) 499-9910
Fax: (303) 727-7245

Transpersonal Hypnotherapy synthesizes Transpersonal Psychology, Eriksonian Hypnosis, NLP, and Alchemical Hypnotherapy. The institute teaches a variety of methods to help practitioners determine their clients' needs and apply the most appropriate technique, providing brief therapy with long-lasting results. Although eleven levels of certification are available, the institute recommends that before practicing professionally, students receive their Hypnotherapist (fourth level) certification, which includes a Marketing and Case Supervision home study course. Advanced certifications include Clinical Hypnotherapist I, II, and III, Transpersonal Hypnotherapist I, II, and III, and Master Transpersonal Hypnotherapist.
The institute's Foundational Course teaches inducing and moni-

toring trance states, hypnotherapeutic communications, transpersonal journey work, shamanic soul retrieval, abreaction reframing, past life regression, phobia cures, shadow work, circle integration, and creating and maintaining your practice. Advanced classes include Experiencing the Transpersonal Self, Eye Movement Therapy, Medical Hypnotherapy, Transpersonal NLP, and a variety of teaching assistant and private practice supervision opportunities.

Classes include both on-campus and home-based instruction.

How long it takes: Hypnotherapist—200 hours
Clinical Hypnotherapist I—250 hours
Clinical Hypnotherapist II—300 hours
Clinical Hypnotherapist III—350 hours
Transpersonal Hypnotherapist I—400 hours
Transpersonal Hypnotherapist II—450 hours
Transpersonal Hypnotherapist III—500 hours
Master Transpersonal Hypnotherapist—1,000 hours

What it costs: Hypnotherapist—$2,990
Each additional 50 hours—$625

Payment plans, student loans, and a limited number of scholarships are available. Credit cards are accepted.

Advanced Neuro Dynamics
615 Pi'ikoi Street, Suite 1802
Honolulu, HI 96814
(800) 800-6463
(808) 596-7765
Fax: (805) 596-7764
and@hypnosis.com
www.hypnosis.com

Advanced Neuro Dynamics certifies NLP Practitioners and NLP Master Practitioners. In the NLP Practitioner program, students learn to help people use the structure of language to create positive thought patterns, overcome procrastination, depression, and phobias, and accelerate personal and professional growth and success. In the Master Practitioner program, students also learn quantum healing techniques, effective presentation and training elements, advanced Time Line Therapy techniques and Erickson, Estabrook, and Elman Hyposis.

How long it takes: NLP Practitioner Certification—1 week

NLP Master Practitioner Certification—2 weeks

What it costs: NLP Practitioner Certification—$1,795

NLP Master Practitioner Certification—$2,695

Credit cards are accepted and payment plans are available.

Hypnosis Institute of the Pacific
One Main Plaza, Suite 504
Wailuku Maui, HI 96793-0990
(800) 927-9618
(808) 242-7000
Fax: (808) 243-9813

HIP offers hypnotherapist certification through a series of four courses. The first course, Professional Hypnotism Training, covers erasing negative beliefs, preinduction interviews, trance management, direct and indirect suggestions, developing rapport, and waking hypnosis. The second course, Principles and Practices of Hypnotherapy, teaches traits of an effective therapist, laws and ethics, identifying root issues, stress management, overcoming compulsions, behavior modification, and transformation therapy. The third course, Hypnotherapist Training, includes courses in elevating self-esteem, overcoming procrastination, smoking cessation, eliminating test anxiety, success motivation, and how to build and promote your practice. The fourth course, Healing the Mind, Body, and Spirit, includes classes in pain management, allergy relief, injury recovery, painless childbirth, accelerating postoperative healing, expanding intuition, accessing higher consciousness, and finding the healer within.

How long it takes: 200 hours

What it costs: $3,200

The institute offers financing and accepts credit cards.

The Hypnotherapy Training Company
P.O. Box 2038
North Chelmsford, MA 01863
(800) 497-1807
(978) 251-1737
www.ultranet.com/~twtpub/htc.htm

The Training Company offers three levels of certification training. The first, Basic Clinical Hypnotherapy, teaches students to use hypnotic suggestions, induction, relaxation, visualization, and anchoring. It also provides hands-on training, supervised student practice, and instruction in how to begin a practice. The second level, Advanced Clinical Hypnotherapy, teaches multiple induction techniques, advanced color therapy, encapsulation procedures, psychic self-surgery, regression therapy, and soul retrieval techniques. The advanced course also prepares students to work with the medical community, obtain medical referrals, and effectively research diseases. The third level, Metaphysical Hypnotherapy, trains students to safely use psychic awareness techniques, chakra systems, "masked" regression techniques, spirit guides and guardian angels, and therapeutic dowsing techniques.

The Training Company also offers a Hypnotherapy Instructors' Certification course, which trains students how to make a living as an instructor of hypnotherapy. This course requires a minimum of two years of active experience as a Hypnotherapist.

How long it takes: Basic Clinical—3 days
Advanced Clinical—3 days
Metaphysical—3 days

What it costs: Basic Clinical—$449
Advanced Clinical—$495
Metaphysical—$295

Credit cards are accepted.

Infinity Institute International
4110 Edgeland, Suite 800
Royal Oak, MI 48073-2285
(248) 579-5594
Fax: (248) 549-5421
aspencer@infinityinst.com
www.infinityinst.com

The institute offers a hypnotherapy certification program that consists of three classes: Basic Hypnosis, Advanced Hypnosis, and Hypnoanalysis. The Basic Hypnosis class covers suggestibility testing, preinduction talk, stress management, induction methods, weight loss, smoking cessation, and setting up a practice. The Advanced Hypnosis course includes classes on rapid inductions, age regression, the Hickman method, posthypnotic suggestions, glove anesthesia and dentistry, and the Elman method. The Hypnoanalysis training covers word association in hypnosis, dream analysis, spiritual cleansing, time line, sexual disorders, releasing negative energy, and regression therapy.

How long it takes: 120 hours

What it costs: $1,710

The institute occasionally offers scholarships to currently enrolled college students.

DoveStar Institute
50 Whitehall Road
Hooksett, NH 03106-2104
(603) 669-5104
(603) 669-9497
Fax: (603) 625-1919

120 Court Street
Plymouth, MA 02360
(508) 830-0068
Fax: (508) 830-0288

39 Main Street
Attleboro, MA 02703
(508) 222-1683
Fax: (508) 222-3691

4C Northridge Drive
Hilton Head Island, SC 29928
(803) 342-3361
Fax: (803) 342-3639

The institute offers three levels of hypnotherapy training, which prepare students to become Hypnotherapists, Alchemical Hypnotherapists, and Transformational/Alchemical Hypnotherapists.

The Hypnotherapy program includes six hypnotherapy classes that cover trance induction, emotional clearing, etheric plane communication, regression, finding inner guides, rescuing the inner child, using shamanic and modern techniques, communicating with different aspects of the personality, and facilitating behavioral change. The training also includes a Four Forces class that discusses the Universal Forces that involve all consciousness, four electives, and three practicums.

The Alchemical Hypnotherapy course includes all of the above plus attending additional elective courses, receiving twenty-two hours of hypnotherapy sessions, and assistant teaching the six foundational hypnotherapy classes. Electives include Alchemia Breathwork, Inner Harmony, Inner Alignment, and Four Forces Counseling.

The Transformational/Alchemical Hypnotherapy course trains students in Alchemical Synergy, which helps clients connect with the "inner master" to develop optimal potential and self-mastery. Coursework includes all of the Alchemical Hypnotherapy requirements, plus additional electives and supervised practicums and receiving forty-four hours of hypnotherapy sessions.

The institute also offers training programs in breathwork and colon hydrotherapy. See the appropriate sections for more information.

How long it takes: Hypnotherapy—3 months
Alchemical Hypnotherapy—4 months
Transformational/Alchemical Hypnotherapy—
6 months

What it costs: Hypnotherapy—$2,355
Alchemical Hypnotherapy—$2,715
Transformational/Alchemical Hypnotherapy—
$4,075

The institute accepts credit cards, and some work-study positions are available.

Academy of Alternative Therapies
1229 Saint Francis Drive, Suite A
Santa Fe, NM 87505
(505) 983-1515

The academy offers Master Hypnotist and Hypnotherapist certification training courses. The Master Hypnotherapist course covers hypnotic induction, visualization methods, atheoretical hypnosis, parts therapy, creating hypnosis tapes, and how to develop a successful hypnotherapy practice. The Hypnotherapist training includes classes in regression therapy, gestalt techniques, attitude restructuring, pain management, hypnotic dreamwork, hypnotherapeutic psychoneurophysiology techniques, and past life regression. The academy offers students the opportunity to take continuing education classes from teachers with backgrounds in various healing modalities, including rebirthing, focusing, and NLP. The academy also offers a practical skills internship program, during which students complete twenty-five hours of supervised sessions.

How long it takes: 325 hours

What it costs: $2,888

Payment plans are available.

Hypnosis Career Institute
10701 Lomas Northeast, Suite 210
Albuquerque, NM 87112
(505) 292-0370

The institute offers a client-centered certification training that consists of four modules: Professional Hypnosis, Advanced Hypnosis, Hypnotherapy, and Hypnotherapy Certification. The Professional Hypnosis course includes classes on induction techniques, deepening techniques, handling resistance, permissive methods, and indirect methods. The Advanced Hypnosis course covers age regression, abreactions and contraindications, Eastern and Western techniques, meditative approaches, and metaphoric learning. The Hypnotherapy course includes classes in client welfare, interprofessional relations, habit control, self-improvement, relationship counseling, and developing a successful practice. And the Hypnotherapy Certification course is a practicum that discusses case studies and offers students an opportunity for in-depth supervised practice.

How long it takes: 200 hours

What it costs: $1,780

Credit cards are accepted and there is a discount for early registration.

Ohio Academy of Holistic Health
3033 Dayton-Xenia Road
Dayton, OH 45434
(800) 688-8211
(937) 427-0506
oah@earthlink.net

The academy offers certification training in Clinical Hypnotherapy. The program consists of four core courses: Basic Hypnotherapy, Psychology for Hypnotherapists, Advanced Hypnotherapy, and Hypnotherapy Preceptorship. Basic Hypnotherapy teaches professional ethics, specific therapeutic techniques, marketing, and interview techniques. Topics in the Psychology for Hypnotherapists course include states of consciousness, memory conditioning, stress, personality theories, and other areas of psychology that may aid the effective practice of hypnotherapy. The Advanced Hypnotherapy course covers Eriksonian techniques and language patterns, hypnotherapy for children, regression techniques such as imagery and metaphor, hypnotherapy in the medical and dental realms, ethics, and referral parameters. And the Hypnotherapy Preceptorship includes on-site training, with observation, supervision, case studies, and review. Other required courses include Medical Terminology, First Aid/CPR, Anatomy and Physiology, and Therapeutic Communications.

How long it takes: 212 hours

What it costs: $3,180

Institute of Integrated Healing Arts
2113 18th Avenue South
Nashville, TN 37212
(615) 383-4449

The institute offers a clinical hypnotherapy certification course that focuses on Integrative Hypnosis. This is a method of hypnotherapy that allows clients to access their own deep levels of knowing and experience their own psychological power over themselves, rather than surrendering to therapist-generated suggestions or images. Integrative Hypnotherapy makes it possible to contact childhood memories, clear emotional blocks, strengthen internal resources, change life scripts, heal damaged self-esteem, and create a new self-image. Courses include suggestibility testing, trance induction, creating effective suggestions, NLP techniques, tracing root issues, therapeutic models for emotional clearing, connecting mind/body, and noninvasive procedures.

How long it takes: 12 weeks

What it costs: $4,500

Credit cards are accepted and a payment plan is available.

Dallas Hypnosis Training Institute
1522 West Airport Freeway, Suite 208
Irving, TX 75062
(972) 570-7747

The institute's training program includes five levels of professional instruction, including courses in induction techniques, one-session stop-smoking programs, sports hypnosis, and using the mind to heal. The program also gives students the opportunity to work with clients under the supervision of a professional hypnotherapist. Upon successful completion of each level, a certificate of completion is given. After completion of four levels, students are eligible for certification as hypnotherapists, and after completion of the fifth level, they are eligible to become clinical hypnotherapists.

How long it takes: Each level is 50 hours. Hypnotherapy certification is available after 200 hours, and Clinical Hypnotherapy certification after 250 hours.

What it costs: Tuition per level—$500

Heartsong Hypnotherapy Center
4314 West Lovers Lane
Dallas, TX 75209
(214) 358-3633

Heartsong offers a clinical hypnotherapist certification program that consists of five levels of study. In the first level, students learn about suggestibility testing, removing hypnotic suggestions, instant trance techniques, ideomotor responses, and controlling the depth of trance. The second level covers age and lifetime regression, subpersonality work, time line techniques, childbirth hypnosis, healing addictions, and marketing your skills. The third level teaches students intuitive hypnotherapy, script writing, reality therapy, shamanistic hypnotherapy, and how to deal with compulsive disorders and sexual dysfunction. The fourth level covers emotional clearing, Eriksonian and Gil Boyne techniques, advanced pain control, childbirth hypnosis, and grief therapy. And the fifth level is an advanced course dedicated to clinical practice with clients and a review of the first four levels. Heartsong also makes a special offer: At any time after completion of the course, former students may take the course again at no cost.

How long it takes: Per level—50 hours

What it costs: Per level—$550

Eastern Institute of Hypnotherapy
P.O. Box 249
Goshen, VA 24439
(800) 296-6469
(540) 997-0325
Fax: (540) 997-0324

The Eastern Institute offers hypnotherapist and master hypnotherapist training programs that emphasize Transpersonal Hypnotherapy. The training includes individual demonstrations, experiential participation, audio/video, lecture, and independent study. Classes in the Hypnotherapy certification course include Induction Methods, Mind/Brain Testing, NLP Therapy, Hypnoanesthesia, Deepening Trance, Suggestive Therapy, and Stress Management. The Master Hypnotherapy certification includes advanced training in reperceptual versus cathartic methodology, emotional clearing techniques, retrieving fragmented selves, generational time lines and forgiveness, strategic therapy and the multisession format, and achieving homeostasis.

How long it takes: Hypnotherapy—100 hours
Master Hypnotherapy—125 hours

What it costs: Hypnotherapy—$950
Master Hypnotherapy—$950

Credit cards are accepted.

The BodyMind Academy
1247-120th Avenue, Northeast
Bellevue, WA 98005
(425) 635-0145
(425) 367-9060

The academy offers a BodyMind Counseling Hypnotherapy Practitioner program that incorporates Jungian and depth psychology, counseling skills, Trustwork, inner character relationship work, and information on family dynamics, stages of development, abuse, and addiction. The course is divided into three major subject areas: Relaxation, Stress, and Trance; Imagery and Your Inner World; and Vision, Guidance, and Suggestion Programs. Relaxation, Stress, and Trance covers the healing process, resonance, case studies, progressive relaxation, trance and suggestion, working with injury and abuse, and developing and maintaining healthy boundaries. Imagery and Your Inner World includes discovering and working with the Inner Child, regression, healing past events, working with pain, case studies, cancer, chemotherapy, asthma, AIDS, birth trauma, phobias, and resistance. Vision, Guidance, and Suggestion Programs covers substance addictions and pattern addictions (which include workaholism, compulsive sex, and procrastination), Professional Addiction Cessation Programs for tobacco, food, alcohol, and drugs, shamanic vision quest, personal mythology, and personal power.

The academy also offers a Breathwork Practitioner training course. See Breathwork and Rebirthing for more information.

How long it takes: BodyMind Counseling Hypnotherapy
Practitioner—234 hours

What it costs: BodyMind Counseling Hypnotherapy
Practitioner—$2,406

Credit cards are accepted and payment plans are available.

Hypnotherapy Institute of Spokane
2732 North Nelson Street
Spokane, WA 99207
(888) 327-4465
(509) 327-4465

The institute offers certification programs that train Master Hypnotists, Hypnotherapists, and Clinical Hypnotherapists. Students first take a comprehensive basic training that teaches techniques for emotional clearing, healing the inner child, contacting inner guidance, clearing issues from past lives, transcending additions and phobias, bringing subpersonalities into harmony, and establishing a successful professional practice. After completion of the basic training, students become certified Master Hypnotists. The Hypnotherapist training requires the additional completion of classes such as Group Processes, Pre-op Clinical, Allergies, Phobias, Sexual Abuse and Hypnotherapeutic Bodywork. And Clinical Hypnotherapist certification requires additional coursework in subjects such as quantum hypnosis and psychoenergetics, group facilitation, in-depth inner child work, abortion, and using hypnosis to fight disease.

How long it takes: Master Hypnotist—150 hours
                             Hypnotherapist—200 hours
                             Clinical Hypnotherapist—250 hours

What it costs: Master Hypnotist—$1,750
                             Hypnotherapist—$2,500
                             Clinical Hypnotherapist—$3,200

Credit cards are accepted and early registration discounts are available.

Institute for Therapeutic Learning
9322 21st Avenue Northwest
Seattle, WA 98117
(206) 783-1838
jelias@sprynet.com
http://home.sprynet.com/sprynet/jelias

The institute offers Transpersonal Clinical Hypnotherapist and Master Clinical Hypnotherapist training and certification. The program emphasizes the insights and principles governing the nature of mind and communication upon which hypnotherapy, NLP, shamanism, and all transformative techniques depend. Classes include transmutation and discharge of unresolved emotion, subpersonality work and hypnotic regression therapy, hypnotic anesthesia for surgery, dental work, and childbirth, comprehensive treatment planning, and future progression hypnotherapy. The training provides practical tools and guidelines to help students achieve the level of skill necessary to confidently begin a counseling career.

The institute offers in-person classes, correspondence training, and various combinations of both on-line and distance learning options.

How long it takes: Transpersonal Clinical Hypnotherapist—150 hours
                      Master Clinical Hypnotherapist—300 hours

What it costs: Transpersonal Clinical Hypnotherapist—$1,800
                  Master Clinical Hypnotherapist—$3,390 (approximately)

The institute offers several options that combine the in-person trainings with the taped courses and independent studies to make up the 300 hours necessary for advanced training. Mentorship classes and supervision are also available.

There is a substantial early payment discount.

Miscellaneous Therapy ◆ ◆ ◆

This section includes a handful of schools that teach shamanism and shamanic counseling, another handful that teach movement and dance therapy, and an assortment of other programs that teach various alternative therapies. Some of these, such as Focusing or sexual surrogacy, are not too far removed from traditional therapy. Some, such as astrological counseling and women's wisdom, are rooted in more ancient, and more alternative, systems. If you want to help people integrate their psyches, become happier and more self-aware, or just resolve some problems, check out all of these programs—they cover a very wide range.

Movement Expression
622 Las Lomas Avenue
Pacific Palisades, CA 90272
(310) 454-5335

Movement Expression synthesizes various dance styles, theater, spirituality, and creative, primitive, and subtle movement in a unique art form that revitalizes energy, heightens sensuality, expands creativity, and enhances the quality of relationship. It is a process for transformation that integrates body, mind, and spirit through movement. In the Movement Expression Teacher Training Program, students learn how to teach basic techniques and principles through various forms (such as Fluid, Beat, and Integration), articulate concepts, present exercises, develop leadership skills, organize and promote workshops, and conduct private movement sessions.

How long it takes: 1 year, meets once per month

What it costs: $600

Movement Expression
13749 Riverside Drive
Sherman Oaks, CA 91413
(818) 788-3740
(310) 476-7016

Movement Expression combines a series of unique movement exercises with guided imagery, allowing people to release stress, inhibitions, and self-criticism, experience greater energy and freedom of expression, and become more centered and self-confident. Movement Expression offers a Teacher Training Program, which trains students to explore various forms of movement, examine the relationship between mind and body, discover how to read body language, and learn specific individual, partner, and group exercises. Teachers in training also learn how to structure a class and a series of classes, develop leadership skills, and create their own unique teaching style.

How long it takes: 4 weekends

What it costs: $1,100

Tamalpa Institute
P.O. Box 794
Kentfield, CA 94924
(415) 461-9479
Fax: (415) 457-7960

The institute offers a certification program in Expressive Art Therapy, a therapeutic approach that integrates dance and the expressive arts with techniques and principles of creativity. This process builds on the belief that dances created in response to real life experiences and needs have great transformative power. It addresses the four levels of human experience: the physical through movement and dance; the emotional by examining autobiographical content through movement and therapeutic processes; the mental through communication skills, creative writing, presentation of theory, and RSVP Cycles; and the spiritual is inherently addressed when the previous three levels are embodied and integrated.

There are three levels of training. In Level I, students attend an Expressive Art Therapy intensive that focuses on applying the Expressive Art process to therapy. Students also explore the relationships between art, therapy, somatic awareness, and the creative process. Level II training has five parts: Somatics in the Expressive Art Process, the Movement Ritual Teacher Course, Expressive Art Therapy Guiding Skills, Group Process and Community Building, and Dance and Ritual in the Natural Environment. Level III is designed to help students build the strong skill base and methodology needed to do Expressive Art work on a professional level. It consists of observation, tutorials, discussion groups, advanced seminars, and community work.

How long it takes: Level I—2½ months
                      Level II—2 months
                      Level III—1 year

What it costs: Level I—$3,525
                      Level II—$3,600
                      Level III—$5,500

Credit cards are accepted.

International Professional Surrogates Association
P.O. Box 4282
Torrance, CA 90510
(213) 469-4720
ipsa1@aol.com
http://members.aol.com/ipsa/home/html

The association offers a professional sex surrogate training course that combines experiential exercises, lectures and reading assignments, individual counseling and group processing, and daily journaling. The curriculum includes four major areas of study: Human Sexuality, Sex Therapy, Clinical Issues, and Professional Issues. The Human Sexuality classes cover anatomy and physiology, the sexual response cycle, sexually transmitted diseases, contraception, sexual and lifestyle variations, and sexual dysfunctions. The Sex Therapy coursework includes discussion of treatment modalities, behavior modification theory, relaxation methods, sensate focus philosophy and exercises, and communication skills development. Clinical Issues covers interview procedures, body imagery, client resistance, surrogate self-care, surrogate/client emotional attachment, the role of the supervising therapist, working with the differently abled, sexual orientations and gender issues, and working with same-sex clients. And the Professional Issues section covers the ethics of a responsible surrogate, generating referrals, interviewing with therapists, and other business aspects of running a private practice. The training ends with an internship in which students are placed with experienced therapists who understand the surrogate therapy process and facilitate the intern's learning with additional hours of consultation and supervision.

How long it takes: 60 hours in 12 weeks or a 10-day intensive

What it costs: $1,000

Bryce Britton
1847 Euclid Street
Santa Monica, CA 90404
(310) 450-5553
bryce@lainet.com

Bryce Britton is a board-certified sex therapist, a diplomate and clinical supervisor for the American Board of Sexology, and is certified by the American Association of Sex Educators, Counselors, and Therapists. She offers a Sensual Guide/Surrogate Training Program. The training program includes classes on theory, bodywork, sensate focus training, sensuality exercises and Tantra techniques, as well as a supervised internship. Specific coursework focuses on various sex therapy models, human sexual response cycle, masturbation awareness, gender issues, coital variations, STDs, counseling techniques, breathing techniques, ethics, professional boundaries, burnout, and business. After students successfully complete the course, a letter of referral is written to other therapists who may be interested in working with a trained sensual guide/surrogate.

How long it takes: 44 hours, not including the internship

What it costs: $1,800

The Foundation for Shamanic Studies
P.O. Box 1939
Mill Valley, CA 94942
(415) 380-8282
Fax: (415) 380-8416
www.shamanism.org

The foundation offers training in core shamanism, the universal and near-universal shamanic methods of entering nonordinary reality for problem solving and healing. The basic workshop, The Way of the Shaman, is a prerequisite for the Harner Method Shamanic Counseling course that leads to certification as a Shamanic Counselor. In the Way of the Shaman, drumming and other techniques are used to initiate participants into shamanic journeying and the shamanic state of consciousness, and to awaken their dormant spiritual abilities. In the Harner Method Shamanic Counseling course, students learn how help clients undertake a shamanic journey and, with the help of the shamanic counselor, become their own practitioners of divinatory shamanism. Shamanic counselors do not provide answers or interpretations for the client, but instead are experienced shamanic facilitators who provide encouragement and advice based on their own experience of journeying and divination.

Additional certification requirements include participation in a shamanic drumming group, the completion of at least 120 additional hours of shamanic training, submission of 25 hours of audiocassette records of shamanic counseling work, and completion of a five-day teaching examination.

How long it takes: The Basic Workshop—2 days
                    Shamanic Counseling—5 days
                    Complete certification program—6 months

There is also a 3-year program, for intensive training in rare and little-known shamanic methods.

What it costs: Basic Workshop—$100 to 200
                    Shamanic Counseling—$690
                    Complete certification program—$620

The above does not include the additional 120 hours of required training. Tuition varies depending on the sponsoring organization.

PsychoShamanism Training
P.O. Box 18722
Encino, CA 91316-8722
(800) 308-4372
(818) 782-6869

PsychoShamanism combines shamanic processes, the rituals and ceremonies of the ancient mystery schools, and contemporary therapeutic techniques such as Gestalt, Reichian breathing, NLP, guided imagery, deep body therapies, energy work, and EMDR. This approach is designed to treat the body, mind, and spirit as an integrated whole, helping people increase their self-worth, improve their health, and enhance their sexual pleasure and intimacy. The professional training course begins with an introductory workshop—Beginning PsychoShamanism Training—and is then divided into four modules: Taking Your Power, Healing the Wounds, Creating through Imagination, and Teaching Your Wisdom. Taking Your Power includes classes on becoming a spiritual warrior, opening the energy body, bodywork basics, diagnostics, power animals, sacred spirituality, and rattles and drums. Healing the Wounds includes classes in becoming a healer, opening to your guides, using energy work, inner family council imagery, hypnosis, and medicine cards. Creating through Imagination covers an introduction to the visionary, opening the higher centers, relationship energetics, trance and nonordinary realities, and medicine tools. And Teaching Your Wisdom includes instruction in teaching and learning styles, shamanic techniques, and more medicine tools.

How long it takes: Beginning Training—2 days
Taking Your Power—9 months
Healing the Wounds—9 months
Creating through Imagination—9 months
Teaching Your Wisdom—9 months

What it costs: Beginning Training weekend—$425
Each 9-month module—$1,550

Payment plans are available.

Big Heart
P.O. Box 31902
Seattle, WA 98103
(206) 517-2728
jnorrgard@artic.edu

Big Heart offers a Shamanic Healing Apprenticeship Program that trains students in a variety of shamanic methods. The curriculum includes power restoration healing, divination work, empowerment counseling, ritual work, extraction healing, peacemaking, death and dying, and soul retrieval healing. Trainees learn to create rituals for specific healing purposes, journey for information for others, safely remove spiritual intrusions, work with grief, and safely bring lost soul parts back to the client's body. Other lessons discuss shamanic ethics, practicing in a multicultural society, and shamanizing in a psychologized culture.

How long it takes: 10 months

What it costs: $3,000

The Focusing Institute
34 East Lane
Spring Valley, NY 10977
(914) 362-5222
Fax: (914) 362-5222
info@focusing.org
www.focusing.org

Focusing is a gentle, safe way of paying attention to a bodily sense of a situation, problem, or creative project. This awareness allows creative change in thinking, bringing clarity and inner transformation. Certified teachers of Focusing learn how to teach and organize the key elements of the Focusing process, how to use experiential exercises to show the difference between feedback and criticism, how to design their own teaching modules, and how to set up classes and workshops. Students of the institute learn guiding steps and process suggestions, the value of listening empathically, how to help clients interpret their dreams as a growth step, and strategies for dealing with the critic in themselves and their clients.

To be certified as a Focusing teacher, students must attend five levels of standard workshop training and one specialty workshop, assistant-teach at one workshop, and complete an Advanced Certification Workshop. It's also possible for prospective students to arrange an individualized training program with a Focusing Institute certifying coordinator.

How long it takes: Per Standard Workshop—2 days
Specialty Workshop—2 to 3 days
Certification Workshop—6 days

What it costs: Per Standard Workshop—$225 to $275
Specialty Workshop—$225 to $295
Advanced Certification Workshop—$900

Credit cards are accepted.

Focusing Resources
2625 Alcatraz Avenue, #202
Berkeley, CA 94705-2702
(510) 654-4819
Fax: (510) 654-1856

Focusing Resources trains students to teach Focusing. Graduates help clients master this body-centered process that brings clarity to life issues and leads to an immediately felt inner transformation, finding a way of knowing without always having to look to outer authority or other people's opinions.

Focusing Resources' certification program is offered in cooperation with The Focusing Institute (above): costs and course length are comparable. But note that the certification program offered by Focusing Resources is flexible enough to be followed anywhere in the world. After completing workshops, you become a Trainer-in-Training by making agreements with two mentors, one usually being the director of Focusing Resources and the other being a trainer near you.

The Wellness Center for Research and Education
13050 San Vincente Boulevard, Suite 107
Los Angeles, CA 90049
(310) 656-7117
Fax: (310) 656-7112

The center offers the Wellness Course, which trains students to become certified Self-Development Trainers and authorized teachers of the

Reality Management Program. The Wellness Course consists of two parts: Wellness Course I and Wellness Course II.

Wellness Course I introduces the fundamentals of self-development, including belief management, homeopathy, transpersonal psychology, hypnosis, nutrition, and kinesiology. Students are taught to use such tools and techniques as Identity Integration Procedure, Goal Manifestation, Obsessive Behavior Pattern Detoxification, NeuroPhysical Reprogramming, Therapeutic Fasting, and Neuro-Emotional Remedies.

The Wellness Course II offers additional tools to travel into cellular consciousness, explore the unconscious mind, fully develop intuitive skills, and handle deeply buried issues. Classes include Advanced NeuroPhysical Reprogramming, Color and Sound Therapy, Biological Age Testing, Advanced Body Reading, and Bio-Compatibility Testing.

Once certified as a Self-Development Trainer, students can offer the Reality Management Program—a series of simple tools, including NeuroPhysical Reprogramming sessions, that empowers clients to choreograph their lives, deepen their awareness of who they are and what their mission and purpose in life is, and strengthen their sense of oneness with their innate intelligence.

How long it takes: Wellness Course I—5 days
                       Wellness Course II—5 days

What it costs: Wellness Course I—$1,500
                       Wellness Course II—$1,500

Credit cards are accepted.

The Astrology Institute

Chiron Healing and Education Center
17 Locke Lane
Lexington, MA 02173
(781) 861-0349
josephc637@aol.com

The institute offers two certification trainings: one is for aspiring professional counseling astrologers who begin with a very limited knowledge of astrology, and the other is a more in-depth training that teaches advanced counseling techniques to those who have already mastered the basics.

The curriculum for the professional certification course includes everything from beginning astrology to complex applications such as timing life transitions, relationship comparisons, and counseling techniques. Classes include hands-on exercises and a practicum, and students obtain a comprehensive working knowledge of astrological symbols. They also receive an in-depth theoretical and practical training in gestalt and psychosynthesis techniques, childhood and adult development, and personality theory and family systems.

The counseling training program covers topics such as gaining comfort in the consulting situation, adult and child development, transpersonal psychology, and the relevance of conventional psychoanalytic thinking and methodology. This course emphasizes brief therapy skills, as the institute considers them most appropriate for the majority of astrology clients who enter into counseling to deal with a single issue or problem.

How long it takes: Professional Certification—2 years
Counseling Training—2 years

Students may enroll in both courses simultaneously.

What it costs: Professional Certification—$3,000
Counseling Training—$3,000

Payment plans are available.

C.O.R.E. Counseling Program
American Society of Alternative Therapists
P.O. Box 703
Rockport, MA 01966
(508) 281-4400
Fax: (508) 242-1144
asat@asat.org
www.asat.org

C.O.R.E. Counseling is a unique therapeutic approach to identifying and changing the destructive beliefs and life patterns that cause mental, physical, emotional, and spiritual problems. Practitioners help clients exercise their unlimited capacity for conscious creation of life by transforming their lives of struggle, pain, and fear into ones of elegance, dignity, and fun. The society trains C.O.R.E. Counselors with both home study and classroom trainings. Lessons include Breaking the Cycle of Cause and Effect, Understanding and Applying Parts Therapy, Morphogenic Field Alignment, Accessing and Interpreting Unconscious Information, and Setting Fees, Record Keeping, and Low Cost Marketing Strategies. The home study course consists of twelve videotaped lessons. Additionally, home study students may telephone an instructor if they need help or feedback.

How long it takes: Classroom course—3 weekends
Home study course—students work at their own pace.

What it costs: $995

Credit cards are accepted.

The Option Institute
2080 South Undermountain Road
Sheffield, MA 01257
(413) 229-2100
Fax: (413) 229-8931
happiness@option.org
www.option.org

The institute offers an Option Process professional training program that certifies Option Process mentors and Son-Rise Program teachers. Option Process mentors use Option Process Dialogue to help adults and verbal children become happier and more loving and face challenges in their lives with hopeful, optimistic solutions. Son-Rise Program teachers work with special-needs children (with autism, ADD, multiple sclerosis, cerebral palsy, epilepsy, and other neurological and muscular disorders) and their families, implementing parent-directed, child-centered home-based programs that create maximum opportunities for the child's growth.

Both certifications require that students complete Living the Dream, an intensive program that gives them the basic skills to use the Option Process with themselves and introduces them to sharing it with others. Living the Dream teaches Option Process Dialogues, Shortcuts to Happiness, Active Meditation, A Vision to Live By, and a range of activities such as art, drama, movement, and visualizations. Advanced study is taught on an individualized, apprenticeship basis.

How long it takes: Living the Dream—8 weeks
Option Process Mentor Training—about 2 years
Son-Rise Program Teacher Training—about 2 years

What it costs: Living the Dream—$8,750

The advanced trainings are available both as full-time work-study programs (which include tuition and offer a small stipend) and part-time paid programs (for which the tuition is variable).

Cost includes housing and meals. Credit cards are accepted.

The Human Design System
New Sun Services America
P.O. Box 195
Taos, NM 87571
(505) 758-2909
Fax: (505) 758-3925
zc@humandesignsystem.com

The Human Design System is a tool for self-analysis and self-knowledge that leads to the acceptance and mastery of one's life. It synthesizes aspects of two families of science: the ancient systems (astrology, I Ching, the chakras, and the Kaballah), and contemporary disciplines (physics, astronomy, genetics, and biochemistry). It provides a clear language to describe, and a graphical map to help understand, the mechanisms of people's unique circumstances.

To become a Human Design Analyst, students must first complete the Basic Training that teaches students to study their own charts on a regular basis, and to recognize the constantly changing influence of the planets and other people in their lives.

Students who want to provide Human Design services professionally by becoming licensed analysts must then complete the Advanced Training, which includes extensive training materials, study sessions, a practice overview analysis, and an examination. Advanced professional courses and teacher training courses are also available.

How long it takes: Basic Training—2 days
Advanced Training—6 days

What it costs: Basic Training weekend—$320
Advanced Training—$745

Bearpaw Counsel
HC 1, Box 104
Bearsville, NY 12409
(914) 679-1082
Fax: (914) 679-3021

Bearpaw Counsel offers training in Intenergy, a healing teaching that encourages deep psychological and spiritual change, the emergence of healthy ego, and reconnection with the innate capacity to reflect our spiritual origins in movement. The training teaches students to work with the Life Story, to see the evolution of the "inner child" and "inner parent," to employ the many dimensions of "Body," and to consciously link human psychological/spiritual health with the universal web of life. The curriculum focuses on the spiritual foundations of character, freeing and transforming energetic blocks through bodywork, and the aspects of relationship as a force in healing.

How long it takes: 6 months (part-time)

What it costs: $1,900 to $2,350

Trainings are offered in New York and Alaska.

Rapid Eye Institute
581 Lancaster Drive Southeast, Suite 270
Salem, OR 97301-5642
(888) 399-1181
(503) 399-1181
Fax: (503) 373-3606

The institute teaches Rapid Eye Technology, a natural, safe, and quick way to release stress and remove emotional trauma by simulating the eye movement of REM sleep. Rapid Eye practitioners help clients release false messages taken into the subconscious, quickly remove the effects of mental and emotional trauma, create lasting change in their lives, and develop new skills for living. There are two phases of training. Phase I defines RET and teaches wand techniques, which practitioners use to direct clients' eye movements. Phase II integrates the basic skills taught in the first phase with coursework on releasing patterns, addictions, and deep dysfunctional core beliefs. The institute requires that students receive six RET sessions before attending the training, and complete a one-hundred-hour practicum before they receive their certificates.

Phase I can be completed on campus or as a home study course. Phase II must be completed on campus.

How long it takes: Phases I and II, on campus—10 days
                      Phase I, home study; Phase II, on campus—6 days

What it costs: $3,190

Credit cards are accepted and a payment plan is available.

Unergi Center
P.O. Box 335
Point Pleasant, PA 18950
(215) 297-8006

The center offers a certification training course in Unergi, an integrated therapy method based on gestalt therapy, the Alexander Technique, the Feldenkrais Method, the Rubenfeld Synergy Method, the healing forces of nature, and creative expression. Unergi practitioners help clients release habitual movement patterns, and use touch to invite a dialogue between body and mind that accesses and processes deeply buried memories and emotions. Specific skills used in Unergi include mindful movement, listening touch, energizing and connecting the chakras, dream work, creative expressions such as painting, doodling, and dancing, communing with nature and a healing community, and guided visualization and meditation. In addition to the residential training modules, certification requirement includes sixty private Unergi sessions, regional supervision sessions between training modules, and a certification project.

How long it takes: 1 to 3 years (part-time)

What it costs: $9,000

Payment plans are available.

Woman Wisdom Mystery School
Heart of the Goddess
10 Leopard Road
Berwyn, PA 19312-1808

(610) 695-9494
Fax: (610) 408-0146
merrymaid@aol.com
www.voicenet.com/~artemis

The Woman Wisdom Mystery School offers a Professional Teacher Certification program. Trainees learn to organize and teach their own Woman Wisdom Mystery Schools, offering classes about Women's Blood Mysteries, Initiation of the Chakras, The Faces of the Goddess, Wise Woman Healing, and Directional Ritual Masks. Clients come to the school for healing, to activate their creative talents, and to discover their true purpose in life. They journey to the core of their female psyche, and find a transformational work and a sacred community in which to midwife their authentic selves.

Teacher trainees first study at the school at the student level—learning what it is they'll soon be teaching to their own students. Then they receive the teaching manuals for home study prior to attending a practicum that covers teaching and ritual skills and business and marketing strategies. The course includes training, certification, ongoing mentoring, teaching manuals, student handouts, resource lists, and marketing materials.

How long it takes: 3 weeks

What it costs:　　$6,200

Index